Spotlight

on
Teaching Chorus

Spotlight
on
Teaching Chorus

The National Association for Music Education

*MENC would like to thank the MEA state editors throughout the country,
who facilitate the distribution
of essential information to MENC members in their states.*

Production Editor: Elizabeth Pontiff

Contents

Introduction 1

Section 1: Rehearsal Strategies

A New Beginning
John L. Baker. 5

Teaching Music in the Ensemble Rehearsal through Multiple Intelligence
William I. Bauer 5

Classroom Management in Choral Settings
Judy Bowers 8

For the First-Year Teacher: Planning Your Rehearsals
Patrick K. Freer 11

Planting a Seed: Singing in Tune
Doris R. Granum. 14

Finding Flow in the Choral Rehearsal
Leslie Guelker-Cone 15

Vocal Energy in the Choral Classroom
Chris Hendley. 17

Hearing Students, Sign Language, and Music: A Valuable Combination
Steve Kokette 18

How Do You Have the Time to *Not* Teach Theory?
Wayne Lackman 20

What Really Counts
Suzan M. McKinney 21

Using the International Phonetic Alphabet as a Teaching Tool for Children's Choir Directors
Deborah A. Mello 23

A Disruptive Force in a Choral Ensemble
Clarence Miller 25

Tips on Teaching the Elementary School Chorus
Karen A. Miyamoto 25

About Sight-singing:
   The Literature Says …
   Grace Muzzo with Joni Hunnicutt and Dawn McCord. 28
   Georgia Teachers Say …
   Dan Lane, Judy Spears, Joyce Edwards, Kenya Snider, Mary Busman, Doug Looney, Susan Cotton, and Eva Jameson 31

Twelve Habits of Highly Effective Choral Music Educators
Michael Nuss 35

Sight-reading—A Joy!
Steve Peter 38

Teaching Tips
Lynn Talbot and Peggy D. Dettwiler 39

Section 2: Selecting Repertoire

Selecting Quality Choral Literature in the High School Setting
Angela L. Batey **43**

Choosing Choir Music for Children
Angela Broeker **46**

Why Teach SATB Music to Eighth-Grade Chorus?
Cheryl Davis **48**

A Perspective on Literature for Young Choirs
Al Holcomb **49**

Programming Concerts to Educate Students and Parents
Peggy Leonardi **51**

How Do YOU Select Literature for Your Choirs?
Willard Minton **52**

Who's Afraid of Contemporary Music? Educational Strategies for Coping
and Conquering
Melanie A. Mitrano **54**

Political Correctness vs. Artistic Freedom
Jonathan C. Rappaport **57**

Choral Music by Women Composers
Edgar Scruggs **58**

Section 3: Vocal Technique

Alexander Technique as a Method of Body Awareness in Singing
Kathy Enervold **63**

The Singing Voice in K–5
JoAnne Greene-Beatty **65**

Imagine This ... The Use of Imagery in Vocal Production
Debbie Looney **68**

Section 4: Program Development

Establishing an Out-of-the-School-Day Elementary Choir: Getting Started
and Beyond
Karen Baldwin **73**

Ten Steps for Creating or Adding Vitality and Improving the Quality of Your Choir
Tina Bull **76**

Using a Cultural "Broker" to Enhance Your Concert Program
Regina Carlow **78**

Student Conductors: A Tool for In-depth Teaching and Student Empowerment
Lucy E. Carroll **79**

Using Student Evaluations to Help Improve Teaching and Learning
Jeff Doebler **80**

Obtaining and Organizing Your Choral Library
Patrick K. Freer 81

Starting an Elementary-School Choir
Martha Howeiler 84

High School Male Chorus: Rare Bird, Strange Beast, Definite Challenge
Allan Hoke 87

Effectively Involving Band Parents—Tips for Beginning Band Directors
(Choir and Orchestra Directors, Too!)
David Maccabee 88

Concert Etiquette, or How Does Your Audience Measure Up?
Deborah A. Mello 89

Keeping Junior High School Boys Singing
Mark Munson 91

A Choir Retreat in Your Classroom
Michael Ross 95

Teaching Music in the Urban Setting: Point of View
Annice M. Schear 96

More Room at the Top
Christopher Shay 98

Where Have All the Accompanists Gone?
Donald Speer 99

Survival of a Music Program: Six Steps to a Successful Program
Barry Talley 100

A Recipe for Successful Recruitment and Retention
William H. Yoh, Jr. 102

Adopt an Audience Member
Catherine J. Young 104

Section 5: Conducting and Score Study

The Choral Conductor: Reflections of a Singer
Peggy D. Dettwiler 107

Better Preparation Equals Better Performance: Score Study and the
Choral Conductor
Leslie Guelker-Cone 108

Negation: Try it. You'll Like It!
Clarence Miller 109

Section 6: Performance

Checklist for a Successful Elementary Music Program or Concert
Lori Kipfer 113

So You Can't Hear Your Show Choir … So What's New?
Rick Whitney 114

Section 7: Copyright and Recording

An Educator's Guide to Recording for CD Release
Jerome Bunke **119**

School Concerts, Cable TV, and Music Licenses
Corey Field **120**

How to Record Your Performing Ensemble
Lee Walkup **121**

Section 8: Adjudication and Competition

Preparing Students for All-State Choir Auditions
Steve Meininger **127**

Preparing Your Choir for Adjudication
William J. Naydan **130**

Section 9: Inspiration

No Excuses!
Leslie Guelker-Cone **133**

Looking to History for Colleagues
Anna Hamre **134**

Getting It All Together
Howard Meharg **135**

Tell the Truth! Create a Disturbance! Make a Difference!
Fred Ritter **136**

Dear Denise
Beth Smalling **137**

Make Them Champions!
Carl Vuncannon III **138**

The Spotlight series comprises articles that have appeared in magazines of MENC state affiliates over the past several years. The purpose of the series is to broaden the audience for the valuable work that is being done by music educators across the country. Were it not for the dedication of the state editors and article authors, this series would not be possible. MENC would like to thank these individuals for their contributions and to encourage others to share their expertise through MEA and MENC publications.

Introduction

"Chorus is the best part of music, I think."
—Matt Skrinjar, 5th grade[1]

One of a child's first group musical experiences is likely to be singing. If children have good early choral experiences, they may continue to sing in choruses throughout their lives. Choral singing has always been an important part of American culture. More than 150 years ago, Lowell Mason, with one concert, showed that all children—and not just the talented few—could perform music with the singing voice, and music became a regular part of the public school curriculum.[2] This book, *Spotlight on Teaching Chorus,* can help music educators everywhere continue that legacy.

Sections of *Spotlight on Teaching Chorus* cover topics like rehearsal strategies, with suggestions for how to make rehearsals more efficient, effective, and rewarding. Learn new ways to make your program better. Read hints on recruiting and diversity. Get new insights for choosing choral literature.

Should you select music based on what your students would like, what they need to learn—or should you balance the two? Your students can learn to sing with proper vocal technique, and there are hints to help you teach them. Some articles have recommendations about how to teach your chorus new music and how to improve your conducting technique. There are tips for better performances, and there is essential information about copyright and recording and how to prepare your students for contests. There are also articles to inspire you and encourage you to think about what you do and why you do it.

These articles were gathered from music educators throughout the MENC family. May this book and this series inspire further sharing among music educators in settings such as MENC journals, online communities, and division and national conferences; lifting music educators toward higher goals and greater accomplishments.

Notes

1. MENC, *Kids Voices: Young People Talk about Music* (Reston, VA: MENC, 1996), 47.

2. Michael L. Mark and Charles L. Gary, *A History of American Music Education,* 2nd ed. (Reston, VA: MENC, 1999), 145.

Section 1

# Rehearsal
Strategies

The authors in this section share some of their strategies for effective rehearsals. Here are ideas on how to plan rehearsals, how to improve vocal energy, how to use sign language with hearing students, and many others.

 Section 1

Rehearsal Strategies

A New Beginning
John L. Baker

"Prepare" for your new beginning!

Sometimes as music educators the last thing we think about is rehearsal, and one of the last things we do is plan for a rehearsal. Using *A Choral Directors Handbook* by Walter Ehret and *How to Successfully Market Your Choir* by Tom Janssen, I've compiled a list of helpful hints or reminders to help better prepare ourselves and our students for rehearsal and performance.

1. Start rehearsals on time.
2. Selections to be rehearsed should be listed on the board.
3. Give the music to the accompanist before the rehearsal.
4. Plan sectional rehearsals.
5. Stand up occasionally.
6. Sing for, but not with, the group.
7. Study and mark your score.
8. Encourage your students.
9. Each rehearsal should conclude with a feeling of accomplishment.
10. Talk little, sing much!
11. Create a choral calendar.
12. Use a narrator for your concert.
13. Begin your concert with an a cappella piece from the back of the auditorium.
14. Invite other groups to be a part of the concert.
15. Use printed programs.
16. Write a student handbook.
17. Assign one student to serve as historian.
18. Develop a logo for your choral department.
19. Plan a choral retreat.
20. Communicate with parents.

John L. Baker teaches music at Enterprise High School in Enterprise, Alabama. This article originally appeared in the October 1996 issue of the Alabama's Ala Breve. *Reprinted by permission.*

Teaching Music in the Ensemble Rehearsal through Multiple Intelligence
William I. Bauer

With the publication of his milestone work *Frames of Mind,*[1] Harvard psychologist Dr. Howard Gardner challenged the traditional view of intelligence as a single number which could be derived from a paper-and-pencil test. Gardner proposed a theory of multiple intelligences, which he identified through psychological and psychometric documentation, by examining brain physiology, and by confirming the existence of a symbol system for each intelligence. For music educators, perhaps the most exciting among these intelligences is the musical/rhythmic intelligence. However, an understanding of all the intelligences, along with an awareness that each student differs in his or her intelligence strengths, could enhance the music teaching/learning process. The following is a brief exploration of some ways in which Gardner's multiple intelligence theory might be utilized in an ensemble rehearsal. While the techniques listed are by no means exhaustive, it is hoped that the suggestions provided will stimulate thinking about ways in which we can teach to all of our students' intelligences.

Verbal/Linguistic Intelligence
Verbal/linguistic intelligence pertains to one's abilities with written and spoken language. While verbal/linguistic types of instruction are often useful and efficient ways to teach, the key for music educators is to avoid overreliance on verbal/linguistic techniques while also seeking creative ways of activating this intelligence during music learning.

Ensemble teachers/conductors might provide short biographical sketches of composers or summaries of musical eras and styles of compositions being studied for students to read. Using solfège and rhythm syllables during rehearsals can provide a verbal/linguistic link to musical sounds. The teacher/conductor could engage students in conversations about different aspects of the music being practiced and the rehearsal process itself. Questioning techniques can be an especially effective conversational procedure. Consistent use of proper musical vocabulary when referring to aspects of a composition and/or performance issues and expecting students to do the same will help to develop students' musical vocabularies.

Logical/Mathematical Intelligence

When people exhibit a high degree of logical/mathematical intelligence, they can recognize abstract patterns; are good at inductive, deductive, and scientific reasoning; are able to see relationships between things; and can execute difficult calculations. Teachers could activate this intelligence in students by providing information on the theoretical elements (time signatures, intervals, chord/scale construction, the rules of harmony, etc.) of music being worked on. Having students critique and analyze performances of themselves and others requires logical thinking skills. Ensemble directors who tape-record rehearsals and play them back for their students to critique are developing this intelligence. Working with students to enable them to recognize stylistic elements and provide a musical interpretation of a composition that is stylistically appropriate is another process requiring the use of logical/mathematical intelligence.

Visual/Spatial Intelligence

Strong visual/spatial intelligence is often characterized by the ability to mentally picture a concept, idea, or object; the ability to read and construct graphic models; and a good sense of direction. To use the visual/spatial intelligence in the ensemble rehearsal, the teacher/conductor could make use of similes and metaphors to assist students in visualizing the performance and interpretation of composition. Providing students with charts and diagrams of the form and structure of music being worked on could help develop an understanding of a composition's individual parts and how they combine to function as a whole. A time line across the front of the classroom where the compositions, composers, and dates of works

performed throughout the year are placed could provide a visual aid to the flow of music history. Allowing students to sit in different areas of the band, choir, or orchestra other than their normal seats might provide an understanding of the acoustical reasons why instruments and voices are traditionally placed in a certain location in an ensemble's setup.

Body/Kinesthetic Intelligence

Persons with excellent control of body movements exhibit high body/kinesthetic intelligence. Focusing student attention on the role of the body in performance (posture, breathing, instrument holding position, etc.) and creating activities to explore these fundamentals are essential for fine musical outcomes. Movement activities categorized by Dalcroze as movements in place (clapping, swinging, turning, conducting, bending, and swaying) could help solidify rhythmic concepts in any ensemble. Simple pat-clapping techniques are a means to assist students' understanding of meter. Having half of an ensemble tap a subdivision on their legs while the other half performs a tricky rhythmic passage, and then reversing the roles, can instantly clear up precision problems. Asking students to "sizzle" a musical passage by hissing air (articulating on an air stream) can help alleviate articulation and style problems by focusing students' attention on the role of breath support and the air supply. Traditional music ensembles where the body/kinesthetic intelligence is significantly utilized include marching bands, strolling strings, and show choirs.

Interpersonal Intelligence

Verbal and nonverbal communication, sensitivity to other people's moods and feelings, and the ability to work as part of a group are all facets of interpersonal intelligence. Good ensemble skills require good interpersonal skills. Students must constantly be aware of and sensitive to what other ensemble members are doing to achieve uniform style—good balance, blend, intonation, and so forth. Teachers can foster this awareness by constantly emphasizing listening skills. Occasionally allowing students to work on ensemble music in small groups or sections requires their use of interpersonal communication and cooperation. Peer teaching—allowing stronger students to work with weaker students on a musical passage or technique—could also strengthen this intelligence. Sensitizing students to the gestures of conducting should heighten their awareness of the nonverbal aspects of musical communication. Being able to give and receive constructive feedback on their own and others' performances can also build students' interpersonal intelligence.

Intrapersonal Intelligence

A person with well-developed intrapersonal intelligence is aware of his or her own feelings and emotions and can fully express him or herself. Aesthetic education, which many music educators hold as a primary philosophy and rationale for school music, is very much linked to the intrapersonal intelligence. Teachers/conductors could have students write a narrative, author a poem, draw, paint, design a sculpture or collage, create a dance, or use any of their other intelligences to provide a representation of the personal meaning, feeling, or effect of a composition. Improvisation, a means for students to be spontaneously creative, could be included as a frequent rehearsal activity for ensembles. Projects involving composition are another outlet for personal expression of feeling. Another part of intrapersonal intelligence is cognizance of personal strengths and weaknesses. For music students, an awareness of the aspects of their individual parts to a composition that needs improvement and an understanding of the way to practice in order to achieve this improvement would fall under this category. Maintaining a portfolio of class work could also help students to develop an awareness of their personal strengths and weaknesses and to progress as musicians.

Musical/Rhythmic Intelligence

Musical/rhythmic intelligence involves a sensitivity to aural phenomena, and includes the ability to recognize, create, and/or reproduce a melody or rhythm and to be sensitive to tonal characteristics. Hopefully, nearly everything we do in an ensemble rehearsal sensitizes and develops this intelligence. Some activities that specifically focus on the recognition and use of tonal and rhythmic patterns, along with the development of an individual's sensitivity to other musical elements, might include the following: Sequential instruction in tonal and rhythm patterns as advanced by Edwin Gordon's *Music Learning Theory* could comprise a section of the daily rehearsal, perhaps as part of warm-up procedures. Pointing out or assisting students in the discovery of patterns used to create musical form can be another way to increase their understanding of the ways sounds are combined and manipulated by composers and arrangers. By selecting music literature that features many different textures, styles, orchestrations, dynamics, etc. and then focusing students' attention/listening on these features, the teacher/conductor provides the setting and instruction necessary to facilitate the development of musical sensitivity. If students primarily perform music that is mostly tutti in its construction or music in only a few genres or styles, they will not be exposed to the variety of sonorities and ways of arranging and manipulating sounds that composers utilize, and the students' musical/rhythmic intelligence will not be challenged to develop.

Summary

Recently Gardner has indicated there may be other areas that meet his criteria as discrete intelligences. As new findings occur, music educators should continue seeking ways to fully utilize students' intelligences in order to assist them in discovering ways in which music can be a lifelong, meaningful part of their lives. Moreover, Gardner's research supporting a musical intelligence is a powerful statement for the inclusion of music as a part of every child's education.

Many of today's schools are primarily oriented toward the linguistic and logical/mathematical intelligences. To provide students with a well-rounded education that will enable them to function in the many different roles they may encounter in life, they need opportunities for learning in all of the intelligences. If one of the basic ways of thinking, learning, and knowing about the world is through the use of a musical intelligence, students must be provided the opportunity to develop this intelligence to their fullest capability.

Notes

1. Gardner, H. (1983). *Frames of Mind: The theory of multiple intelligences.* New York: Basic Books.

William I. Bauer is assistant professor of music education at Case Western Reserve University in Cleveland, Ohio. This article originally appeared in the September 1998 issue of Indiana's Musicator. *Reprinted by permission.*

Classroom Management in Choral Settings

Judy Bowers

Achieving excellence in the music classroom/rehearsal hall is a goal both novice and experienced teachers strive to accomplish. This achievement of excellence, i.e., effective teaching, seems to be a composite of many varied teaching behaviors. One important part is successfully managing students. Becoming skilled at classroom management seems to be a developmental process for most teachers, and experiential learning ("baptism by fire," some might say) certainly plays an important role. The research community can also provide valuable guidance as teachers continuously diagnose the problem, prescribe a treatment, and hope to cure student-related problems, while maintaining a high level of academic and performance accomplishment. Teachers have long been aware that the greater the level of student engagement, the higher the student achievement level. How teachers accomplish student involvement and engagement seems an important part of effective teaching in any instructional setting, because student engagement often prevents student misbehavior.

Developmental Teaching Sequences

Research Idea. One common cause of inappropriate student behavior is having too great a disparity between what is being taught and what all the students are capable of learning. Unfortunately, it is almost impossible to ability-group students for choral ensemble in many school settings. While students cannot control the quality or amount of vocal talent they possess, they can develop vocal technique and music literacy. In a perfect world, musically illiterate students would not be placed in a choir with highly advanced students. However, such problems as the shortage of male singers, scheduling problems, and extraordinary talent (sometimes paired with extraordinary lack of musical knowledge) force teachers to either incorrectly assign the student to an ensemble or lose the student, resulting in choral instructional settings with a huge range of student training. This training disparity should probably affect how a teacher instructs the group.

One strategy suggested for keeping mixed ability groups involved and succeeding is to use a developmental sequence (i.e., determining the task analysis for each goal) to build vocal and music skills (Bowers, 1999). A strength of this approach is that all students are participating together (thus avoiding long stretches of waiting for "their turn" with the teacher). In addition, moving through all steps involved in accomplishing a task allows a quick review for the advanced student and at least some introductory experience for the novice. The very talented or highly trained students can continue to work on similar goals, but operate at a different level of Bloom's taxonomy, as appropriate. This approach would support the goal of maintaining high student engagement, which seems to coexist with higher student achievement.

Research into Practice. One important skill for inexperienced choral groups is developing independence so students can maintain multiple voice parts and sing harmony as well as sing in unison. The developmental sequence for this skill involves eight steps (Bowers, 1999) accomplished in a sequential fashion with almost all students actively participating at all times (thus supporting good classroom management).

Skill building sequence for singing harmony:
1. Sing a melody
2. Add an ostinato (rhythmic, melodic)
3. Sing partner songs
4. Sing songs with descants
5. Sing phrases or sections of a round
6. Sing rounds and canons
7. Sing "transitional pieces"
8. Sing 2–4 part music

Teacher Talk

Research Idea. One element which has been carefully scrutinized for over a decade is how much "teacher talk" occurs in rehearsal and how effectively that talk functions in efficiently meeting performance goals and affecting student attitudes. A general statement summarizing the many, many studies examining this topic could easily be: *We all talk too much!* Furthermore, much teacher talk is unrelated to academic or performance issues.

An effective tool for self study is the 1-2-3 direct instruction model, where "1" indicates teacher talk; "2" indicates student response, activity, or performance; and "3" indicates teacher feedback to student performance. Yarbrough and Price (1989) have consistently reported that approximately 40% teacher talk, 55% student engagement, and 5% teacher feedback support good instruction and high student engagement in music instructional settings. Though these percentages seem reasonable, they are not generally reflected in rehearsal until the teacher makes a conscious effort to use talk efficiently.

Research into Practice. Some method of direct instruction analysis will enable the teacher to isolate teacher talk amounts and decide if they seem appropriate. The question "Is teacher talk present in lengthy clumps rather than alternated with student activity throughout the rehearsal?" can be quickly answered.

While there are a number of rather sophisticated analysis procedures generally associated with this process, simply timing the 1, 2, 3 categories occurring in a videotaped rehearsal can provide some rehearsal insight. Another "quick and dirty" use of the direct instruction model is to simply observe a taped rehearsal and record each number category to look for patterns of instruction (write down "1" during teacher-initiated talk, then "2" for student performance, "3" for teacher response without timing or classifying beyond the 1, 2, 3 label). If few 1-2 or 1-2-3 patterns are present, then likely there exists lots of 1 (teacher instruction, directions) and 3 (teacher feedback about student performance). If there are extended periods of 1 (teacher talk) with limited evidence of 2 (student involvement), then student off-task behaviors are being encouraged. Lengthy teacher monologues invite students to become disruptive or bored or both.

Another strategy for excessive teacher talk is to simply make a conscious effort to add active student learning. Give some directions, briefly explain the academic task, and then let the students become actively involved.

Student Motivation

Research Idea. One important factor related to high student motivation is a student's past successes. Thus, if teachers want non-motivated students to become motivated, they must first insure that a student has actually experienced success, and this is not always an easy task to accomplish. Madsen (1983) suggests an 80/20 success ratio as a healthy environment for nurturing motivation. If about 80% of instruction is attainable, then students should not become discouraged when they face challenges or even failure on the remaining 20% of instruction. Hopefully, the high success level will establish enough self-confidence to provide a stable context for the inevitable failures that come when tackling new tasks.

Research into Practice. One immediately apparent drawback to implementing the 80/20 success ratio in any classroom, but particularly in choral ensembles with widely ranging levels of ability and training, is that instruction will not function identically for all students. What is easily accomplished by some students might well be part of the 20% challenging material for others. (This seems to support developmental instruction, keeping all students engaged while working through a learning sequence.)

Assessment apparently plays a large role in maintaining the 80/20 success ratio. Each year should begin with some method for determining student achievement levels in vocal, choral, and music literacy curriculum. This approach suggests that performance repertoire be selected on grounds other than "the teacher likes the song." A part of repertoire selection should include whether the students are developmentally ready to learn the music. The 80/20 approach may also rule out beginning each year with the same worksheets, lessons, and activities. If 100/0 exists for many students, they will become bored and perhaps uncooperative. If 50/50 or 30/70 exists, then students may become discouraged and probably disruptive. Teachers must start where most students can function successfully and then accommodate those ahead or behind this point. Periodic assessment throughout the year seems essential in maintaining vocal, choral, and music literacy progress for all ensemble members.

Another important question raised by the success ratio idea pertains to class size: "How large can a choir be without interfering with the teacher's ability to guarantee student learning, motivation, and classroom management?" While it may be exciting to have developmental choirs of 80, 100, or larger as performance forces, there seems to be an expensive price tag attached to groups this size. A teacher must *know* what each student can do in order to structure individual progress and assessment, and to continually maintain the 80/20 success ratio. Each teacher will ultimately decide how many students he or she can manage, but the idea that bigger numbers mean better programs might warrant more study. Music teacher accountability requires much more than conducting an exciting concert. Along with the great joy of rehearsing and performing choral music comes the responsibility for each member to progress toward being an independent, literate musician who will value and support the arts, and hopefully gain skills to remain a lifelong music maker.

Teacher Intensity

Research Idea. For more than a decade, research has helped isolate the role teacher intensity plays in effective music teaching (Madsen, Standley, and Cassidy, 1989; Cassidy, 1990). Madsen and Geringer (1989) defined teacher intensity as "sustained control of the student/teacher interaction evidenced by efficient, accurate presentation and correction of the subject matter with enthusiastic affect and effective pacing." Thus, teacher delivery and accurate information become key parts of effective teaching. Of particular interest to teachers is the finding that almost anyone can identify effective teaching, from elementary students and non-music majors right up through music majors and experienced teachers (Byo, 1990). Less comforting is the finding that delivery of information plays so important a role that even wrong information was overlooked when the presentation was dynamic (Kaiser, 1998). Study of teacher intensity focuses attention on the importance of teacher delivery in instructional settings.

Research into Practice. Two important strands of teacher intensity include dynamic delivery and accurate information. Professional conferences, inservice, continued study toward advanced degrees, and healthy interaction with colleagues all contribute to a teacher staying current and presenting accurate information. Even festival ratings can provide an assessment of musical accuracy.

Teacher delivery can be self-assessed by observation of videotaped rehearsals, and use of the direct instruction model (1-2-3) supports well-paced teaching and effective delivery. Self analysis also can pinpoint pacing and delivery issues. When determining that delivery and pace are inadequate, a teacher may want to implement the Three Es: Energy, Enthusiasm, and Eye Contact.

Energy can be affected by more physical movement, more vocal inflection, or even just varying speech between fast and slow—not all fast and not all slow. Enthusiasm is that nebulous excitement students read to mean "this teacher likes being here, likes us, likes teaching, etc." A simple rule for enthusiasm might be: if you are not excited, you must still act excited.

Eye contact is perhaps the single most powerful behavior a teacher can use to achieve appropriate classroom management. Again, videotape a rehearsal and count any glance sustained for three seconds as eye contact. Surprisingly, eye contact takes real practice to master. The three-second rule prohibits eyes continually focused on the keyboard or the score. This suggests that teachers must know the music and be able to use a keyboard comfortably without watching the hands. Eye contact is an invaluable tool in developing teacher intensity to support and maintain good classroom management.

Conclusions

1. Good classroom management is an essential skill for effective teaching.
2. Using a developmental approach may prevent off-task student behavior because all students are engaged and succeeding to some degree at all times.
3. Extensive teacher talk is a less effective method for keeping students on task and involved in the learning. Use of the direct instruction model can assist a teacher in self-assessing the amount and appropriateness of teacher talk in rehearsal, thus increasing the likelihood of good classroom management.
4. Students are motivated to succeed by succeeding. Teachers can structure this success by striving to maintain an 80/20 ratio of successes and challenges in music instructional settings.
5. Teacher intensity implies accurate information is well delivered, and the 3 Es (energy, enthusiasm, and eye contact) support effective delivery.

Works Cited

Bowers, J. (1999, January). Developing inexperienced singers into independent musicians. Invited address, Florida Music Educators Association, Tampa, FL.

Byo, J. L. (1990). Recognition of intensity contrasts in the gestures of beginning conductors. *Journal of Research in Music Education, 38,* 157–63.

Cassidy, J. W. (1990). Effect of intensity training on preservice teachers instructional accuracy and delivery effectiveness. *Journal of Research in Music Education, 38,* 164–74.

Kaiser, K. (1998). The effect of differentiated high versus low intensity teaching on band musicians evaluation of teacher effectiveness. *Dissertation Abstracts International.*

Madsen, C. K., & Geringer, J. M. (1989). The relationship of teacher "on-task" to intensity and effective music teaching. *Canadian Music Educator, 30,* 87–94.

Madsen, C. H. Jr., & Madsen, C. K. (1998). *Teaching/discipline: A positive approach for educational development* (4th ed.). Raleigh, NC: Contemporary Publishing Company.

Madsen, C. K., Standley, J. M., & Cassidy, J. W. (1989). Demonstration and recognition of high and low contrasts in teacher intensity. *Journal of Research in Music Education, 37,* 85–92.

Yarbrough, C., & Price, H. E. (1989). Sequential patterns of instruction in music. *Journal of Research in Music Education, 29,* 209–17.

Judy Bowers is associate professor of choral music education at Florida State University in Tallahassee. This article originally appeared in the October 1999 issue of the Florida Music Director. Reprinted by permission.

For the First-Year Teacher: Planning Your Rehearsals
Patrick K. Freer

What Is the Rehearsal for, Anyway?

Well, that's a dumb question if I ever heard one! You may be right, but consider that the rehearsal may serve a broader function than simply learning the music for the next concert. Stop for a moment to think of your next (or first) concert as part of a long educational process beginning with kindergarten musical play, progressing through elementary music class, and including sharing the first ensemble experience with the elementary school chorus, being prepared for the eventual demands of high school choral repertoire, and choosing lifelong participation in choral music.

How does our next concert fit into the plan? At the middle school level we need to be certain that we are not only preparing students for the music at hand, but giving them the skills to maintain their interest in choral music. The rehearsal is where we teach the physical skills of producing the sound, the intellectual skills to analyze choral performances, the technical ability to make sense of printed music notation, and the skills associated with reflecting on music and our role as musicians.

One of the focal points of the middle school rehearsal is to guide students toward viewing their voice as an instrument. Doing so will help deflect some of the insecurities adolescents will have when aware that others are evaluating their singing. When band students talk about their instrument, they are talking about a physical object they manipulate to create sound. The choral student can only talk about his voice—and we need to make absolutely certain that any criticism of the voice is directed toward the voice as instrument and away from the voice as a person.

Our goal as middle school choral directors must be to allow students to sing freely and with confidence. This usually requires that the director build opportunities into the rehearsal process where students can be observed individually, whether singing alone or with a small group. Asking the student questions such as, "What do you notice about the position of your jaw?" or "How did that feel?" will do more to focus attention on the vocal instrument than stating, "Your jaw was too far forward" or "That note was flat."

You'll also need to be aware that all students learn in slightly different ways. Some students simply have different preferences for how they learn music (seeing the printed page, hearing the phrase before singing it, etc.). Other students will have physical limitations on what they can see and do in the rehearsal and performance. All of these considerations need to be accounted for when planning the rehearsal.

Designing the Rehearsal

"That conductor knows what she wants and knows how to make it happen!" A comment like this is often used to describe the rehearsal techniques of successful choral directors. Directors of choral ensembles may often see effective rehearsals as simply the byproduct of a conductor's personality or organizational skills rather than the result of detailed planning with specific academic and musical goals for every second of rehearsal time. A successful conductor and teacher will carefully study and plan the rehearsal, monitor the rehearsal as it happens, and then reflect upon what actually happened. The goal is that each rehearsal will bring you and your choir closer to your objectives using the most effective and productive strategies.

Sequence Your Teaching. One common way to approach the teaching of a concept in the rehearsal is to think of the process as having three steps:

1. Presentation (of the information or task)
2. Student Interaction (with the information or task)
3. Conductor Feedback to the Students

In a complete teaching unit, the conductor tells the chorus what to do, lets them try it, and then tells them how well they did. Try not to interrupt the flow of this sequence by focusing your singers on one task (breath control of a long phrase) and then giving feedback on something different (the third note of the phrase was flat). As always, keeping students focused on single tasks allows you to minimize your own talking in the rehearsal. Middle schoolers quickly discover that if it's OK for the director to talk, it's OK for them to talk, too!

By planning ahead for the tasks you will give to your choruses, you are truly directing the learning of the ensemble members. That doesn't mean that you are giving students every piece of information or that you are necessarily prescribing the method through which each student will learn the information. You have merely decided the task ahead of time. When a conductor waits until an ensemble is rehearsing to decide on the task, the chorus members have become the determiners of class content. Instead of reacting to students' incorrect behaviors, successful directors need to lead students to correct responses through a well-planned rehearsal presentation which includes appropriate feedback.

Organization of the Rehearsal. There are at least three primary ways in which you can organize the 40 highly prized minutes of time you call the rehearsal. Try each of these rehearsal designs to see which one works most effectively for you and your students:

1. The ABA Rehearsal
   Beginning of Rehearsal: familiar music
   Middle: slower-paced presentation of new and detailed work
   End: familiar, enjoyable music
   Principals and supervisors tend to approve of this structure because it mirrors teaching models in other content areas.
2. The Golden Proportion Rehearsal
   The rehearsal is designed to have the most intensity approximately two-thirds of the way through the allotted time.
3. The Alternating Rehearsal
   Frequent changes of pace in the rehearsal are facilitated by alternating the musical tasks according to familiarity, difficulty, genre, or mood. Middle schoolers generally like this design the best!

Cooperative Learning in the Rehearsal

What would happen if the teacher occasionally stepped back from the direct method of instruction, and instead provided an appropriate context within which the students could discover, analyze, and critique through a group process? The result would probably be very much like cooperative learning.

In a true cooperative learning venture, several distinct elements must exist: a functioning relationship among all members of the group, both individual and group responsibilities, face-to-face communication, the refinement of cooperative skills, and time for group processing.

Cooperative learning is not simply group learning. Heterogeneous groups must be carefully selected by the teacher to incorporate students with special abilities, personalities, learning styles and interests. Each student should have a role in the organization, such as the Spokesperson, Encourager, Materials Manager, Recorder (writes down decisions), Timekeeper, etc. Groups of two or three students will necessarily function differently than larger groups.

TIP #1: Before the First Rehearsal

1. Know where students are to sit when they come into your room, even if the seating is unassigned.
2. Determine your quiet signal (suggestion: sing a sustained comfortable pitch on an "ooh" vowel; each student who hears it joins until the entire chorus is singing the same pitch).
3. Rehearse your introduction to the students (Who am I?).
4. Rehearse your description of student expectations, including basic classroom procedures and attendance policies.
5. Rehearse your outline of the year ahead, describing some of the work necessary to achieve the performance goals.
6. Decide on what role students will play in the administration of the chorus. If there are to be choir officers, announce these positions on the first day along with the anticipated selection procedure. This will ensure that students feel you want their involvement even before they've asked for it!
7. Make certain the physical conditions of the room convey the first impression you intend.
8. Plan an achievable musical task for the first rehearsal. Try to steer away from singing something taught by the former teacher (this will invite too many comparisons). Be utterly realistic in planning this first rehearsal—provide structure, provide a goal, achieve the goal, and give information about what to expect during the next rehearsal.
9. Plan to do voice testing or placement on any day other than the first rehearsal!

There will be two outcomes of a cooperative learning experience: one regarding the subject matter and another involving social interaction toward a common goal. The group processing/reflection element is crucial if students are going to be able to approach the next project in a better and more effective manner. It is perfectly acceptable for students to not have achieved their group's goal, if in the process they have internalized how to come closer to the target next time.

Long-Range Planning

One of the most important things you can do to help retain your sanity amidst the flurry of activity which accompanies any middle school is to plan your major rehearsal goals over long periods of time. Much as the general music teacher (hopefully!) has a curriculum which states the material to be taught and the sequence in which topics are to be presented, the choral director also looks at his or her schedule and plots goals over time.

The Three-Year Plan. If you teach in the typical middle school, you will see these students for three years. What they learn in grade six prepares them for grade seven, and so forth. If you're able to, look at the curriculum being taught in the elementary schools—or better yet, talk to an elementary music teacher. Find out what the kids know and have experienced. Then, make a list of concepts and/or musical genres you want the students to accomplish by the time they leave your care. Begin looking at a three-year process of learning rather than simply trying to survive from rehearsal to rehearsal. You may find that it keeps your mind focused on the real goals at hand!

The One-Year Plan. Do much the same as in the three-year plan, except that you can begin to fill in the specific concepts and repertoire selections with which you will be dealing. You may organize your plan by semesters or by concert. Ask yourself if the students are prepared to successfully accomplish the demands of your repertoire by concert time or year's end. If not, how and when will you structure the rehearsal experiences so that the students arrive at the concert ready to showcase their knowledge and skills? Looking at a yearly plan will also give you a good idea of how many rehearsals you have per concert. You'll then be able to judge whether or not you've programmed the appropriate amount of repertoire and difficulty levels.

The Concert or Semester Plan. Depending on how your schedule is organized, you can now fill in the detailed goals for every rehearsal. It is advised that you write down the plan as close to the beginning of the school year as possible— then, if you vary from the plan, you always know how far you've strayed! The goal of each of these plans is to insure that you are providing the intended learning experiences for each student in a way which is structured and sequential.

The Weekly Plan. The requirement of turning in copies of lesson plans to the principal or supervisor is commonplace for beginning teachers. It will be much easier for you to complete your plans each week if you've gone through the arduous task of developing the long-range plans described above. The amount of time you invest early in the school year to plot your path will be greatly appreciated each Friday when you have to turn in your lesson plans by 3:00!

Patrick K. Freer is education director of Young Audiences of New Jersey Inc. This article originally appeared in the March 1998 issue of New Jersey's Tempo. *Reprinted by permission.*

Planting a Seed: Singing in Tune

Doris R. Granum

"Plant a seed before the sense of wonder has been dulled and self-consciousness imprisons the child."
—Ruth K. Jacobs

"Everything depends on the leader."
—Zoltán Kodály

One student casually reported to me that he liked his new school because at his previous school they only had "silent music." For the life of me, I couldn't figure out how one could conduct a music class silently. I finally realized the teacher was having a knee-jerk reaction to being evaluated by the principal in a situation that seemingly was "out of control." Evidently children singing somewhat boisterously (enthusiastically) was not perceived by the principal as a controlled educational environment—so the teacher had eliminated the participation component of the class. Thus … "silent music." Help! Have we become such slaves to so-called classroom management techniques that the children are not allowed to sing? Please, let them sing and sing a lot!

The one resource available in all music classrooms for every student is the human voice. All children can and will sing naturally when given ample opportunity to exercise the vocal mechanism. I love using the Orff instruments; we "rhythm band" weekly, and we often "fly around" to the "Flight of the Bumblebee"; but the majority of my class time is spent learning musical concepts through songs because every child can participate. And because we sing often, it is easy and pleasant to produce very musical sounds at all grade levels. However, the musical sounds don't happen by accident. Just as one doesn't become Horowitz by randomly striking the keys of a keyboard, the child doesn't become an in-tune singer by singing a lot. It won't happen without exercise, and purposeful exercise is a must. My classes are at an advantage because, as a vocalist, I love to sing and am comfortable modeling the sound I want. If you are not a voice major though, that does not mean that good singing can't happen in your classroom. To the contrary, musicians who are not overly trained often model *better*. By this I mean that a simple, pure vocal tone is a much more desirable sound than a wobbly, operatic sound. One doesn't have to produce a totally *senza vibrato* sound, but clarity of melodic line is essential! Also,

the pure vocal sound is infinitely preferable to the Hollywood, pop, guttural sound. Though a child can reproduce that sound, it is a short-lived career at best. (Has anybody heard any vocal recordings from Andrea Quinn lately? She was the thirteen-year-old "Annie" who retired after a one-year run on Broadway because of nodules.) The first step to guiding children to singing on pitch is to provide a model of clear, simple, well-produced melodic singing.

This Olympic year will provide a wealth of fresh motivating examples for the second step in producing good singers—vocal warm-ups. I have long been an advocate of equating the singer to the athlete—treating the vocal cords as if they were another set of muscles that need stretching and refining. Every class period from kindergarten through fifth grade begins with about five minutes of warm-ups (see vocal warm-ups below). In addition to explaining how the cords work, I share the analogy of blisters and muscle cramps suffered by football players and their need to be prepared to play. Once the students understand the why of warm-ups, they are seldom questioned or pooh-poohed. Below are some simple exercises for K–5 that I have found to be very effective:

- Any short, small-ranged song that loosens the cords without stretching too far initially. This is especially important for classes early in the day. Examples: "Hello, Everybody" and "The Alphabet Song."
- Descending scale passages (5-4-3-2-1) moving up by half-steps after each sequence sung on vowels (e.g., mee-meh-mah-moh-moo) or any nonsense syllables (nah; moo, etc.).
- Singing "The Alphabet Song" in F minor to emphasize harmonic changes, modality, and intonation.
- Singing the entire alphabet on a single tone with a single breath. Add staccato, legato, faster, slower, other rhythmic variations (triplet feeling, dotted rhythms, etc.)

Because a set of such exercises consistently begins our classes, it provides the added bonus of letting the children know we have begun the lesson and it is time to focus.

And focus they will—and produce they will—if the final two pieces of good teaching are in place: appropriate materials or repertoire and specific listening objectives. Over the last fifteen years, most of the music series and curriculum packets have been including songs that are appropriate both melodically and rhythmically. Use the series! One does not have to invest in expensive octavos for children to teach good repertoire. And don't shy away from the high stuff. Children can produce e" and f" beautifully and easily. We adults just need to drink a second cup of coffee and take a deep breath! Those notes are really not that high! Conversely, do stay away from music that dips below middle c on a regular basis. What feels quite comfortable for you early in the morning is not a good diet for children if you want them to produce a beautiful tone consistently.

Once you have found these appropriate songs, use them to develop good listening skills in the students. Have you caught yourself saying this? "Listen to this great song." Period. Nothing specific to listen for. A better statement might be: "Listen to the first line of this song. Is the music moving from high to low or staying mostly on the same note?" Or when the students are singing in class, ask them, "Is your neighbor singing the same tune as you are?" Or say, "Follow the piano and make sure you're moving in the same direction or making as big a leap with your voice as that octave jump." Recently, in a recording session, the conductor kept saying, "Let's do another take," rather than explaining the problem and fixing it. I guess he hoped that after enough repetitions he might accidently get what he wanted. Children, as well as adults, can be guided into producing a very musical sound if told what to listen for and what to reproduce.

Because I want my students to become good lis-

teners and producers of good melodic sound, I try not to use many of the canned or electronic accompaniment tapes/records/CDs provided with most textbooks. It is very difficult for them to hear a clear melodic line when a full, synthesized orchestra and rhythm component is added on top. Besides, the children tend to oversing (scream) to match the sound on the tape. Though the exciting and interesting accompaniments give the students a professional sound initially, in the long run singing with a tape/record/CD is detrimental to their overall musicianship. In summary, your students don't have to be gifted or even exceptional to become on-pitch, in-tune singers. You do, however, have to:

- give them plenty of opportunity to sing
- consistently model appropriate, clear, head-voice tones
- begin lessons with vocal warm-ups that attend to flexibility, melodic direction, intonation, and breathing
- use appropriate repertoire with carefully guided listening and singing activities.

There is nothing magical about the process, but the feeling is nothing short of magical when your students ask to sing "that beautiful song" again.

Doris R. Granum is music specialist at Oglethorpe Elementary School in Athens, Georgia. This article originally appeared in the Fall 1996 issue of the Georgia Music News. *Reprinted by permission.*

Finding Flow in the Choral Rehearsal
Leslie Guelker-Cone

In his book, *Flow,* psychologist Mihaly Csikszentmihalyi describes the characteristics of what he calls optimal experience and *flow.* According to the author, "what makes experience genuinely satisfying is a state of consciousness called *flow*—a state of concentration so focused that it amounts to absolute absorption in an activity. … People typically feel strong, alert, in effortless control, unselfconscious and at the peak of their abilities. Both the sense of time and emotional problems seem to disappear, and there is an exhilarating feeling of transcendence. … On the rare occasions that it happens, we feel a sense of exhilaration, a deep sense of enjoyment that is long cherished and that becomes a landmark in memory for what life should be like. This is opti-

mal experience." As musicians and performers, we have been fortunate to experience this concept of *flow* and, in fact, Csikszentmihalyi uses the idea of musical performance as an obvious example of a *flow*-producing activity.

While the experience of *flow* happens most for us in the performance setting, I have been wondering how we can achieve this more often in the rehearsal setting; how we can make the day-to-day experience of making music something that is genuinely satisfying and absorbing for us and our students. Csikszentmihalyi believes there are several components that must be in place in order for us to be able to create *flow*-producing activities, whether in extraordinary situations or in our daily lives. These include: setting clear goals, matching skills to actions, providing immediate feedback, encouraging deep concentration, allowing participants to exercise a sense of ownership, and encouraging enjoyment of the moment. While he isn't speaking about music specifically, I believe these components are extremely pertinent to the pursuit of music making, and attention to them can help us find *flow* in the daily rehearsal setting.

Setting Clear Goals

This requires thorough preparation on our part as conductors. We must know where we are headed both in the short- and long-term, and we must be able to articulate these goals to our students so that they can feel a sense of achievement as they accomplish them in the rehearsal setting. Goal-driven activity can help us focus more readily on the task at hand, making it more specific and understandable.

Matching Skills to Actions

In the rehearsal setting, we must constantly balance activities and expectations with student abilities. We want to challenge but not overwhelm, providing an environment in which students can succeed but will constantly be pushed to greater levels of achievement. In Csikszentmihalyi's words, "The best moments usually occur when a person's body or mind is stretched to its limits in a voluntary effort to accomplish something difficult and worthwhile. … By stretching skills, by reaching toward higher challenges, a person becomes an increasingly extraordinary individual."

Providing Immediate Feedback

Of course, music provides much of its own feedback. We both hear and feel what we are doing, and know, at least to a certain extent, whether or not what we hear and feel is good. As conductors, one of our major roles is to provide additional feedback that reinforces what the music itself tells us. By providing positive and constructive feedback, we give students the opportunity to focus in on specific opportunities for action and help them come closer to the goals that have been set.

Encouraging Deep Concentration

The hectic and often fragmented lives both we and our students lead often make the achievement of deep concentration difficult. Learning to put away other thoughts and to really concentrate on the task at hand can be aided by constantly making students active participants in the music-making experience—not just passive doers, but listeners, evaluators, and decision makers in the musical process. When we become truly involved in the process, concentration becomes easier and we often find that, as stated above, the normal passage of time disappears—an hour of rehearsal can seem to pass in minutes.

Allowing for Ownership

This is an extension of the above. The more we allow students to be true partners with us in music making: setting goals, providing feedback, the more they will feel a sense of ownership and control over their environment—the rehearsal setting. As students focus in on self-created goals, an intrinsic reason for concentration and participation is created. Allowing for student-directed feedback creates stronger, more involved musicians.

Encouraging Enjoyment of the Moment

The idea of being "in the moment" is one that often eludes us—and our students—as we find ourselves bombarded daily with both school-related and personal demands and worries. Concentrating on rehearsal goals and feedback, working to our fullest capabilities, and being personally involved in the music-making process all can help focus us in the moment. In addition, as conductors, we shouldn't be afraid to share with our students moments in the rehearsal that are particularly meaningful or enjoyable for us.

In Csikszentmihalyi's view, concentration on the above components creates an environment in which *flow* can be experienced, in which optimal experiences may be achieved. During such experiences, concern for the self falls away. Yet when the activity is over, the self emerges stronger and more complex than before. In the author's words, "an activity that produces such experiences is so gratifying that people are willing to do it for its own sake, with little concern for what they will get out of it, even when it is difficult."

We are so fortunate to be involved in such an activity! May we create classroom environments that encourage deep enjoyment and challenge, and that pave the way for the creation of optimal experiences. May we find *flow* in our rehearsals and in our lives.

Leslie Guelker-Cone is director of choral activities and coordinator of vocal studies at Western Washington University in Bellingham. This article was originally published in the May 2000 issue of Washington's Voice. *Reprinted by permission.*

Vocal Energy in the Choral Classroom
Chris Hendley

When adjudicating young choirs, I am constantly amazed at the number of times I write, "Work for more energetic tone," or "Tone lacks energy." In fact, I find myself saying the same thing to my own college choir often enough. This problem is not limited to high school and middle school groups; it seems to occur at one time or another in all choirs, regardless of experience or ability.

We all work diligently to secure the basics of choral tone: accuracy of pitch and rhythm, blend and balance, uniformity of vowels, diction, tone quality, expression, and so on. Once everything is in place, we evaluate, and occasionally we think, "Something's still not right! The tone still lacks energy." In an attempt to find a solution to this problem, I began to ask such questions as, "What is vocal energy?" "Where does it come from?" "How do I teach it?"

Discovering and maintaining vocal energy will always be an important task in my own quest for the perfect choral tone, partly because I have struggled so to find the solution to this frustrating problem. It is my hope that in reading this article, other choral directors will benefit from my experience as well as join me in trying to find new and innovative methods to teach the concept of vocal energy.

First, what is vocal energy, and what is its source? In singing, energy can refer to the presence of breath and how breath is effectively controlled. Energy can also be found in the elements of expression, and for my purposes, rhythm. I have decided that energy requires a complex mental operation as well. The list could go on, but the point is there is no simple answer to the question. Several aspects of choral tone production affect vocal energy.

A choral director must be a voice teacher, instructing the singers how to breathe correctly and efficiently, as well as how to manipulate the vocal process. Every singer needs individual vocal instruction, but this is not a realistic possibility for most of us. The director can encourage the singers to seek voice lessons but must rely on group instruction for the most part. While this is possible, it does take longer to establish the basics of vocal pedagogy, so the process must be gradual (weeks, months, years). If your choir's vocal problems go beyond your pedagogical skills, have guest specialists work with the singers. (It is a good idea, however, to seek instructors who share your philosophy of vocal pedagogy.) In trying to establish these essential vocal habits, don't neglect the simple effectiveness of demonstration. By vocally demonstrating the difference between an energetic tone and a nonenergetic tone, you can help singers learn to use their aural gifts to find the correct tone, possibly saving a great deal of time in the developmental process.

In searching for vocal energy, I have also found myself using means of expression as a tool. Rhythm is especially helpful for choirs having difficulty achieving an energetic tone. I particularly like to use spirituals for this purpose. The vitality of the rhythm patterns and the fast-paced tempos found in spirituals can help the singers identify with the energetic tone needed in choral singing. Once the choir has achieved an energetic tone, move on to slower, less rhythmic selections, attempting to carry over the same energetic tone in a slower (and possibly softer) setting. It is these latter selections that tend to be more difficult in the long run, as the choir must create the energy itself as opposed to relying on the inherent rhythm of the piece. This type of challenge is very important to the maintenance of an energetic choral tone. When all is said and done, energy is basically a mental operation. It is very similar to pitch, in that a choir can be given all the correct solutions to maintaining correct pitch, but in the long run the choir simply has to focus and think consistently. This concept is probably the most difficult to teach as well. Basically, the idea is to develop exercises that will make the students conscious of their tone. So far, I have found success through such techniques as motivational vocalises, aesthetic sensitivity awareness, and linking conducting gestures or other physical movement to tone production.

Begin to develop exercises and vocalises geared to motivating the singers to work both physically and mentally. It is important to vary the selection of vocalises and incorporate fun into the warm-ups. Figure 1 is a vocalise I developed for the sole

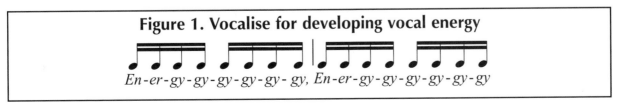

Figure 1. Vocalise for developing vocal energy

En-er-gy-gy-gy-gy-gy-gy, En-er-gy-gy-gy-gy-gy-gy

purpose of achieving vocal energy. It is based on the motivational "chanting" that many athletic teams engage in. Sing it in unison, quarter note = 72. Take the vocalise both up and down chromatically. Vary the tempo and dynamics, and strive to maintain a unison blend and balance. In addition to the rhythmic benefits, this vocalise encourages team playing and a common goal. This mindset is very important to the success of a choir.

I also emphasize the aesthetic value of the music. Students who can relate to the meaning of the piece may find it easier to maintain an energetic tone. It goes without saying that for a choir to work well as a whole, the individual members must love what they are doing. I have discovered that relating the importance of aesthetics to the singers really improves the morale and ultimately the quality of the group.

By linking a physical movement with tone production, you can help singers develop a concrete idea of what they are working for. I have, on occasion, had the choir stand up and move to the music. I have even given them some physical motions to perform while singing and have experimented with conducting gestures that encourage energetic tone production. Not only does this get the whole body involved, but it also

seems to help with the connection of a physical and mental energy working together. The singers are more likely to grasp the concept of energy if they can associate it with something tactile. Finally, be sure to continue to provide positive feedback when the singers demonstrate the energetic tone you are working for.

As we have found, there is no single way to teach the concept of energy. One must continue to strive for new and different methods of achieving energy and be willing to vary the teaching style when current methods are no longer effective. Above all, remember this: once the choir finds the energetic tone, they won't soon forget it. It becomes a part of them, and the director finds that before long, the choir and the director are feeding from the energy of one another and, ultimately, functioning as one entity.

Chris Hendley is assistant professor of music at Georgia College and State University in Milledgeville where he teaches voice, vocal related courses, and courses in music literature. He is also the former director of choral activities at GC&SU. This article originally appeared in the Spring 1998 issue of the Georgia Music News. *Reprinted by permission.*

Hearing Students, Sign Language, and Music: A Valuable Combination
Steve Kokette

For many years now it has been widely recognized that students benefit from being encouraged to move to music. In this brief essay, I wish to propose that the use of American Sign Language (ASL) with hearing children may be a beneficial form of such movement. My reasons for making this suggestion stem from the proven value of using bodily movement in teaching music, especially applications of the Dalcroze method and the proven effectiveness of signing in teaching language arts to children who have no hearing impairment

As early as the 1800s, some educators working with children who had hearing impairments advocated that sign language be taught to children without such an impairment, because they noticed that the hearing siblings of deaf children often developed better skills in reading, spelling, and writing if they were exposed to sign language at home. Teachers who knew sign language and used

it while teaching in the classroom observed that children paid greater attention to the lesson. Music teachers noticed that children paid greater attention and learned lyrics better if the teacher were signing while singing the text. They further observed that children seemed able to recall lyrics more readily, even weeks or months later, if the music educator used sign while teaching.

Few educators today will raise an objection to the introduction of "signs" or "signing," the nearly universal terms for skill in the use of American Sign Language, for use by children who do not have a hearing impairment. In addition to the advantages noted above, additional benefits to using sign language with hearing children include the fact that even the most rudimentary knowledge of sign allows some level of communication with the hearing impaired community, and many hearing-impaired students are being mainstreamed into regular classrooms. Next, a knowledge of sign allows the hearing student to develop a beginning awareness of the linguistic richness of sign language and, thus, of language in general. Indeed, some have argued that American Sign Language is not merely English conveyed by signs, but something more: a unique cultural heritage and a fully developed language having its own syntax and rules. While some educators presume, because of the reasons just given, that the use of sign should be introduced to hearing children in an arts or cultural enrichment program, evidence shows that the use of sign language is useful in teaching vocabulary, phonics, and language arts, as well as in classroom management.[1]

Similar arguments are made for the use of bodily movement and dance in educational programs, especially, but not solely, in the process of teaching music. The combination of music and movement, some educators noted at the end of the nineteenth century, seems to lead to an improved understanding of other subjects. For instance, in the early 1900s, Emile Jaques-Dalcroze, the leading theoretician of this approach, wrote:

> Twenty years ago I wrote some little songs, and set children to punctuate them with bodily movements. I frequently noticed that children who did not care for music, and detested singing, came to love the songs through their love of the movements.

Dalcroze theorized that lessons in rhythmic gymnastics helped children in their other lessons, for they seemed to develop keener powers of observation and analysis, greater understanding, and more acute memory. Teachers of subjects other than music, according to Dalcroze, often found that rhythmic training to music made students more responsive, more elastic, not only in movement but in personality.[2]

More recently, Phyllis Weikart, another theoretician and practitioner, has written that movement in music helps young children succeed in school because it can aid in providing basic coordination skills for the young child who is still mastering the coordination of physical movement; it can aid in developing the child's awareness of the body as a unique physical object occupying time and space; it can strengthen aural comprehension and visual perception skills; it creates an awareness of "basic timing" as the child learns to move to the beat; and it aids in the development of a positive self-concept.

Movement, Music, Sign

Given the proven advantages of learning and using sign, it is possible that music instruction may be one of the best methods to introduce students to sign, because it is an educational form that involves the body more than most and, given the proven advantages of bodily movement to music education, it is quite likely that skill in signing what they sing will enrich students' appreciation of music and may well enhance their performance in other courses. Young people have an abundance of energy, and most of them love to mimic physical movements. These natural levels of energy and talent allow students to learn quickly the relationship of signs to words.

I am not suggesting that the music teacher has to become proficient in ASL. There are some simple songs that might well be learned partially in sign. In teaching songs having repeated key words, as do many folk songs and songs for children, or a refrain, it is possible to have the students learn to sign only the key word or possibly the entire refrain. The booklet, *Signing for Reading Success,* shows teachers how easy it is to learn some sign language without ever taking a course.[3] In many communities it is also possible to identify a practitioner of American Sign to function as a resource person.

The music teacher who is willing to explore the use of sign in music may well be in for some surprising dividends. Barb Rogers, a teacher at Kinzie School in Chicago, asserts that her students learned music better because of sign. She states that her classes watched the video *Sign Songs* twice and knew the songs thereafter.[4] However, her students came with some familiarity with sign, for Kinzie School mainstreams more than one hundred hearing-impaired students.

Students who are learning songs together are often participating in a relatively new experience of working cooperatively. Learning signs with words and music enhances the experience of working together. If the students become adept at signing, it enhances the beauty of the song's performance. Sign can improve the motor skills of young people, and indeed it is good exercise for people of all ages. In his classic statement of the theory of eurythmics, *Rhythm, Music, and Education,* Jaques-Dalcroze suggests that movement with music might be beneficial in preparing students to play musical instruments with greater dexterity.

Preparing for the Future

Lastly, I wish to suggest another but perhaps more somber benefit of introducing general music students to sign at an early age. We are now very much aware of hearing loss among the general population owing to exposure to blaring rock music, to say nothing of the damage to hearing from the general noise pollution existing in our cities and industrial areas. An introduction to sign may well enable students, should they suffer severe hearing loss, to pick this language up again without difficulty later in life.

Music classes are part of general education for life, and they have always concentrated on the joy of hearing. It is possible that music combined with sign may make a contribution beyond the joy of hearing and keep communication skills alive, even when hearing is no longer possible.

Notes

1. Jan C. Hafer and Robert M. Wilson, *Signing for Reading Success* (Washington, DC: Clerc Books, Gallaudet University Press, 1986). This publication shows teachers—even those who have never taken a course in American Sign—how to test students for the positive value that signing can bring to the classroom. Hafer and Wilson also point out how easy it is for teachers to learn some sign without taking any courses. The book is available from the Aylmer Press, www.signit2.com.

2. Emile Jaques-Dalcroze, *Rhythm, Music, and Education,* trans. Harold F. Rubenstein (London: B. M. Dalcroze, rev. ed., 1967).

3. Hafer and Wilson, *Signing for Reading Success.*

4. For confirmation of this experience, see the review of *Sign Songs* in the September 1995 issue of *Catholic Music Educator* (4:2) 29.

Steve Kokette is the president of Aylmer Press, publisher of videotapes and books about the value of using American Sign Language with hearing children. This article is reprinted from the April/May 1996 issue of the Maryland Music Educator. *It originally appeared in the November 1995 issue of* The Catholic Music Educator. *Reprinted by permission.*

How Do You Have the Time To *Not* Teach Theory?
Wayne Lackman

Some years ago a colleague from a large city school district in another state and I got into a spirited discussion about teaching music theory in our choir classrooms. The discussion boiled down to two basic views on the subject. View one was: "How in the world do you have time to teach theory when we are expected to do so much performing?" And the other was, "How in the world do you have time to *not* teach theory, when you are expected to prepare so much music for performance?"

Often we train our choirs the same way we train a dog. "Sit!" "Stay!" "Play dead!" Well, we use different phrases like "Attack!" "Cut!" "Crescendo!" But the result is the same. We have performers who are able to master any command we send their way without much understanding of the underlying musicality. As tempting as it is to ignore all that inconvenient theory work, it is absolutely essential to develop musicians and not just train singers. When your students are actively involved in the process of creating music every day, rather than waiting for you to fix all the problems, rehearsals become energetic and creative. If you let your students know that you expect them to be musicians, it is truly amazing how much responsibility they will accept.

So, how do we develop that sense of individual responsibility? I don't know if there is a "magic

bullet" that will cure all the woes, but I believe there are some strategies that will head our students in the right direction.

First of all, allow them to correct their own mistakes. Looking at a piece for the first time? The temptation is to show them how to do it from the very beginning. Let them try it first. Then, rather than fixing the mistakes right away, let them try it again and see if they can "get a few more notes than last time." The message is that you trust them as musicians and even more that you expect them to recognize and correct their own errors. It doesn't take long for them to realize that they have as much stake in correct notes and rhythms as you do.

Try to develop questioning strategies that promote thinking rather than rote memorization. Instead of always using questions that have only one answer (Who wrote … ?), try mixing in a few that are more open-ended (What can you tell me about … ?). You'll be surprised at the wealth of information that flows forth. Less informed students also get the message that there is a lot of information available from many sources and that maybe they should check it out. The teacher is not the only one who can share information. Give all of your students, not just the fast ones, the opportunity to be right. Instead of asking, "Susie, what key is this piece in?" how about saying, "Raise your hand when you know what key this is in." And then give them time to figure it out. You can even have fun with it. "It looks like all of the sopranos know, but only half of the altos so far … " Don't underestimate the power of taking a little time after the question to allow students to find the answer.

Let your sections have some autonomy during rehearsals. In our choir, we use "section circles" or "mini-sectionals" during class. This is what I do: Let the sopranos (or other section) go to a practice room (hallway, etc.) for a short sectional (7–9 minutes) to work on a specific spot in the score. Assign a different person each time to listen and keep the sectional on track. Then have them report in when they get back. There are lots of messages there: (1) You and your section can and should be responsible to identify and correct problems. (2) I trust you to get this done. (3) There is a different listener each time. That means everyone is responsible for improvement—not just the director or section leader. (4) We expect that you will be able to report progress when you check back in—even if that just means you now really know where the problem is. I've often been pleasantly surprised at the creative solutions students develop in these mini-sectionals when I let them.

Hold them responsible for the information.

It's all right to do theory quizzes. Assign younger students or those with less experience to a theory buddy to help them through the music. Relate all of that theory information to pieces you are rehearsing. When you discuss a piece, expect that they will look at the music and know what directions are written there.

Finally, be in it for the long haul. Responsibility and musicianship don't happen in one class period or during one week, but eventually it does sink in. When it does, it's worth it.

When your students get the message that they are also responsible for the musicality of the group, rehearsals become more of an act of creation and development than one of pounding through the notes and fixing problems. They are interesting and energizing, and they remind us of why we thought this would be a good way to spend our careers.

Wayne Lackman teaches music at Gig Harbor High School in Gig Harbor, Washington. This article originally appeared in the May 1997 issue of Washington's Voice. *Reprinted by permission.*

What Really Counts
Suzan M. McKinney

What difference does it make if you have a masters degree in vocal tone production? What difference does it make if you've been playing instruments all your life? To this choral director, none whatsoever, if you don't have the respect and admiration of your students.

If you don't know how to control your classroom or keep your students focused, your knowledge of music is down the tubes. Maintaining behavior involves certain rules that I try to keep in my classroom. Before I can share what works for me, I will address the issue of how to build admiration and respect from students. On the first day of school, I give my "testimony" to my students, conveying my passionate love for young people and music. I share with them my past—what brought me to them, my hopes, dreams, and most of all my high expectations for them musically. I challenge them to become committed with me to grow as a musician and person. You may say, "But this has nothing to do with classroom management!" Oh, yes it does! It sets the stage and tone for allowing me to establish behavior control with a purpose for the students to rise to the occasion

for what I demand from them. I live by my motto: "Reach' em—then you can teach' em." I think that says it all. It sets the stage for the best possible director-student rapport/relationship. (I'm banking on my motivation and drive being contagious.)

As a choral director, I very quickly establish the rules of my craft with my students. Body language and momentum say it all! Here are some tips:

1. Demand eye contact and focus from students at all times during the entire rehearsal. I refuse to speak to the side of someone's face. I tell my students to use their zoom lens, or that we have a laser beam connecting our eyes together. I insist on it and don't let up for one minute. Every minute has to count! (You say that is impossible. Please read on to find my only exception to this rule.)

2. Do not raise your voice. I don't have an attitude with my voice, but I *do* with my eyes. If you can give a stern look, the visual message will be stronger than wearing out your voice and losing your students' respect by yelling. The softer you speak, the more they will strain to hear you and sit on the edge of their seats. (I've had some friends who teach with a microphone. I can't stand for someone to yell at me. So I feel it only reasonable to show that same respect for my students.) That only gives the student more freedom to make noise. (You might want to practice making faces in the mirror until you have the look you need to communicate what you want.) *Trust me! It works!*

3. Make "lag" your enemy. Refuse to lose a second from one point to the next. I tell my students that when I stop, it is to tell them something—not for them to talk or remove their focus. If you are *consistent* and demand this, they will become conditioned to it and hang on your every word. Now for the exception to rule Number 1: If we have spent a good thirty minutes in rehearsal without letting up for one second (don't forget that I'm teaching middle school), then I give my students the referees' signal for *time-out* and my students earn sixty seconds of relaxation and visiting with their neighbor. After sixty seconds have been spent, I play I-V^7-I chords on piano, and students must snap back into singing position and focus once again on me. (We practice this several times in the beginning of the year and make a game out of it.) With time and determination, they will become very accustomed to it.

4. Smile as often as possible. One principal I had would tell his staff *not* to smile—that it would signify to the students that your guard is down. Much to the contrary for me!!! When it is not warranted, *don't do it,* but take every chance you can get to smile. My smile balances out my stern "you'd better get with it" look. It also lets the students know that I don't hold grudges and that I can move on after having to be the disciplinarian, not to mention what it does to the student's mood.

5. Use a tape recorder for maintaining behavior offenses that occur in the classroom. I use a small handheld recorder, call the student's name and offense out loud. This informs the student that I am acknowledging the misbehavior that he chose to demonstrate. Then, by hearing his name called, he realizes that his grade just dropped—that he lost points. This system keeps me from having to look down at my grade book, thus taking my eyes off of my students. I don't believe in ignoring misbehavior. Then, it only grows. I make the student own what he has chosen to do or not to do. At the end of the day, I have a trustworthy, supportive parent play back my tape recorder and record the points in my grade book.

6. Never teach in a bad mood. If I'm having a bad day, I make it my goal to fake it for my students. They chose my class as an elective, and I take it as a compliment that they want to spend this time with me. I don't want them to regret it, and I don't want to regret my actions either—so I stay as bright and happy as I possibly can on a low day. Plus, they will sing flat if my spirit is down. They mirror you! If you force a smile, before you know it, you will even make yourself feel better, not to mention your students!

7. Give students a visual and audible direction to begin class. Don't ever deviate from it each day. I walk to the piano and play three chords—the same three chords to begin every day with every classroom group.

8. Keep the same lesson format and structure every day so that the students know the routine and what to expect. When format and structure are changed, it opens the door to chaos and confusion. For example, my daily plan is: roll, warm-ups, sight-reading, work repertoire, review musically or reflect verbally on what has been accomplished. I try to never deviate from this plan!

9. Let the students know what ticks you off (ahead of time!) Giving them these parameters gives them some advance warning. You will find that most students want to stay out of that area if they know in advance what upsets you.

10. Give consequences for undesirable behavior before the offense and remain consistent in upholding those consequences.

11. Make class fun. Keep humor present while learning. When boredom sets in, you've got problems. Singing is supposed to be fun! I work constantly on this. It doesn't come naturally for me, but it can be done and makes a huge difference. And it does make teaching so much more enjoyable for me. As the old saying goes: "When Mama ain't happy, ain't nobody happy!"

On a personal note, I am in this profession due to a high calling and strong convictions. These ideas come from twenty years of trial and error combined with lots of determination to succeed. Classroom management can make or break you. Good classroom control warrants maximum time efficiency and lowers the stress level of the director. Who doesn't want that? I hope that you can take some of what has worked for me and form your own recipe based on your personality/situation to maximize your classroom control in your own classroom. Have a musically *wonderful* year!

Suzan M. McKinney teaches chorus and handbells at Chain of Lakes Middle School in Orlando, Florida. This article originally appeared in the October 1999 issue of the Florida Music Director. *Reprinted by permission.*

Using the International Phonetic Alphabet as a Teaching Tool for Children's Choir Directors

Deborah A. Mello

How many of you continually strive for uniform vowel color with your choir? How often do you find yourself reminding your singers to sing the beginning and ending consonants of words more clearly? Have you noticed that a great deal of your choir's intonation problems are directly related to the production and sustaining ability of the vowels that are being sung? Have the regional idiosyncrasies of speech become an everyday part of your choirs singing sound? These are problems directly related to diction, the pronunciation of words, the enunciation of vowels or syllables, and the articulation of consonants.

The following comments deal directly with several views and suggestions from various leading choral directors:

Linda Swears suggests a poster, banner, or bulletin board theme might include the following motto: Vowels make the sound—consonants make the sense. An analogy that Sally Herman uses can also be valuable for students:

"Think of the vowels as being a stream of water pouring out of a faucet. The consonants want to cut through the stream of water without interrupting the flow. Pass your hand through the water quickly and precisely. If you let your hand linger too long under the water, the water will splash in your face. We want our musical phrases to be clean and flowing, not splashed."

The idea of consonants "cutting through" should be emphasized as being powerful and quick. Most choirs sing correct consonants, but many times they are too soft and without energy. An example that I have used with my choirs has been, for instance, on the word "crying." Ask the choir to pronounce the word "courage" in the way the Cowardly Lion in *The Wizard of Oz* speaks it. They usually try to outdo each other in the exaggeration of the letter C. If pronounced correctly, ask the choir to pronounce the word "crying." Isolate the word in the text and ask the choir to sing the word "crying." Place it back into the context of the piece and sing the phrase and the entire song.

Vowels, on the other hand, vary a great deal from singer to singer. If you can agree on a unified vowel sound for every vowel sung, the transformation of the choir's sound will be astounding! The International Phonetic Alphabet (IPA) can

assist you in the unification of vowel sounds. These are the sustainers and shapers of your choir's tone quality.

The IPA is a universal system for all languages. It assigns one symbol for each vocal sound, regardless of the spelling. As choral director, you can establish those sounds for yourself and mark them in your music. This will quickly isolate the individual sounds for your choir as you teach them. It will save you a great deal of time in rehearsal and will help to unify your choir's sound. As the singers converge on a common enunciation of vowels, their intonation will also be affected. You will find less flatting and sharping of notes. Combining good posture, singing technique, and uniform enunciation and articulation will produce positive results. As you begin to notice a difference, encourage your singers to be aware of these differences:

- Ask the choir to produce a particular vowel sound or word in two contrasting ways. Ask them which one is the most desirable for singing.
- Model some examples for the choir and ask them to evaluate and choose the better example.
- On a rotating basis, ask a few students to sit out in front of the choir and listen. Ask these students to give specific constructive remarks. Point out examples well done and those in need of improvement. Try a few of their suggestions.
- Ask students to model a sound, syllable, word, or phrase.

Another invaluable use of IPA is for foreign language songs. Particularly in languages that may be unfamiliar to you or have unfamiliar symbols or sounds inherent to that language, the IPA can assist you in teaching the language. Mark the symbols directly under each word. See Figure 1 for some examples to consider.

Figure 1

English	O MU-SIC (o mu-sik)	David Brunner Boosey & Hawkes 6798
French	Je Danse La Pol-ka (ʒə dãˇs la pɔlˑ-ka)	Herrington & Glick Intrada Music P1051
Latin	Ju-bi-la-te De-o (ju-bi-la-te de-o)	*arr.* Rao Boosey & Hawkes

Figure 2 International Phonetic Alphabet

(a sampling)

IPA Symbol	Sample Word
Five Basic Singing Vowels	
[i]	tree
[e]	chaotic
[a]	father
[o]	note
[u]	too
Short Vowels	
[æ]	cat
[ɔ]	call
[ɛ]	egg
[I]	sit
[u]	full
Neutral Vowels	
[ʌ]	up (stressed)
[ə]	alone (unstressed)
Voiced Consonants	
[g]	go
[ð]	the
[z]	rose
[ʒ]	fusion
[dʒ]	judge
Unvoiced Consonants	
[θ]	thin
[s]	sing
[ʃ]	shine
[tʃ]	cha-cha
[ŋ]	sing

Take the time to learn the symbols and their sounds. As with most methods, the more you employ it, the more adept you will become in using it. Will this be the answer to all your choir's diction and intonation problems? Absolutely not! Nothing can replace the ears, eyes, and musical intuition of the conductor. The use of IPA can enhance what you are already doing and strive to cut down on wasted rehearsal time. I have found it to be a valuable tool when teaching children in any context, whether it be school, church, or community.

References

Choksy, Lois. (1981). *The Kodály Context*. Englewood Cliffs, NJ: Prentice-Hall, Inc.

Decker, Harold A. & Herford, Julius. (1973). *Choral Conducting, A Symposium*. Englewood Cliffs, NJ: Prentice-Hall, Inc.

Herman, Sally. (1994). *In Search of Musical Excellence: Taking Advantage of Varied Learning Styles*. Dayton, Ohio: Roger Dean Publishing Company.

Marshall, Madeleine. (1946). *The Singer's Manual of English Diction*. New York: G. Schirmer.

McRae, Shirley W. (1991). *Directing the Children's Choir: A Comprehensive Resource*. New York: Schirmer Books/Macmillan.

Phillips, Kenneth H. (1992). *Teaching Kids to Sing*. New York: Schirmer Books/Macmillan.

Pohjola, Erkki. (1993). *Tapiola Sound*. Ft. Lauderdale, FL: Walton Music Corporation.

Rao, Doreen. (1993). *We Will Sing*. New York: Boosey & Hawkes.

Roe, Paul F. (1970). *Choral Music Education*. Englewood Cliffs, NJ: Prentice-Hall, Inc.

Swears, Linda. (1985). *Teaching the Elementary School Chorus*. West Nyack, NY: Parker Publishing Company, Inc.

Thomas, Kurt. (1971). *The Choral Conductor*. New York: Associated Music Publishers.

Deborah A. Mello teaches general and choral music at McKeown Elementary School in Hampton Township, New Jersey. She is also the founder and artistic director of the Children's Chorus of Sussex County, New Jersey. This article originally appeared in the May 1996 issue of New Jersey's Tempo. *Reprinted by permission.*

A Disruptive Force in a Choral Ensemble

Clarence Miller

This is one of several letters Professor Miller wrote to the Concert Choir during his 36 years as its conductor.

Webster defines disruptive as "tending to break up: causing disruption." There are no stars in a choral ensemble, including the conductor. In any given choir, Webster's definition could start with the conductor not knowing the music, missing cues, talking too much, blaming the entire ensemble for the faults of a few, preaching instead of teaching, and yelling instead of telling. What conductor would admit to one, two, or even three of the above? This conductor will, but his attempt to improve is constant and continuous.

What then is the disruptive force from the opposite side of the music stand? Let's name a few. Not looking at the music from one rehearsal to the next ... at least 10–20 minutes; not studying difficult passages and preparing oneself for the arrival of such; waiting for the other person to learn the music, then scabbing and borrowing from that person's energy and talent; complaining about too much to do, when no one was forced to be in the ensemble in the first place; worrying about someone else's personality differences or strange characteristics and not realizing perhaps one's own personality is just as strange; singing physically, but allowing the mind to be somewhere else; concerned about where one sits instead of doing one's own thing and taking care of one's own choral space; not leaving petty problems outside the rehearsal room; talking about others for gossip's sake rather than for the good of the ensemble; blabbing one's mouth before one's brain gives permission; feeling that the conductor is picking on one when commenting or making a general correction to a section or the whole group; or constantly thinking that what the conductor says does not apply to you; using the ensemble as a prestige symbol, but not wanting to be a prestigious member; only joining because of an awesome tour and only for a social experience, not a musical one; constantly thinking what the conductor has to say when stopping the group is nothing but air escaping out of the bottom part of the anatomy; joining the crowd and not realizing the crowd is only effective if each member is responsible.

It takes much to be part of an outstanding ensemble. The question is ... do you have *"much"*?

Clarence Miller is professor emeritus at Glassboro State College/Rowan University, New Jersey. This article originally appeared in the January 2001 issue of New Jersey's Tempo. *Reprinted by permission.*

Tips on Teaching the Elementary School Chorus

Karen A. Miyamoto

Developing Good Singing Posture

Good, alert posture is essential for good singing. This is a commonly overlooked component when teaching the elementary school chorus. It is seldom stressed, and most students have no idea of what we mean by "correct singing posture."

I.   Helpful Guidelines When Seated (Campbell & Scott-Kassner, 1995)
  A. Sit away from the back of the chair.
  B. Place feet flat on the floor.
  C. The back is straight, and the head feels as if it is suspended from the ceiling by a string attached to the crown of the head.
  D. The chest is held high while the chin is down.

II. Helpful Guidelines When Standing
  A. The spine is straight with the chest held high.
  B. Feet are slightly apart with one foot a few inches ahead of the other.
  C. The balance of the body weight is slightly forward.
  D. The arms are relaxed and held comfortably at the sides.
  E. Knees should be relaxed and not locked. A light bouncing in place, one knee alternating with the other, and then both knees, can eliminate tightness and tension.
  F. Shoulders are held back slightly and down. Shoulder rolls are helpful: rotation of the shoulders forward, down, and up will decrease tension. The reverse movement (backward, down, and up again) can also be helpful.
  G. Arms and hands should hang easily down at the sides. This can be achieved at the

end of the spinal stretch or "breast stroke" gesture, although attention may need to be called to the position of the arms and hands.

III. Helpful Tips on Teaching Good Singing Posture
   A. Help students to think of their bodies as musical instruments. Just as a flautist or violinist must learn to hold his or her instrument correctly, the singer must do the same.
   B. Use analogies to describe what happens when the body is not properly aligned for singing. One example is a garden hose—what happens to the flow of water when it is bent? When it is straight? The same principle holds true for singers. Poor posture interferes with the flow of air through the windpipe and can diminish the sound produced.
   C. For children who tend to slouch, have them pretend their spines are as straight as yardsticks. Ask students to clasp their hands behind their backs. This will automatically bring the chest up and prevent the shoulders from drooping. Ask students to release their hands slowly, keeping the chest and shoulders in correct position.

Teaching Deep Breathing

Breathing needed for singing is called deep breathing. This involves taking the air into the lowest part of the lungs first. As this occurs, the area around the lower rib cage should expand while the chest is held high and the shoulders remain stationary. As the air is expelled from the lungs, it passes through the windpipe and causes the vocal cords to vibrate. This vibration produces the singing tone.

Helpful activities for teaching deep breathing (Campbell & Scott, 1995; Swears, 1985):

1. Children can take in air as they would sip soda through a straw: with puckered lips, they slowly sip the air in a gentle manner similar to drinking. Because sipping is an easy and gentle action, there should be no tension involved in the exercise.

2. Taking the image of a balloon, children can compare the expansion of their own lungs to the fullness of a blown-up balloon. They can imitate the roundness of a balloon as they breathe in through their mouths, with their arms curved in front of them and their fingers touching. The more air they inhale, the wider the balloon becomes; their arms move out more widely so that their fingers can no longer touch. As the air of a balloon is slowly released, they can slowly release the air without producing a vocal sound, and their fingers touch again. The inhaling and exhaling process can challenge children physically, especially when the instructor demonstrates the appropriate vocal sound to which the exercises lead.

3. Help children become aware of the natural breathing process by asking them to place one hand just below the breast bone. Ask them to describe what they feel in this area as they inhale and exhale. Most children will be able to explain that the area expands as they inhale and flattens as they exhale.

4. Demonstrate deep breathing for singing by standing so that the students see your side profile, and place your hands on the area just below the rib cage. Inhale deeply, showing the children how this area expands as the air is taken in. Have the students repeat the exercise several times. Explain to the children that breathing for singing is identical to this process except that the breath needs to be fuller in order to support a long musical phrase.

5. Some children want to lift their shoulders as they inhale. This is incorrect and produces shallow breathing. To avoid this, ask them to clasp their hands behind their backs. At the same time, ask them to arch the roof of their mouth as they inhale. They should feel a "cold air" breath pass through the back of the throat, filling the lowest part of the lungs first.

6. Imagery is often useful when teaching breathing. Here are some examples:
   a. Pretend you are filling an inner tube around your waist as you inhale.
   b. Take a breath as if you saw a ghost.
   c. Begin your breath as if you are about to yawn.
   d. Stretch your lower ribs as you sing.
   e. Pant like a dog.
   f. Say the words "ho, ho, ho!" like Santa Claus.

Vocal Exercises and Warm-ups

Warm-ups are a necessary part of each rehearsal. Spend at least the first ten minutes of your rehearsal doing warm-ups and vocal exercises. This will lead to increased quality vocal production. Warm-ups are designed to correct specific weaknesses and prepare for skills needed for new repertoire.

Warm-up tips (Telfer, 1985): Keep your warm-up session as short as possible; a warm-up should be a fast, concise way to physically warm up the voice and to teach new concepts. Move on to repertoire as quickly as possible. Use some physical exercises of your own between warm-ups or in mid-rehearsal (e.g., rolling shoulders, shaking arms, rotating neck, shaking out legs, etc.). Do not use any warm-up for longer than six rehearsals in a row; either start on a variation or switch to another warm-up. Familiarity breeds sloppiness.

Spacing, Formation, and Choral Sound

The choral formation is an often overlooked component in the production of choral sound. Choral methods materials routinely endorse various choir formations and seating arrangements. Kohut and Grant (1990) state that "noticeably different" changes in choral sound occur by moving sections of the choir, relocating individual singers, or singing in mixed quartets. While such comments are rampant among choral music educators, little empirical research is available regarding choir formations. There is still less empirical evidence with respect to spacing of singers and choral sound. In a 1999 study by James F. Daugherty, the spacing and formation of the choir in performance was evaluated for its choral sound. The results were that 95.6 percent of choristers thought that spacing had some influence on choral sound. Ninety percent of choir members reported that they could hear and monitor their own voices better with spread spacing than with close spacing. Seventy-five percent of choristers reported that they could hear and monitor the sound of the ensemble as a whole better with spread spacing than with close spacing. Auditor results indicated consistently significant preference for excerpts sung with spread spacing and no consistent preference for formation.

To sum up this new research, it is better to have your choir stand with spread spacing (space between each individual) rather than bunched up and close together. It allows for better sound/acoustics, listening, and performance.

References

Campbell, P., & Scott-Kassner, C. (1995). *Music in childhood: From preschool through the elementary grades* (pp. 133–135). New York: Schirmer Books.

Daugherty, J. F. (1999). Spacing, formation, and choral sound: preferences and perceptions of auditors and choristers. *Journal of Research in Music Education, 47,* 224–238.

Kohut, D. L., & Grant, J. W. (1990). *Learning to conduct and rehearse.* Englewood Cliffs, NJ: Prentice-Hall.

Swears, L. (1985). *Teaching the elementary school chorus* (pp. 66–71). West Nyack, NY: Parker Publishing Company.

Telfer, N. (1985). *Contemporary warm-ups: Ideas for choral conductors and solo singers* (p. 5). Newmark, Ontario, Canada: Stuart Beaudoin.

Karen A. Miyamoto teaches music at Kapalama Elementary School in Honolulu, Hawaii. This article originally appeared in the April 2000 issue of Hawaii's Leka Nu Hou. *Reprinted by permission.*

About Sight-singing
The Literature Says …
Grace Muzzo with Joni Hunnicutt and Dawn McCord

Music educators agree that the ability to sight-sing—to hear in one's mind the sounds that the notation represents and reproduce these sounds vocally—is a vital asset for both choral and instrumental musicians. It is also generally agreed that the teaching of sight-singing is underemphasized in middle and high school music classes. Although many ensembles demonstrate high levels of achievement in performance, individual students may be, and often are, very poor sight-readers. What reading may have been begun in elementary school with Orff or Kodály methods is rarely reinforced or continued at the upper levels of public school.

Choral teachers who have a rigorous performance schedule tend to resort to rote learning (Daniels, 1988), because it appears to be the most expedient way to teach new literature. Under the immediate pressure of preparing performances, it is tempting to neglect general music skills—to the long-term detriment of the program and the singers themselves. Choral students may easily pass through an otherwise fine program without ever learning how to sight-sing. Colwell (1963) observed that the error-detection skills of high school choral students actually declined as the year progressed—a fact that he attributed to an emphasis on performing at the expense of reading fundamentals. As Paul Cappers (1985) succinctly puts it, "Once the students reach the elective choral program … music learning stops and singing takes its place."

Instrumental students usually possess some degree of sight-reading skill—at minimum, they are expected to count rhythms accurately and to play correct pitches. But the ability to sight-read an instrumental line is not sufficient to produce a really fine instrumental musician. Many authorities emphasize the benefits of sight-singing in instrumental classes, pointing out that sight-singing trains students to hear pitches in the mind rather than simply pressing the right keys. The ability to audiate provides a concept of tonality that leads to meaningful music reading (Dunlap, 1989). A solid body of research has shown that singing improves instrumental performance (e.g., Burton, 1986; Elliott, 1974). Harris (1991) found that one of the factors in achieving superior sight-reading ratings at band festivals was the use of ensemble singing in rehearsal. For fifth- and sixth-grade wind stu-

dents, a program of training using solmization was found to be effective for developing aural recognition of major and minor tonality and melodic sight-reading (Grutzmacher, 1985).

It is clear that regular sight-singing practice benefits both choral and instrumental ensembles. Why, then, does it receive mere lip service in secondary music classes? Time pressure is unlikely to be the only factor. Taggart and Taggart (1994) found that college music faculty disagree strongly about the best method of teaching sight-singing in theory classes. They speculate that this lack of uniformity at the university level indirectly affects public school music programs, because preservice teachers receive very little training in sight-singing pedagogy. They are thus inadequately prepared to teach sight-singing with confidence and authority.

Is There a "Right" Method?

Researchers have shown considerable interest in the competing claims of the various sight-singing methods: fixed *do,* movable *do,* and scale degree numbers. Henry and Demorest (1994) assessed the effects of method on group sight-reading accuracy. They found no statistically significant difference between the sight-reading skills of a choral group trained using fixed *do* and a group using movable *do.* Within the groups, individual differences were broadly distributed, indicating that group performance was not a valid indicator of individual achievement. Indeed, Henry and Demorest (1994) concurred with several other studies (e.g., Colwell, 1963; Demorest and May, 1995; Tucker, 1969, cited in Dwiggins, 1984) in finding that individual sight-singing skill correlated most strongly with piano instruction. (This finding refutes the commonly held notion that playing the piano is, at least in the early stages, a kinesthetic skill that has little to do with audiation.)

All the methods have their proponents. More (1985) advocates the Kodály movable *do* because it emphasizes ear training and sight-singing simultaneously, but acknowledges that movable *do* is not well adapted to atonal music. Smith (1987) maintains that good singers adjust intervals, especially tritones, depending on the scale function of the two pitches; using movable *do* therefore produces better intonation. Jordan (1987), contending that true intonation cannot occur without Edwin Gordon's concept of the "resting tone," supports the use of the movable *do* system. Powell (1991) argues that choirs sing far better in tune if they sight-read on solfège syllables; singing *ti-do,* for example, will provide a higher leading tone than singing a "generic" half step. Middleton (1984) advocates a mixed approach: he concedes the effectiveness of movable *do* for young children, but feels that advanced students must move to the fixed *do* system, "the ultimate tool for pitch/tonal reading." However, Demorest and May (1995) found that choirs using movable *do* performed better than choirs using fixed *do;* but the fact that the students in the fixed *do* groups had learned movable *do* in elementary school may have affected the results. Roe (1983), in his textbook on choral music education, recommends the use of numbers with high school students and cites the ineffectiveness of movable *do* with twelve-tone rows.

According to Winnick (1987), all the methods have advantages and limitations. Fixed *do*, the system used in the Paris Conservatory, promotes the development of absolute pitch, but it is unsatisfactory for highly chromatic music and must therefore be accompanied by drill in intervallic singing. Movable *do,* as previously noted, is well suited to tonal music but is difficult to use with atonal material. Scale degree numbers, popular in American public schools, function in much the same way as movable *do*. The number system is simpler but less flexible than movable *do*, because it offers no reasonable options for accidentals, modulations, or minor melodies. The intervallic approach, in which the sound of each interval is memorized and "called forth" during music reading, is time-consuming to teach and detracts from the sense of tonality and the overall aesthetic experience of singing.

In sum, no one method is perfect, nor is any method totally without merit. Although most published sources seem to favor relative solmization, the use of any method on a regular, systematic basis is an improvement over the haphazard way in which sight-singing is often approached in the rehearsal.

Just Do It!

In teaching sight-singing, method matters less than determination (Daniels, 1988). Teachers who are persuaded of the importance of sight-singing but are uncertain how to go about it may find ideas in the following summary of strategy tips gleaned from the published literature (Dettwiler, 1989; Middleton 1984; Telfer, 1993). This list is not comprehensive or even necessarily coherent (some suggestions may actually contradict others), and some recommendations are better adapted to choral than to instrumental groups. Not everyone would agree with every item in the list, but even experienced teachers may find a few fresh hints.

- Regardless of method, consistent daily work, even for only a few minutes, is essential.

- Keep sight-singing sessions short (ten minutes or less).
- Include materials with lyrics.
- Identify the tonic and dominant for every example.
- When working with choral groups, change the normal seating arrangement to avoid dependence on fellow singers.
- Be aware that many students can appear to be sight-reading when they are actually imitating—listening and responding almost instantly to another singer's pitch and rhythm.
- Insist on "silent singing" before singing or clapping.
- The creative use of solos, duets, and group or partner work can create variety and encourage independence.
- Use the vocal warm-up to expand the aural experience of the singers (too many vocalises are sung in the major mode).
- Elements for effective warm-up and sight-singing sessions include (1) sound before sight; (2) singing-speaking experiences; (3) tonal solfège; (4) tonal elements separate from rhythmic elements; (5) use of rhythm syllables; (5) use of kinesthetic experiences.
- Tonal patterns based on the church modes are effective in aural training. For better retention at the middle school level, include sight-singing in at least two class meetings per week.
- Practice solfège at the beginning of each rehearsal.
- Exercises done in two parts are more rewarding for singers, but younger students may find two-part material confusing.
- Sight-reading materials can be chosen from literature being rehearsed and/or from sight-reading materials, but careful sequencing and repetition are essential.
- Students should have the reading material in their own hands.
- Use familiar material while introducing small changes; balance the predictable with the unpredictable.
- Try tuning harmonies from the top down; if the chorus is audiating the resting tone, the chord will be easier to hear from the soprano down.
- With instrumental groups, both singing and playing intervals are more effective than either singing or playing alone.
- Encourage students to become involved in other forms of music; instrumental experience benefits choral singing and vice versa.

References

Burton, J. B. (1986). A study to determine the extent to which vocalization is used as an instructional technique in selected public high school, public junior college, and state university band rehearsals: Alabama, Georgia, Louisiana, and Mississippi. *Dissertation Abstracts International, 47* (08), 2937A.

Cappers, R.K. (1985). Sight-singing makes middle school singers into high school musicians. *Music Educators Journal, 72*(2), 45–48.

Colwell, R. (1963). An investigation of musical achievement among vocal students, vocal-instrumental students and instrumental students. *Journal of Research in Music Education, 11,* 123–130.

Daniels, R. D. (1988). Sight-reading instruction in the choral rehearsal. *Update, 6*(4), 22–24.

Demorest, S. M., & May, W. V. (1995). Sight-singing instruction in the choral ensemble: Factors related to individual performance. *Journal of Research in Music Education, 43,* 156–67.

Dettwiler, P. (1989). Developing aural skills through vocal warm-ups: Historical overview of pedagogical approaches and applications for choral directors. *The Choral Journal, 30*(3), 13–20.

Dunlap, M. R. (1989). The effects of singing and solmization training on the musical achievement of beginning fifth-grade instrumental students. *Dissertation Abstracts International, 51* (02), 444A.

Dwiggins, R. R. (1984). Teaching sight-reading in the high school chorus. *Update, 2*(2), 8–11.

Elliott, C. A. (1982). The relationships among instrumental sight-reading ability and seven selected predictor variables. *Journal of Research in Music Education, 30,* 5–14.

Grutzmacher, P. A. (1985). The effect of tonal pattern training on the aural perception, reading recognition and melodic sight reading achievement of first-year instrumental music students. *Dissertation Abstracts International, 46* (05), 1221A.

Harris, B. P. (1991). Comparisons of attained ratings to instructional behaviors and techniques exhibited by band directors in sight-reading performance situations. *Dissertation Abstracts International, 52* (8), 2852A.

Henry, M. L., & Demorest, S. M. (1994). Individual sight-singing achievement in successful choral ensembles. *Update, 13*(1), 4–8.

Jordan, J. M. (1987). The pedagogy of choral intonation: Efficient pedagogy to approach an old problem. *The Choral Journal, 25*(9), 9–16.

Middleton, J. A. (1984). Develop choral reading skills. *Music Educators Journal, 70*(7), 29–32.

More, B. E. (1985). Sight singing and ear training at the university level: A case for the use of Kodály's system of relative solmization. *The Choral Journal, 23*(8), 9–22.

Powell, S. (1991). Choral intonation: More than meets the ear. *Music Educators Journal, 77*(9), 40–43.

Roe, P. F. (1983). *Choral music education.* Englewood Cliffs, NJ: Prentice Hall.

Smith, T. A. (1987). Solmization: A tonic for healthy musicianship. *Choral Journal, 28*(1), 16–23.

Taggart, C. C., & Taggart, B. F. (1994). Sight-singing systems: A survey of American colleges and universities. *Southeastern Journal of Music Education, 6,* 194–209.

Telfer, N. (1993). Sight-singing in the choral rehearsal. *The Choral Journal, 34*(1), 39–40.

Winnick, W. (1987). Hybrid methods in sight-singing. *The Choral Journal, 28*(1), 24–30.

Georgia teachers say …

In practice, method counts less than motivation and consistency. Every successful teacher has a strategy that works for him or her, and no two are quite alike. Here's what some think:

Dan Lane

We have all been there, and few of us liked it! We have survived and vowed that we will do a better job with it next year. We have all blamed the key, or the tessitura, or the harmonic progression when

vocal warm-ups (this is where the students learn to sing!); 10–15 minutes of sight-reading work, where specific sight-reading techniques are taught; and 20–30 minutes of literature work.

During the physical and vocal warm-up, I progress from the simple to the complex, using a variety of vocalises to facilitate vocal development. I also plant seeds here for aural development, necessary for a successful sight-reading experience. As part of this warm-up, we always sing a major, minor, and chromatic scale and do various number interval exercises. See figure 1.

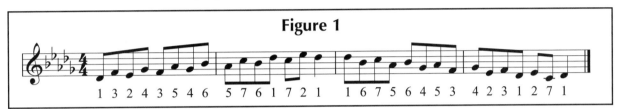

Figure 1

1 3 2 4 3 5 4 6   5 7 6 1 7 2 1   1 6 7 5 6 4 5 3   4 2 3 1 2 7 1

our students did not perform as well as we thought they could.

Festival sight-reading. What is it about this fifteen minutes of the year that causes so much dread and concern for so many teachers? Is it uncertainty about what the rules allow and what is taboo? Is it lack of preparation on our part? Is it the fear of the unknown obstacles lying in wait for us in that ominous sight-reading book? Is it all of the above?

Many years of participation in festivals and several years of judging sight-reading have given me a chance to observe many teachers coaching their groups during the allotted five minutes of preparation time. The most successful seem to have two things in common: they have obviously invested a great deal of time before the event, and they have a well-tuned method to use in the sight-reading room. These actually go hand in hand.

Though I do not claim to be an expert in the teaching of sight-reading, my students and I have enjoyed quite a bit of success in the choral sight-reading room. I am happy to share with you what I do to prepare my students for a successful sight-reading experience at festival.

The Sight-Reading Routine. I include sight-reading in the rehearsal every day beginning with the first day of school, so that by festival time the students are very comfortable with sight-reading. Also, my sight-reading methods are carried over into all rehearsal activities, so that my students see the connection between sight-reading and vocal development and literature. Sight-reading is not something we do to be successful at festival; it is something we do to be successful as choral musicians. A typical rehearsal consists of 15–20 minutes of physical and

These kinds of exercises are repeated daily to train the ear (and actually the brain) to hear and be able to recall the sound of specific intervals.

Next, I move on to teaching specific concepts that the singers can use when sight-reading a new piece. There are quite a few decent sight-reading method books, but I have found the best sight-reading examples for my classes are the ones I create myself. Nobody knows the strengths and weaknesses of your choir better than you—so who better to write examples to provide remediation for your choir than you? (When writing examples, do not be afraid of giving the eighth note the beat, especially in compound meter. If students can read simple meter solidly, they will catch on to this very easily.)

Typically, through the first three weeks of October, I write three unison sight-reading examples each day using the *GMEA Handbook* criteria for All-State auditions. When we approach a new line, we discuss challenging intervals or rhythms and analyze the key, identifying the starting and ending pitch numbers. We then set up the tonality by singing the tonic pitch, singing up the scale (major or minor, depending on the example) to the highest pitch in the example, back down the scale to the tonic, and then down the scale to the lowest pitch in the example and back up to the tonic. We then sing the arpeggio, and then the students sing their starting pitch. I then allow them 45 seconds or so to study the example aloud independently. It sounds somewhat like an orchestra warming up!

After the study time, I play the tonic triad and the starting pitch again, and the students then sing the example. I use a slow tempo (about quarter note = 50) to allow time for the brain to process all of this information, and I keep an auditory (snapped) steady beat so that the students feel the pulse of the beat. After they sing, we go back over places that could have been better and sing the example again until they are successful. The entire procedure is repeated for each example. This takes quite a bit of time when it is first introduced, but in the long run it saves time, because the choir learns literature much faster with these newly acquired skills.

Toward the end of October, I move to part sight-reading using examples from past GMEA sight-reading books (GMEA sells the previous year's book at All-State—it is a great resource), from old hymn books that have been donated by local churches, or from examples I have written myself.

The method I use for part sight-reading is basically the same as unison, with minor changes. The procedure I use in class is exactly the same that I use in the sight-reading room on the day of festival. Since we only have five minutes preparation time in the festival sight-reading room, I try to stick within those parameters in class, especially as festival time draws closer.

When we approach a new piece at this stage, we first identify the key and the individual starting pitch for each voice part. The students then have about 30–40 seconds to study their lines silently. (Notice that I have not yet established the tonality.) During this time, they are to analyze the example, first vertically (key changes, homophonic vs. polyphonic rhythms, places of unison, places of dissonance, dynamics, etc.), then horizontally (rhythmic problems, challenging intervals, places in other parts that will help their part, etc.) We then spend about 30 seconds singing the tonic pitch, analyzing and singing up the scale to the highest pitch in the example, back to the tonic, on down to the lowest pitch in the example, and back up to the tonic. If it is appropriate for the example, we then will sing arpeggios or any of the number exercises that we have rehearsed in class. Each section then sings its individual starting pitch, and the students rehearse independently for two or three minutes. (In the sight-reading room I seat the sections separately.) Meanwhile, I circulate from section to section and briefly discuss the *horizontal* problems they found in their individual line. When time is up, I play the tonic triad, and each voice sings their individual starting pitch again. We then say a quick prayer (just kidding), and sing the example a cappella rather slowly.

Again, we analyze the problems and continue to work the example until we are successful.

And on to Literature. After sight-reading we move to literature work, but we definitely do not leave sight-reading behind. Every piece we sing is introduced using our sight-reading method. One thing I really detest is teaching notes and rhythms, so I try to make that the students' responsibility as great as possible. Every section in every choir has a section leader whose job it is to rehearse notes and rhythms.

Before introducing a new piece, I decide on the smaller focus of the day (for example, pages 1–3). Because the rhythms in the literature are often more complex than the sight-reading examples, we begin by speaking the text of the piece in rhythm. If the piece is homophonic, everyone speaks his/her own rhythm simultaneously. If it is polyphonic, everyone speaks the bass rhythm, then the tenor, and so on. This keeps everyone involved and gives everyone more practice in recognizing various rhythmic patterns. After we have established the rhythm, we set up the tonality and individual starting pitches as we did during sight-reading. The sections then separate to learn the pitches and rhythms (on pitch numbers) of the day's focus. (After initially "speaking the text," we use just numbers until the pitches and rhythms are solid, adding the text only when I feel that it won't "throw" the singers.)

When reading literature that is not diatonic, we call any altered tone a half step above the diatonic pitch "sharp" and any pitch a half step below the diatonic pitch "flat," no matter how it is marked (e.g., in the key of C minor, we call the B-natural leading tone "sharp" because it is a half step higher than the diatonic B-flat). If the key signature does not indicate the actual key of the section, it is necessary to give the choir that information (pointing out that the section is in D major, for example, even though the key signature denotes G major). Adjust the numbering accordingly. The accidental C-sharps would be called "7" instead of "sharp." We adjust so that the aural intervals they have learned (5-7, 2-7, etc.) remain constant. For the same reason, I always base minor sections on 6, so that aural intervals remain constant.

As the sections rehearse separately, I circulate from group to group, helping with any problems that arise. Everyone in the class is involved at the same time. I am simply a facilitator; the students are actually learning on their own. Again, the classroom sounds like an orchestra warming up, but the singers are used to this sound and are quite capable of tuning out the work of the other parts. After about 10 minutes, we come back together as a group and sing our parts simultaneously.

Usually (and sometimes surprisingly) it works! The singers have learned the pitches and rhythms of that section, and no one has had to sit idle while I plunked out notes on the piano or taught one section at a time. Furthermore, choirs trained in this way sing better in tune, because their aural skills assist them in proper placement of pitch intonation. The students find class much more interesting, and I have fewer discipline problems because they stay actively involved and truly have ownership in what they are learning. And yes, the younger classes are just as successful as the more advanced classes. I simply spend a bit more time teaching sight-reading concepts to the younger groups.

By the time we get to festival, sight-reading is second nature to my students, and it causes them very little anxiety. The choir is a well-tuned machine ready to tackle any sight-reading example, because we have had numerous "dry runs" in class. In fact, the students enjoy "showing off" and love to encounter challenging examples!

Follow exactly the same procedure in the sight-reading room as you do in the classroom; students perform better if they are comfortable with the procedure. And do not be apprehensive about "the rules." Nothing in the procedure I have explained violates any festival guidelines. A good rule of thumb is that you can *say* anything, but you can *demonstrate* nothing. If you follow a plan such as this, you will not need to demonstrate. The students will know what to expect, they will be well equipped to handle the situation, and your blood pressure will stay thirty points lower.

Judy Spears

Students must feel the pulse and duration of rhythm in their large muscles before they can begin to understand rhythm in the abstract. Therefore, we begin with familiar body movement before we ever discuss actual notation or counting. The chart below provides an example in 4/4 time.

You may wonder about the visual distinction between half and whole rests. First, you tell a story about these two gentlemen long ago in London who dressed in top hats. One of them, upon meeting a lady, would merely lift his hat and say, "Howdy, ma'am." The other would bow from the waist, sweeping his hat from his head to acknowledge the lady. Therefore, his hat would be turned upside down. Obviously, anyone could distinguish the half gentleman from the whole gentleman. Of course, students must make all the right moves with their pretend top hats as they read the half and whole rest.

This made-up "movement" system works very effectively with all ages (See figure 2.). The element of playfulness is entertaining, so the students enter into the spirit of the "game" without realizing at first how quickly they are learning the fundamentals of rhythm reading. My freshmen "tell their feet what to do" in reading the rhythms of the actual literature they are going to perform for the entire first semester. (I never use separate sight-reading simultaneously. We always read rhythm first before considering pitch, since the right pitch in the wrong place becomes a wrong pitch.)

Syncopation is taught as "hip notes," so your imagination can certainly conjure up how that looks in action. This builds in crisp accents and feels very natural. We would say "hip note and" for an eighth-quarter-eighth pattern, a very common-

Figure 2		
Symbol	**Motion**	**Verbal Response**
quarter note	walk in place	walk
eighth note	run in place	run-run
half note	side step and close	giant step
whole note	side step and drag to close on 2-3-4	split-2-3-4
dotted half note	side step/close and tap toe	giant step dot
dotted quarter	side step/close and	
followed by eighth	side step back (last motion quickly)	walk dot and
quarter rest	kick	shh
eighth rest	quick breath	(sound of audible breath)
half rest	lift hat	howdy ma'am
whole rest	bow from waist (rest-2) and return	rest-2-3-4
	to upright position, placing hat	
	back on head (3-4)	

ly encountered syncopation. Actually, what words you choose to say for any rhythm are not as important as the physical sensation of moving. I do find the students are much more successful when they speak in combination with movement. Feel free to use your imagination and create a "movement" reading system that works for you and your students. Students love the sense of musical independence when they realize they can read music for themselves.

Joyce Edwards

I favor the solfège system in combination with the Curwen hand signs. I find the additional practice on the pure vowel sounds helps me spend less time on diction when I get to the text of the literature. We sing scales daily in combination with the hand signs. I find the hand signs particularly useful in drilling harmonic intervals. We call it "two-handed singing." We play games where I assign part of the class to each hand. If I see difficult intervals or chord progressions in the sight-singing example, I use the hand signs to practice them. All kinds of shifting harmonies can be practiced in this way with no time spent with *Finale* or the photocopier. I find that "two-handed singing" improves the intonation of the group. The students also enjoy inventing or improvising harmonic drills and leading the practice session.

Kenya Snider

One of my favorite drill routines is:
- Discuss the rhythm with the students.
- Snap the beat and have students tap the rhythm on their knee (no sound, but I can "see" if they are thinking the rhythm correctly).
- Discuss the pitches within the given key, locating those intervals that may cause difficulty.
- Establish the key by *singing* the scale and tonic, subdominant, and dominant triads.
- Using finger signs, briefly drill the difficult intervals.
- Ask the students to audiate their parts on numbers—showing the finger signs (in rhythm) as they mentally read. This process allows me to monitor their thinking and assess their progress as they study.
- Finally, sing the parts aloud on numbers with correct rhythm.

Mary Busman

To help establish tonal vocabulary, I have the students memorize many canons on solfeggio so that intervals will come easily to them. I also use osti-

nato patterns whenever I can to help the students remember intervals and tonal patterns. The repetition is most helpful and the music-making that results is lots of fun. The students also use the Curwen hand signs when singing scales and drill patterns. I try to present sight-reading problems sequentially—never asking them to "read" sounds they don't "have established in their heads" from past musical experiences (this explains memorizing the host of canons). I believe firmly in having students succeed at each step so that they don't fear sight-singing.

Doug Looney

Motivation is not a problem. Students actually learn to love sight-singing when they are successful. They will be successful only if it's a part of every single rehearsal. In the fall, I concentrate on solo material (in preparation for All-State auditions) and give students a chance to sight-read individually in class. This helps them get over being nervous.

For materials, I use actual sight-reading examples I have collected for the last six or eight years from the first round of All-State auditions. I use the computer to transpose and create some variety.

After All-State, we begin to read from the sight-singing booklets that I have bought at All-State. We read anything from one-line M-class to SATB or SSA, and the students switch parts constantly. I also have many of the selections in the computer so I can transpose or rearrange the parts.

Susan Cotton

I find that the "buddy system" works well, especially in groups like the Metropolitan Atlanta Young Singers, which includes members in early elementary school though middle school. The older students find it a challenge to be teamed as "teacher" with a younger member. After I have discussed the challenges of the example and established the key, I let the older members of each team take over the rehearsal phase—the time used to practice rhythm and melody aloud. Then we all sing the selection together. The "buddy system" keeps the older members from being bored with the easier examples used to teach the younger singers; and the younger members are challenged by figuring out the more difficult examples with their older "buddies."

Eva Jameson

We use the foot-tapping system for learning to read rhythms (each beat is a down-up motion) and numbers to aid in reading pitches. Interval drills are done by simply showing the numbers by finger signs (just as hand signs are used in the Curwen/solfège system). We sing the major scale from 1 to 1; the minor from 6 to 6. Arpeggios and chord progression drills are part of every warm-up (i.e., 1-3-5-6-4-2-7-1, etc.).

Grace Muzzo is a member of the Music Education Department at West Chester University in West Chester, Pennsylvania. Joni Hunnicutt taught choral music in public schools in the Atlanta, Georgia, metropolitan area for 20 years. She began teaching at Suder Elementary School in Jonesboro, Georgia, in Fall 2002. Dawn McCord is director of music at Friendship Presbyterian Church in Athens, Georgia. Dan Lane teaches choral music at Starr's Mill High School in Fayetteville, Georgia. Judy Spears teaches chorus at Dacula High School in Dacula, Georgia. Joyce Edwards teaches music at Parkview High School in Lilburn, Georgia. Kenya Snider teaches vocal music at Daniels Middle School in Raleigh, North Carolina. Mary Busman teaches music at Northwestern Middle School in Alpharetta, Georgia. Now retired from teaching, Doug Looney was choral director at North Gwinnett High School in Suwanee, Georgia, for 13 years. He also taught band at the middle and high school levels, directed the Gwinnett County Civic Chorus, and served as a church music director. Susan Cotton taught music in Georgia. Eva Jameson is retired after 32 years of teaching music. This article originally appeared in the Fall 1999 issue of Georgia Music News. *Reprinted by permission.*

Twelve Habits of Highly Effective Choral Music Educators

Michael Nuss

Are you an *effective* choral music educator? Would you consider yourself to be a *highly effective* choral music educator? How many days do you wander home after work, dragging your battered dreams of effectiveness behind you?

No matter what the setting—church, school, college, community—*every* choir director is a choral educator. An ecology of *effectiveness* in teaching and learning must be cultivated between director and singer. This ecology must include respect, love, and encouragement.

Criss-crossing America to conduct festival choirs, present workshops, and teach in-school residencies, it is my great privilege to encounter *highly effective* choral music educators at all levels—elementary, middle, secondary, and collegiate. Their rehearsals ignite the quest for beauty in their singers and, once ignited, these singers trek forth on an intrepid odyssey that will define and enrich their life experiences.

Habits—daily, consistent patterns of action—define our effectiveness as choral music educators. Aristotle said, "We are what we repeatedly do. Excellence, then, is not an act, but a habit." Forming the intersection of knowledge, skill and desire, habits—whether conscious or subconscious—produces our effectiveness. But there are no magic powders, super tricks, or miracle cures. Professionalism in any field is not achieved without enormous personal effort, extraordinary dedi-

cation, and exceptional ability.

You are invited to take a moment to review your own rehearsal habits. Let down your walls and stand naked in front of the glaring honest mirror of self-inventory. Are your habits effective or ineffective?

Extensive personal experience, probing analysis and research, and thoughtful observation have shown me that *highly effective* choral music educators embrace the following twelve habits in some way, shape, or form on a daily basis in an extremely consistent manner.

1. Focus on artistry. Every human being possesses the ability to create beauty, experience beauty, and share beauty. It is this artistic endowment that defines our personhood, develops our individual capacity to feel and imagine, and unlocks our urge for self-expression. Individual artistic potential is awakened and developed through active participation in the creating, experiencing, and sharing of art. A constant, intentional involvement in artistic experience dramatically increases one's artistic facility, enabling the nuance of art to unfold and become meaningful. An absolute focus on artistry provides a rich, exhilarating milieu in which artistic endeavor will flourish, artistic skill will increase, and artistic production will multiply in both quantity and quality. Peripheral concerns will mount powerful assaults on your attention, but if want your choir to sing artistically, *artistry* must be your focus at all times.

2. Specialize in sound. Train yourself and your singers to be specialists in sound. Sound is music's raw material. Each singer must be able to break the "sound barrier" and produce vocal sound from within their own body. Once the sound is produced there are a number of protocols which dictate the soundshaping that will define each choir's "soundprint." Barring physiological impairment, all human beings *can* phonate—but successfully shaping that phonation to create the sounds needed for artistic singing is quite another skill indeed. An intense awareness of one's sound—how it is produced, how it is shaped once produced, how it is managed and monitored—is a critical ingredient of artistic choral achievement. The avalanche of sound we are bombarded with daily has a desensitizing effect on most people. It is this lack of sound sensitivity that creates our greatest obstacles to choral artistry. For example, poor pitch-matching skill is *rarely* physiological. More often than not, singers who lack ability in pitch-matching have a deficit in "soundscape experience." Their ability to aurally focus is lying dormant within them, falling into disrepair from lack of use. Transform your singers into sound specialists with a focus on sound, realizing that your aural acuity will dictate the specific levels of artistic achievement the choirs under your direction will attain.

3. Never stop learning about the vocal instrument. For its size, the larynx is the most complex and versatile mechanical device in the human body and—in addition to its biological behaviors—is the instrument of speech and song. In order to create an artistically successful choral ensemble, directors must possess an extensive, sophisticated knowledge of laryngeal biomechanics (how the voice works) and healthful voice use. Pop music provides few models for healthful voice use, but our singers are powerfully influenced by these ubiquitous vocal models. Additionally, myth and legend permeate much of the vocal pedagogy employed by many choral directors, and several extant choral methods books are actually anatomically incorrect! It is no small wonder, then, that a great deal of confusion and mystery continues to surround the care and use of the vocal instrument. Your understanding and knowledge of the vocal instrument must be more than a passing acquaintance with laryngeal anatomy. If your background and training were bereft of specific, extensive information and experience in this critically important area, seize the opportunity to participate in one of the several exceptional summer voice study programs available in America today. You simply cannot presume to be an effective choral music educator if you are standing in front of seventy-five vocal instruments you know little or nothing about.

4. Listen to your choir. You must listen to your choir at *all* times during your rehearsals and performances. You can't listen if you are talking, singing, playing the piano, taking roll, or doing one single thing other than just listening and focusing on what you hear! You'll be amazed at how your ears will improve once you begin to listen to your choir. And once you hear your choir, you might be surprised by how good (or bad) it really is. But how can you possibly know what work needs to be done, monitor individual vocal instruments, and give corrective feedback if you are not listening to your choir?

5. Rehearse without piano. For choral purposes, the piano is a percussion instrument. It has few properties in common with the vocal instrument, it is an extremely poor tone model for the voice, and it is rarely in tune or voiced properly. Drilling with the piano will not make your singers more self-reliant, improve their tone and intonation, reinforce shaky entrances, or teach them how to sustain sound. In short, there are no advantages to using the piano in rehearsal, even though the perception of advantage persists. Piano use is misleading. It may appear that using the piano during rehearsal—especially with less skilled choirs—facilitates vocal learning and understanding. However, in truth, using the piano simply sustains whatever musical and vocal weaknesses the singers manifest, while actually increasing dependency! After the singers are able to sing with artistic confidence, the parts are learned, and the ensemble understands the basics of choral tone, add the piano whenever you like, but do not deceive yourself into believing that the piano models choral singing, facilitates speedy part-learning, reinforces intonation, enhances vocal skill acquisition, or cultivates artistic choral singing.

6. Eliminate interferences. No matter what amount of time is allocated for your choir rehearsals, you can make much better use of the time you do have if you eliminate *all* unnecessary interferences. Mandated interferences cannot be avoided, but singer-generated and director-generated interferences can. Interferences wear many guises and include unprepared/unfocused directors; inefficient organizational structures; lack of formalized rehearsal routine; and poor rehearsal tenacity on the part of the choir, the director, or both. An elimination of interferences also reinforces your focus on artistry and the specialization in sound.

7. Use invitational language. Singers are human beings and the vocal instrument is flesh and blood. The specific language you use in rehearsal directly impacts the neuro-messages our singers send through their bodies and those messages directly impact their sound, their attitude, their motivation, and their artistry. Do your words *invite* your singers to join you on a quest for beauty or do they simply criticize? Do your words send out "you can do it!" messages or "you'll never get it" messages? Do your words make your singers feel better for making the effort, or regret they even tried? Does your language invite, inspire, and instruct or does it intimidate, inhibit, and insult? Your words are powerful conduits for the experience your singers trust you will provide. Wield that power with awe and respect, always *inviting*.

8. Be consistent. You must model the professionalism you expect from your singers. An integral component of professionalism is consistency. Have you ever sung under a director who drove you like wild horses when he was in the mood to get something accomplished (or in a panic to get something ready for a performance) and then, basically, goofed around at other times? It is very difficult for singers to understand this erratic behavior! It effectively sabotages any good work that is getting accomplished. Although a certain yin and yang needs to be fostered within the rehearsal ecology, your focus on artistry, leadership, and expectations must be consistent. Your own artistic passion must also be consistent. Remember, you are the professional music educator in the room—your students have every right to expect that you will be giving 100 percent at all times, in all situations, and under any conditions. This bedrock of dependability will be the stabilizing force that allows your choir to weather any storm it may encounter, and enable it to grow without self-imposed limits.

9. Maintain a nurturant culture. In the biological sense, a culture is a "place for growing." Your rehearsal is a culture, too. It is a culture for growing minds, spirits, and artistic sensibilities. The direction this growth takes is powerfully influenced by the opportunities, learning episodes, and fields of context created by the director. A nurturant culture is one in which the singers feel safe to take personal risks. These personal risks sow the seeds of artistic stretching, growth, and self-actualization. If your singers feel "safe" to wonder, to discover, and to experience, they will become ignited with the flame of artistic self-expression.

The highly effective choral director is an *encourager*. The only enemy to personal growth is fear, and the antidote to fear is courage. The key goal of encouragement is to stimulate this inner courage. An encourager *enables* rather than *disables*. In a nurturant culture, corrective feedback is phrased in an enabling manner, specific director behaviors are invitational rather than confrontational, and an ecology of encouragement is fostered at all times.

10. Develop metacognitive singers. The ability of knowing, understanding, and taking charge of how you learn and think is called metacognition. The metacognitive singer is self-directed, self-accountable, self-monitoring, and self-motivating. Once a director has given every singer the skills necessary to be metacognitive (and there are *many* skills that must be taught), an atmosphere of high expectations can be effectively embraced, and the choir will actually become an instrument of art.

11. Use effective rehearsal strategies. Every choral music educator has at their disposal a veritable cornucopia of highly effective rehearsal strategies. These time-proven strategies are well-documented, accessible, and easy-to-find (books, colleagues, workshops, journals, professional materials). In his book, *The Seven Habits of Highly Effective People,* Stephen Covey describes a natural principle he calls the P/PC balance. Effectiveness lies in the balance between production (P) and production capability (PC). In the choral setting, directors must maintain this balance in order to achieve effectiveness. For example, thirty minutes of "warm-ups" during a fifty-minute rehearsal is an out-of-balance focus on PC—production capability—and mindless "drilling" on parts without teaching an understanding of pitch and sight-singing is an ineffective focus on production (P). It is imperative that directors understand the importance of the P/PC balance and successfully implement this balance into their rehearsal strategy.

12. Work hard. Education is, perhaps, the most important endeavor on the planet. It holds the key to the future by opening the doors of self-discovery and personal achievement. Choral music educators have the tremendous privilege of being involved with the artistic development of people of all ages. In many ways, this artistic development charts the course and defines the parameters of one's life. It is the ability to express and value that sets the human species apart from all others, and music education's prime directive is to develop every person's natural responsiveness to the power of the art of music. Although artistic sensitivity is a natural phenomenon within each person, developing it in productive ways is certainly not an easy task. As music education professionals, we must work very hard to instill the necessary attitudes and teach the requisite skills needed to effectively access the urges of self-expression that lie deep within each person. Your professional work ethic must include a never-ending quest for knowledge, a con-

tinuing exposure to deeper levels of understanding, and a dedication to effective personal effort.

Michael Nuss is the founder and president of The Arts America Foundation which has developed and produced arts events throughout the world. This article originally appeared in the March 2001 issue of The Tennessee Musician. *Reprinted by permission.*

Sight-reading—A Joy!
Steve Peter

Okay, how do we motivate our students/ singers to become more musically articulate? Or should I ask "Why bother?"

To the "why bother?" my most immediate response would be to pass on the sheer "skill" of it. As singers in choral rehearsals or reading sessions, many of us know the wonderful feeling of being one of the true sight-readers within a section. If you've ever felt the sense of pride at being one of the few singers who nails the unexpected interval, reads that pesky 3/8 rhythm that came out of nowhere, or knew when to come back in after that long accompanied passage, then you know the fun of being recognized for being a skilled sight-reader.

There's the sense of accomplishment that begins to permeate throughout your group when your singers realize that they are beginning to internally "hear" the music before the notes are played or sung for them. Sight-reading is an acquired high-level skill that is most often attained through guided study, consistent teaching, and drill.

When Gary St. John asked if I would share some of my insights with the OMEA readership, he specifically asked that I address the sight-reading session of a league festival or of the State Choir Championships. Having adjudicated at numerous area league festivals as the sight-reading judge, I have developed a fairly standard "line" which seems to work well for me, and for the choirs I work with.

In short, I tell the students and directors that there is little if any science at play when it comes to sight-reading in a pressure situation, but that if they can keep the following elements in mind during the process, they likely will do a bit better as a group: Trust, Attitude, Luck, and Love—or TALL.

TRUST their director, their section, and their overall collective musical intuition to provide the

choir with its very best effort. In most cases, the directors will benefit from a calm group of singers who truly strive to realize the dots on the page in the most musical way they can within this highly charged and often awkward environment.

ATTITUDE is everything! Walk into the sight-reading room with a "can do" mind-set. Realize that every other choir has or will be experiencing the same pressures, and that by being positive and relaxed in the setting, everyone will have a greater chance to do their best work. This is especially true for sopranos who often bear greater "blame" for sight-reading inadequacies since that's the voice part that many of us adjudicators listen for first.

LUCK figures into the equation in all cases. All of us know that our own individual sight-reading skills have been honed through years of singing countless wrong notes and rhythms (and hopefully a few correct ones, too), but most of us still sing! Remind your singers that they ALL read, some may read more consistently than others, but any team needs 100 percent from all the players to do its absolute best. If your section leaders fail to assert themselves for fear of making errors, then you're likely to produce a disappointingly small sound. Not only do your leaders need to push their luck, but everyone needs to "give their all." Remember you've only got one shot. After you've gone through the example once, it's no longer sight-reading—it's rehearsing. Try your luck the first time through.

LOVE is the most important element of all, and this is for the director as well as your singers. The love of this time-honored art form (choral music) is what has placed you and your choir in this situation, so why not let your love of a profession that allows us to produce "art" for a living propel the collective whole to the next level? Take pride in knowing that you and your singers have arrived at this unique moment from completely different angles, and yet you both need each other to realize the moment's true potential. Enjoy each other's accomplishments, and the fact that you're all in it together—what a joy, sharing the choral art with young people who will hopefully be sharing it with others throughout their own lives!

If you share these thoughts with your students prior to a league sight-reading opportunity, they'll probably appreciate having the tangible acronym (TALL) to walk out of the sight-reading room with. It seems to provide them with an extra confidence for their State Choir experience, and, in all frankness, it's not too bad for us directors to keep it and its lessons in mind too.

Best of luck, and SING ON!

Steve Peter teaches music at Cleveland High School in Portland, Oregon. This article originally appeared in the Spring 1997 issue of the Oregon Music Educator. *Reprinted by permission.*

Teaching Tips
Warm-up Tips
Lynn Talbot

This tip is for high school level choirs.

Lynn writes: Although our elementary schools are not totally Kodály based, we use a lot of syllables and hand signing every day in our high school choirs.

All of our students learn to sign the scale and can read and sing syllables with moveable *do*.

I always take a scale chart with me to rehearsals to reinforce the visual and aural aspects of the scale, and we sing many combinations of the scale during each semester.

Some of the student favorites are:

do/do-re-do/do-re-mi-re-do, etc.
do-re-mi/re-mi-fa/mi-fa-sol, etc.
do-mi/re-fa/mi-sol/fa-la, etc.
Sing *do*—hear in your head up to *do*—Add one, etc.
Sing one out loud, hear one, sing one, hear one.

These all work very well as rounds and are great ear-training experiences.

Design Vocal Warm-ups for Specific Choral Works
Peggy D. Dettwiler

This tip is for choral music at any level.

Much can be done within the choral rehearsal to develop the vocal and aural skills of each singer, thereby improving the tone quality and intonation of the entire ensemble. In fact, the choral rehearsal may be the only place where such training takes place, since many choral singers seldom take private voice lessons. Teach voice during your choral warm-up and design the warm-ups so that they relate to the music that will be rehearsed that day. Design your vocalises according to this six-step sequential approach to prepare the singer for the style, mood, key, and technical difficulties of the specific choral work:

1. Start with physical movement for relaxation and stimulation.
2. Incorporate exercises to establish good posture and breathing. Speak consonants using rhythm patterns found in the music.
3. Begin singing by vocalizing with five-tone descending scales or triads in the middle to upper range to encourage head-voice resonance, pure vowels, and blend.
4. Increase the intensity and vitality of the vocalises with dynamic contrasts, faster tempo, and animated facial expression.
5. Develop a vocal technique by expanding the range of the exercises and including stylistic concepts from the music.
6. Vocalize in the mode of the music (major, minor, Dorian, etc.) to establish the tonal center of the music to be rehearsed.

Lynn Talbot teaches music at Stroudsburg High School in Stroudsburg, Pennsylvania. Peggy D. Dettwiler is director of choral activities and professor of music education at Mansfield University in Mansfield, Pennsylvania. This article originally appeared in the Fall 1999 issue of Pennsylvania's PMEA News. *Reprinted by permission.*

Section 2

Selecting Repertoire

The repertoire that you choose for your choirs can be one of the most important decisions you make. Those decisions help keep your program running and your students engaged. This section offers a variety of viewpoints on what makes good literature, what kinds of literature children should sing, and what to consider about specialty literature.

 Section 2

Selecting Repertoire

Selecting Quality Choral Literature in the High School Setting
Angela L. Batey

What music you choose speaks volumes about you as a musician and music educator. The music is the very essence of the choral curriculum. The choice of literature may very well affect many other aspects of the choral program. It is imperative that decisions regarding literature be made with considerable thought. Unsuitable choices will be made unless there is careful attention to such contributing components as ability level, size of the choir, singers' ages, and ranges.

Choosing quality literature is an enormous test of a musician's abilities as well as a time-consuming task. Teachers are bombarded at every turn with free music at reading sessions and samplers from many publishers, complete with compact disc or cassette recordings and perusal copies. There is a great temptation to take the short cuts so conveniently offered to us. How easy it would be to select music by just looking at the beautiful colors and eye-catching designs on the covers! But we should all beware—all that glitters is definitely NOT gold. Those same irresistible covers may hold within them music that is trite or texts that have little or no depth.

The quality of literature chosen by each and every one of us has a direct impact not only on the quality of the students' education but also on the quality of music that is and will be composed and published. We must accept this tremendous responsibility and choose choral literature that is worthy of intellectual scrutiny in both rehearsal and performance and that will enhance students' musical education. Just as a child should not be fed a sweets-only diet—we should not feed our students only popular OR classical music!

Students should be better singers and certainly more intelligent musicians as a direct consequence

of rehearsing the chosen repertoire. One of the first questions that should be asked when considering any given piece of music for the curriculum is: "What will the students gain from exposure to this piece?" Several selections that stretch their skills should be included in each concert. Singers will respond favorably to a challenge put in a positive perspective, but can be stymied by too many. A good balance for any given curriculum is a majority of music at or just beyond their level, several selections that are more advanced, and several that can be refined rather easily. Clausen's "All That Hath Life and Breath" and Starer's "Give Thanks unto the Lord" are two excellent twentieth-century pieces that will challenge most high school choral musicians. Moses Hogan's simple spiritual "God's Gonna Set This World on Fire" can be taught and polished in a matter of minutes, while still giving the singers a satisfying musical experience.

You will most likely be the person governing your singers' experiences in choral music. It is crucial for you to consider their complete musical education and give them the "whole picture," not just music from one or two genres. Over two, three, or even four years in choir, students should have the chance to study, rehearse, and perform a balanced repertoire indicative of the immense legacy that choral music affords.

Diversity in the music curriculum is a worthy objective and can be accomplished by choosing choral literature from different periods that illustrate and exemplify a variety of musical techniques and textures. Music from the various eras of music history as well as spirituals, Broadway musicals, vocal jazz, and ethnic music should be present in the curriculum. Languages other than English should be studied. There should be a balance between a cappella and accompanied, sacred and secular, and serious and light pieces. Instrumental accompaniments other than piano should be used. Students should become acquainted with music appropriate for small ensembles in addition to larger master works. Consider combining all choirs at a concert to perform a work accompanied by orchestra. School choirs may be the only opportunity for some students to participate in such a special occasion. Activities similar to these will build esprit de corps. A unified spirit often becomes a musical benefit to the entire choral program.

Renaissance madrigals can be introduced into the curriculum with Adriano Banchieri's hilarious "Counterpoint of the Animals." To acquaint students with the late Renaissance period, consider Jacob Handl's "En ego campana," a spirited look at the function of church bells in the society of that time. An interesting twist on the music of Johann Sebastian Bach is Ward Swingle's very tongue-in-cheek arrangement, "Bourrée for Bach." David Brunner's arrangement of "Swing Low, Sweet Chariot" is an exciting new look at the genre of spirituals. Seasonal music of France (Richard Donovan's arrangement of "Jacques Come Here"); America (Charles Ives' "A Christmas Carol"); and England (William Walton's "All This Time") make for superb holiday programming. And certainly don't forget the lighter side: Gordon Langford's arrangement of "Jingle Bells" and Walter Ehret's side-splitting "The Sow Took the Measles" are both quality choral diversions. It is important to select music for the curriculum about which you are excited. After all, you will be the one rehearsing it for untold hours! A large dose of enthusiasm is sometimes required to convince choir members of the value of any given piece of music literature. At times you will have to remain resolute. Imagine conjuring up a persuasive argument when you aren't sold on the piece yourself. Students will perceive your absence of dedication to the music in question and will react accordingly. Strive always to expand your comfort zone to embody a diversity of styles, historical eras, and composers.

The introduction of new literature is probably the most critical point in a rehearsal. How you first present a piece to the choir and how they receive it will affect the rest of the rehearsal as well as how they will work on that piece. This is the time that you must sell the piece! At times, students will not respond in a positive manner to a selection even when you are rehearsing it with considerable fervor. If this does indeed happen, it becomes very tempting to simply put the piece aside. The choir is then in the position of selecting the repertoire for the curriculum.

You are the one with the knowledge and experience necessary to make these very significant decisions. If you know, beyond the shadow of a doubt, the piece in question is quality literature, do not be reticent in your defense. On the other hand, if you have made a mistake in selection do not be afraid to remove it from the curriculum.

When choosing literature, you must consider carefully the text and the composer's setting of it. This is perhaps the most important issue for many choral conductors. A majority of choral literature that is printed and purchased today is full of trite, meaningless texts. Quality choral music uses texts that have value as poetry and are full of significance. It must also appeal to the age level of the choir. Always be aware of any guidelines that the school system may have concerning use of religious texts and literature. After considering the value of the text itself, observe the composer's setting of it, including any word painting or stress. If the literature in question is a translation, check to be sure the meaning of the words is true to the original.

Literature that is chosen must be appropriate for the technical level of the singers. Select music that will permit the students' instrument to grow naturally, without pushing the voice. Literature that uses extremes in dynamics and ranges for extended periods is best avoided unless the students are vocally mature enough to handle such demands. Ensembles that are small generally have a lighter, clearer timbre. The Verdi Requiem would not be a good choice for this group!

Choirs can achieve their optimal sound when literature falls within the tessitural boundaries of the singers. Although this is an obvious statement, most pieces do not fit those boundaries. When notes go beyond that spectrum, observe such items as vowels used in the extremities of ranges, how the extremes are approached, dynamics and duration of those notes, and how they are supported (or not) in the texture.

Choose pieces that are not impossibly beyond a student accompanist's level. To do so is inexcusable. By the same token, do not select a piece of music simply to be able to say your choir has sung it. That is an utter disservice to students and smacks of egomania. With arrangements, particularly those of popular music, observe whether it reflects the original's intent. Be careful of transcriptions from one voicing to another. Imagine "Brothers, Sing On" in SSA!

Be sure to keep the audience in mind when selecting repertoire. Programming goes hand in hand with literature choices. Often a subject neglected when choosing literature and designing the flow of concerts, this is what will sometimes "make or break" support you may receive from parents of students. The listener should be an integral part of the concert experience. A diverse audience is usually a part of most public school audiences. You must not only entertain them, but for the sake of the future of the choral art, educate and broaden their musical knowledge. Try to have something for everyone, but your first obligation is to your students' education.

The potency of choral music can be experienced profoundly by both singers and audiences. Aesthetic experiences are always meaningful. Although it may not happen every time, plan for the aesthetic experience in every rehearsal. This positive intrinsic motivation is what will draw singers to your program. If the students study diverse literature, sing it well, are satisfied with their experiences in choir, and have favorable remarks about the program for their peers, teachers, and family, you will never need to beat the bushes to get students interested in the choral program. The reverse is also indisputable. If the feeling on campus and in the community is that the chorus sings "stupid" songs, students do not learn anything, and the experience is mediocre at best, nothing will get students to participate in your program.

The list of repertoire accompanying this article is a good place to start when searching for quality literature. All of the pieces have been used successfully in the high school setting. As you peruse them, keep in mind the general principals of what makes a quality piece of music and the guidelines to determine appropriate music for your singers. Stand up for your students by always selecting music that is quality. They will love you for it. Choose literature wisely, remembering that you are responsible for preparing them for participation in music for the rest of their lives.

Angela L. Batey is associate professor of music and associate director of choral activities at the University of Tennessee in Knoxville. This article originally appeared in the December 1997 issue of The Tennessee Musician. *Reprinted by permission.*

Quality High School Literature That Works!

General

René Clausen
"All That Hath Life and Breath"
Mark Foster MF223

Jacob Handl
"En ego campana"
Roger Dean HCA-102

Robert Starer
"Give Thanks unto the Lord"
E. C. Schirmer 1.2196

David Brunner (arr.)
"Swing Low, Sweet Chariot"
Boosey & Hawkes M05147396

Moses Hogan
"God's Gonna Set This World On Fire"
Hal Leonard 08740286

Seasonal

Richard Donovan (arr.)
"Jacques Come Here"
E. C. Schirmer 1.5021

Charles Ives
"A Christmas Carol"
Presser 342-40121

Gordon Langford (arr.)
"Jingle Bells"
Hal Leonard 08740321

William Walton
"All This Time"
Oxford University Press 84.201

Novelty

Adriano Banchieri
"Counterpoint of the Animals"
Bourne 027546

Walter Ehret (arr.)
"The Sow Took the Measles"
Tetra/Continuo, TC423

Ward Swingle (arr.)
"Bourrée for Bach"
Warner Bros. 64335

Choosing Choir Music for Children
Angela Broeker

Perhaps the single most important factor in determining positive choral experiences for children is repertoire selection. Each concert's pieces contain the potential for vocal development, increased conceptual understandings in music, insights into the music-making experiences of other cultures and historical periods, and the beginnings of a lifetime curiosity and desire to participate in the choral music experience. Choosing children's choral repertoire is, therefore, a daunting task requiring much time and thought from the director. Many hours are spent digging through exhibit bins at conventions, playing through recent perusal octavos sent by music publishers, listening to recordings, attending children's choir concerts, and consulting professional publications for repertoire listings and descriptions. Selection becomes a two-step process. First, conductors must determine the viability of an individual piece, then turn that "storehouse" of appropriate selections into an appealing and worthwhile concert hour. This article addresses the first of these steps: repertoire selection.

Text
When evaluating the appropriateness of a specific text, conductors must work under the assumption that children are intelligent, capable, feelingful, playful human beings able to assimilate many kinds of texts with a variety of subjects and themes. This implies, therefore, that selections using texts that are rich in emotional meaning or historic and cultural insights are equally appropriate. Children are capable of growing from such texts. Beware of contemporary compositions using texts that fail to meet any of these criteria. Trite, poorly constructed texts fail to challenge and satisfy young singers and audiences alike.

Foreign language texts are wonderful singing vehicles for children. Through them, children become part of our global culture. They also master new vowel and consonant sounds that in turn widen the palette of vocal timbres. For less experienced choirs, directors should analyze how much text is used in each foreign language selection. Pieces that repeat a small quantity of foreign language text are much more accessible than those that contain many different verses.

Singability
Most children's choir directors are entrusted with a vast array of relatively inexperienced voices. Many children enter their first choir rehearsal with little or no vocal training, and very few study privately during the elementary and middle school years, leaving vocal development solely in the hands of the choir director. Normally thought of as an area addressed during warm-ups, vocal development can and must continue through the singing of appropriate repertoire. Therefore, selections must include the opportunity for developing both the upper and lower registers of the voice. Directors should balance pieces using lower tessituras with pieces using higher ones. And for the young singers performing two- or three-part music, it is important that choristers alternate between alto and soprano lines on various songs.

Other melodic characteristics also contribute to a selection's "singability." Less experienced singers will have a greater success if high pitches are accompanied by open vowels, specifically "ah" and "oh." As with adult choirs, children will have more difficulty with melodies containing extended use of chromaticism than they will with diatonic melodies containing more predicable patterns. Finally, melodies comprising conjunct motion are easier to sing and easier to teach than those with disjunct motion.

Form
The clearer the form, the more accessible the piece for children. This principle is applicable for the largest and smallest formal elements of a work, from sections such as verses or refrains, to phrases, to specific motives. Clear forms are those that have regular phrase lengths, clearly delineated large sections, and exact repetition rather than slight variation.

Pieces are more easily taught and remembered if they are divided into easily discernible large sections with regular phrase lengths. A two-part piece, for example, is readily absorbed and performed if its two sections each contain four-measure phrases. More important in regularity of section and phrase length is the composer's use of exact repetition and contrast. Children will learn and remember more accurately if themes and motives are consistent throughout a piece. This exact repetition is easier for children than motives classified as "similar." Unless a choir's reading and aural skills are quite sophisticated, motives that are similar are difficult to teach and learn.

This does not mean, however, that children's choir repertoire should be limited to such simple forms. As musical skills develop, so too can the difficulty of formal elements.

Part Writing

Children's choirs should include a sample of unison songs in their repertoire. Much can be learned about healthy vocal technique as well as choral technique through unison singing. Linda Swears, in her book, *Teaching the Elementary School Chorus,* states that "expressive singing can best be nurtured through unison melodic line" and cautions that "good part singing can only occur when students have developed their ability to sing independently."

When directors determine that two- and three-part music is appropriate for their choirs, they should look for pieces with parts that sound like a melody. This includes canons as well as counter melodies and ostinatos. For beginning choirs, it is helpful if these second and third parts have contours, rhythms, and texts unlike the primary tune. Directors often make the incorrect assumption that second parts written in parallel thirds or sixths with the melody are appropriate starting points for part singing. To the contrary, these traditional harmony parts, with the same contour, rhythm, and text as melody, are the most difficult to master. As Swears explains: "It is difficult for many children to hear the difference between parts written in thirds, and if a child cannot distinguish the difference by ear, it is most likely he will be unable to sing it correctly." Inexperienced singers get confused and wander back to the primary melodic line. Therefore, singing in parallel thirds is more appropriate for an experienced chorus, whereas singers more easily achieve imitation or other contrapuntal writing with independent vocal lines with less experience.

In the previous discussion of form, it was determined that inexact repetition of phrases is more difficult than exact repetition of phrases. This principle is equally applicable when discussing imitation between voice parts. If second parts are imitative, they are much easier for children when they exactly imitate the melody. Imitation with expanded or contracted intervals, imitation beginning on a different pitch level, or imitation with slightly different rhythms than the melody will increase the amount of teaching time needed for the piece.

Accompaniment

Treble voices can be enhanced greatly by a beautiful accompaniment. Traditionally, piano and organ are standard accompanying instruments, but other instruments, such as guitar, lute, and harpsichord, work equally well. Many composers have also written for treble voices and obbligato instruments such as flute, violin, or oboe that, along with recorder, provide a beautiful complementing timbre to the treble voice. As with a women's chorus, the continuous treble sounds during a children's concert may be balanced through the use of a bass instrument such as cello or bassoon. Every time a new accompanying instrument is introduced, children expand their knowledge of timbres as well as refine their tuning skills. Often, the addition of a bass instrument gives a harmonic foundation and prepares the unchanged treble voice to eventually sing within a mixed choir. Above all, directors should look upon the use of accompanying instruments as a way of providing variety, a key ingredient in the success of repertoire selection.

Pedagogical Implications

As part of the music education profession, the choral director has an obligation to combine performance with the responsibility for long-term development of the chorister. This development is a combination of musical skills and conceptual understandings that produces an educated musician. Therefore, children's choir directors must also consider pedagogical implications when selecting repertoire. What can be taught from the repertoire chosen? Are there specific melodic, rhythmic, and formal elements as well as societal and historical considerations to be gleaned from the performance of a particular work? What expressive elements are called for in the score? What expressive interpretations might be inferred by the conductor or the student?

Summary

Watching children's faces as choral repertoire becomes part of them is one of the great joys in a conductor's life. This integration of musical meaning and human understanding can only occur if we provide participants with quality repertoire that is developmentally appropriate. The effort put forth in repertoire selection is paid back in full as we share with our choirs and audiences the joy of great music making.

Bibliography

Goetze, Mary. "Wanted, Children to Sing and Learn." *Music Educators Journal* 75 (December, 1988): 28–32.

Goetze, Mary. "Writing and Arranging for Young Singers." *Choral Journal* 29 (March, 1989): 36.

Shrock, Dennis. "An Interview with Jean Ashworth Bartle." *Choral Journal* 31 (September, 1990): 14.

Swears, Linda. *Teaching the Elementary School Chorus.* New York: Parker Publishing Company, Inc., 1985.

Angela Broeker is director of choral activities and associate professor of music at the University of St. Thomas in St. Paul, Minnesota. This article is reprinted from the Fall 1998–99 issue of the Rhode Island Music Educator. *It was originally published in the Spring 1998 issue of the Indiana ACDA newsletter,* The Notation. *Reprinted by permission.*

Why Teach SATB Music to Eighth-Grade Chorus?

Cheryl Davis

And to that question, I respond with, "Why not?" Following a recent discussion with colleagues and friends at a convention, I took a long look at exactly why it is I teach SATB music to my eighth-grade chorus students. My thoughts ran along these lines …

First and foremost, I am a teacher of vocal development. That means I make every effort to find music which offers ranges to match my singers' abilities, while at the same time exposing them to good literature and challenging them to further develop their vocal and reading skills. Although SAB music offers an alternative to those mixed choruses with too few boys to sing a balanced SATB chorus, SAB music also often has a range which may be uncomfortably low for some (but not all) young boys' changing voices. Many times these young men may not even be able to tell that they are not reaching the lower pitches. Some of them have to develop new "ears" along with their new voices.

It has been my experience that I have greater success in singing SATB music, even when I have only a few young baritones in the eighth grade. (Generally, in a group of one hundred eighth-grade students with thirty-five boys and sixty-five girls, I can reasonably expect to start the year with about nine or ten young baritones and finish the year with as many as fourteen or fifteen.) There is a wealth of good literature available in every style which offers a comfortable vocal range for young tenors and baritones. Although more work is certainly involved in teaching SATB music, music can be easily found with ranges that are more reasonable for young male voices than the wider range generally found in SAB music or the limit-

ed range offered in SAT music. When searching for SATB music for eighth-grade students early in the school year, I look for music with a soprano range not exceeding a G, an alto range that does not go lower than an A below middle C, a tenor range within an octave of F below middle C to the F above, and a baritone range from C up to an E above middle C. Many SATB songs have ranges even more limited than this.

We have had wonderful luck with four- and five-part a cappella madrigals, such as:

- "Je le vous dirail!" (Certon-Hirt)
- "Fa Una Canzona" (Vecchi)
- "All Ye Who Music Love" (Donato-Greyson).

These classics are excellent teaching/performance tools for young SATB choruses and can be raised or lowered to better accommodate the vocal needs of the particular group. Other selections with which we have had recent success include:

- "She's Like the Swallow" (arr. Strommen)
- "Troika" (Dave and Jean Perry)
- "Pretty Saro" (arr. Gill)
- "Barbara Allen" (Spevacek)
- "Psallite" (Praetorius)
- "Laudate Nomen Domini" (Tye/Johns), to name a few.

As the year progresses, you will find that the ranges of your young voices will expand, opening up new literature possibilities. Scheduling of choruses varies from school to school. I have taught in junior highs and middle schools where the boys and girls were in separate classes for chorus, and I have taught where they were fully mixed in every class period. After nineteen years of middle school, junior high, and high school experience, I firmly believe it is possible to do an equally fine job of teaching vocal development and reading skills in either situation. I have found that my students enjoy the opportunities offered by performing a broad range of voicings, and we sing girls chorus and male chorus literature, as well as SATB literature, in the eighth grade. Even when my classes were completely separated by gender, I taught some SATB music in addition to treble and male chorus music and put the classes together to give the students this experience. I also selected a madrigal or chamber group and met with them before or after school hours to give them the opportunity to sing SATB literature. The result was well-rounded young musicians with an idea of how each voice part fits into the choral structure of a piece of music and a wide range of experience in singing different voicings and styles.

If you haven't tried an eighth-grade SATB chorus, try one! You may be pleasantly surprised at how well it fits the vocal needs of eighth-grade students. It offers variety and challenge to the students. And besides that, the kids like it.

Cheryl Davis is the choral director at Ruckel Middle School in Niceville, Florida. This article originally appeared in the April 1998 issue of the Florida Music Director. *Reprinted by permission.*

A Perspective on Literature for Young Choirs
Al Holcomb

I will never forget my first year of teaching; after four years of history, theory, conducting, and methods classes, I was ready to make great music with a choir. With *Ceremony of Carols* in the folders, I was excited to begin working with sixth-grade treble voices. To my dismay, rehearsals did not go well. Why couldn't these students learn the music? Didn't these students learn anything in their elementary music classes? I went to other directors for advice. "It's the literature," I was told. "It's too hard. Find some unison and two-part songs and teach them by rote." Rote?! How could I teach songs by rote? It went against everything I had learned in college. "You are doing a gross injustice by not teaching students to sight-read," the voice of my methods teacher echoed in my head. Determined, I decided to find literature that the students could read. After a week of "Hot Cross Buns" and "Twinkle, Twinkle Little Star," the students started to complain. The best singers were threatening to drop choir. Regularly, students suggested that we sing familiar songs as well as songs from the radio. I found out later that the former director told them that they would get to sing pop music if they signed up for choir. "Be careful when using pop literature," the voice from the past reminded. Now I was really nervous. Pop music was certainly not my preference, nor my area of expertise. With a mutiny on my hands, I felt I had no choice. I ordered arrangements of several pop songs that had been on the radio during the past year. "That's not how it goes," the students protested during the first rehearsal. I quickly learned that no matter what was on the printed page, the students were going to sing it as they had first learned it. I had assumed that the students would at least attempt to follow the musical notation that I ordered for them. I decided to try something else. Since they were not looking at the notation anyway, I created word sheets and adapted the music to sound more like the familiar renditions. The students wore black T-shirts and sun glasses for their performance. The students were happy and they even sounded pretty good. The pop program had "worked."

"Let's do a musical," the students suggested the next year. Were they crazy? I had given in to their request of pop music. Couldn't they give me a break? I bargained with them. We would do a musical instead of a pop program. After two months of hard work, it all came together. The students, the parents, and the administration loved it. "It worked," I thought.

Over the next few years, I taught several things that "worked," including show tunes, madrigals, art songs, classical pieces, spirituals, and a variety of arrangements. An unexpected event occurred at the end of my fifth year of teaching. I had decided to allow the students to choose some of the literature for the spring program that year. Assuming that they would choose pop music, I was surprised to find that the students wanted to sing "Cantate Domino" by Pitoni as their final song. "It's cool," they added. I had never been so pleased as I was at that moment. "It worked," I thought proudly.

There are a variety of reasons and criteria to consider in choosing choral literature. We examine text, tonal and rhythmic content, vocal lines, range, tessitura, and style in an attempt to find music that is appropriate for the needs of the students.

Entertainment, variety, audience appeal, and public relations may be considered in programming. We may choose literature based on personal preference or perceived student preference. Literature may also be selected for its cultural, historical, or educational value. There are a variety of musical and nonmusical considerations in choosing literature. Too often we allow nonmusical criteria to dominate decisions. We must not forget that the musical literature is the foundation of the entire teaching/learning experience in choral music.

As choral directors, we benefit by considering our roles as a music educators. Because there are so many types of literature that "work" we may lose sight of artistic and educational goals. The National Standards for Arts Education specify that students should "have an informed acquaintance with exemplary works of arts from a variety of cultures and historical periods" (MENC: The National Association for Music Education, 1994, 19). In choosing an exemplary work of art, we must ask the following questions: Does the literature have artistic value? Is the literature the best possible example of its genre? Does the music express the text appropriately? Does the text fit the vocal lines? Is the text of literary value? Has it stood the test of time? Furthermore, we must ask: Does the literature speak to the human experience? What does the literature say about the culture it represents? Historical period? Literature with historical, culture, and artistic value lends itself to many learning opportunities in music, other art forms, and disciplines outside the arts. Only great music is worthy to be called art. To teach singers to love great music and recognize beauty should be a part of the creed of all music educators. Many students will not have an opportunity to experience great choral music after elementary school. How can students learn to recognize and appreciate art if they have never experienced it? It is doubtful that a student whose closest experience to great music is a Disney medley will attend a performance of Beethoven's *Missa Solemnis* as an adult.

For various reasons, we choose literature that is not of the highest quality. Thinking back to my first years of teaching I now realize that I had become too concerned with pleasing students. This is understandable since I wanted students to enjoy music, like me, and stay in choir. I enjoyed the affirmation from students, administration, and parents by programming musicals, easy arrangements, popular literature, and novelty pieces primarily for their entertainment value. Nonexemplary music,

no matter what its justification, should be used sparingly. Literature for entertainment value should be carefully selected and programmed, remembering that the majority of literature that students study and perform should be quality literature. All choral literature has phrasing, dynamics, and articulation but not all music is expressive. Many arrangements of pop music do not have artistic, educational, or historical value. We must look carefully for the pop arrangements that do. There are many good arrangements of popular music that are vocally well-written and have historical significance in the history of American popular music. An occasional pop piece is fine, as long as students experience a balanced curriculum of music that is artistically and educationally sound. Musical theater literature lends itself to a choral curriculum because of its historical and cultural significance in the evolution of American music. Bad arrangements have no place in the choral experience for children. According to Joseph Flummerfelt of Westminster Choir College:

> For me the most important measure of any music is that it represent superb craft motivated by the most profound human and spiritual impulses. This obviously includes the masterworks, folk songs, spirituals, and the best of musical theater. It relentlessly rules out the slick, the facile, and the superficial. I strongly believe that all people, including today's students, are longing for something beyond easy access and instant gratification, perhaps without their even knowing it. When they are led into a repertoire that springs from a deep well of meaning, they will respond to it and their lives will be changed. (Glenn, 1991, 83)

The last thing we should have to consider in choosing literature is whether or not we think students will like it. Student reaction to literature greatly depends on how it is introduced as well as how they experience the literature. Students will enjoy a choral experience that provides challenges as well as successes. Students will enjoy rehearsals when we make rehearsals enjoyable. It should not be the responsibility of the literature to make the rehearsal "fun."

As educators and musicians we must ask ourselves some difficult questions. Do we have a strong commitment to music education? Do we attempt to provide students with a variety of distinctive literature? Are we careful to maintain the integrity of music while adapting it to suit our individual needs? Are we teaching students to love art through great music? The answers to these questions are telling. As educators we must advocate a child-centered curriculum. As musicians, we recognize music as an art form, deserving integrity and appreciation. I would like to close with the words that hang in front of my desk:

That is Why I Teach Music

Not because I expect you to major in music.
Not because I expect you to play or sing all your life.
Not so you can relax or have fun.
But
So you will be human.
So you will recognize beauty.
So you will be sensitive.
So you will be closer to an infinite beyond this world.
So you will have something to cling to.
So you will have more love, more compassion, more gentleness, more good …
In short, more life.
Of what value will it be to make a prosperous living unless you know how to live?

Author Unknown

References

Consortium of National Arts Education Associations. 1994. *National standards for arts education: What every young American should know and be able to do in the arts.* Reston, Virginia: MENC: The National Association for Music Education.

Glenn, Carole, ed. 1991. *In quest of answers: Interviews with American choral conductors.* Chapel Hill, North Carolina: Hinshaw Music.

Al Holcomb is assistant professor of music at the University of Central Florida in Orlando. This article originally appeared in the Fall 1995 issue of Connecticut's CMEA News. *Reprinted by permission.*

Programming Concerts to Educate Students and Parents
Peggy Leonardi

Concert programming can be our biggest headache. Yet, if done thoughtfully, programming can serve as a guide for curriculum and provide a powerful tool for advocacy.

Our fall concert featured works of the Renaissance, Baroque, and Classical masters. Every choir had the opportunity to sing at least one piece accompanied by string and harpsichord and one a cappella piece from the Renaissance. Junior high school students helped the students and the audience visualize the appropriate time period for each piece by dressing in representative costumes. They stood as mannequins on the sides of the stage, changing position according to the time period of the selection being performed.

With this program, I was able to teach about style and composers. We did extensive listening and discussed compositional techniques unique to each era and composer. Even those students who had initially grumbled about not singing "fun" music at this concert had to admit that singing

with the string ensemble was "cool." This concert also demonstrated the real education that is taking place in my classroom on a daily basis.

I try to do at least one special concert like this per year. We have, for example, done a "Mozartfest" on the 200th anniversary of his death, a fully costumed "Evening on Broadway," a "Medieval Feast," and—my personal favorite—an "Evening Demonstration Concert." The idea for a demonstration concert came from an article contained in a professional journal several years ago (so long ago, I can't remember which journal).

During this program, students demonstrate what they learn and practice in rehearsal. Before singing their prepared pieces, one choir demonstrates warm-ups and technique training, another sight-reads a simple piece using solfeggio, another actually works for a few minutes on a piece "in process" showing steps to creating a musical performance, another demonstrates differences in tone quality (bright and dark, head voice and chest voice, etc.), while another performs ear-training exercises.

Before the technique portion, one student speaks briefly while a video shows the function of an actual larynx while singing. We then relate what we are doing in warm-ups to what they have seen and heard in the video. Each prepared piece is preceded by a brief description of what was learned in studying this particular work.

The audience is given handouts to expedite the process and is asked to join us in several singing exercises. The next time I try this, I may include a small quiz for parents to be collected at the end of the concert and graded by their own child the following day in class.

If you feel that people in your school or community do not view music education as a serious course offering, or if you just want to remind them of the importance of music education, try a demonstration concert. We must eliminate the stereotypes of choral programs in our schools that diminish our educational value. How many times have you heard comments like these: "I had no idea they actually learned things in choir!" "When I was in choir we just sang songs!" "How could my kid get a 'C' in choir?" The opportunity to educate parents in a setting like this is invaluable!

Peggy Leonardi teaches vocal music at Hamilton Middle School and Hamilton High School in Hamilton, Montana. This article originally appeared in the January 1997 issue of Montana's Cadenza. *Reprinted by permission.*

How Do YOU Select Literature for Your Choirs?
Willard Minton

The following article was first published in the Connecticut ACDA Chapter's newsletter Cantabile. *When I wrote the article several years ago, I was a high school choral director, had been so for a very long time, and I was Connecticut ACDA High School Repertoire and Standards Chair. My job changed last school year and I am now a high school band director. Not surprisingly, I still use this checklist for selecting music for my church choir, and I have been able to easily modify it for use in selecting literature for my high school bands to perform. Aside from textual considerations, most every other criteria is just as valid for band literature as for choral. The bottom line is: good music is good music, and bad music is bad music, no matter whether we sing it or play it. We owe our students the best possible material with which to work. If you want to copy my list, go for it! If some of it doesn't work for you, change it! If you want to start from scratch and create a totally different set of guidelines for yourself, do it! But, PLEASE, don't simply accept the often questionable "stuff" which fills our mailboxes every day under the guise of "educational music." Once you find a set of standards which help you provide for your students the best possible music to perform, stick with it and reap the benefits!*

Don't you just love wading through the tons of sample choral music and single copies we have accumulated over the years? Each time I have to build a program or order new music for any of my school choirs or for my church choir, I find myself thinking about a course I took oh, so many years ago when I was an undergraduate at UConn. The course was the mandatory undergrad vocal/choral methods class we all had to take. The teacher was the man who made a lasting impression on me for my life's work, John Poellein. John Poellein was a brilliant choral musician, the director of choral activities at UConn, whose career was cut short abruptly by a stroke. His legacy to choral music education in Connecticut is the large number of choral directors who studied with him and continue to share his enthusiasm and expertise with their own students. Someday, we will have to have a gathering of John's former students who are still teaching in Connecticut—perhaps a real neat choral festival of some kind! But that's another entire article! One of John's assignments for this class was for each of us to prepare a list of criteria for selecting works for our choirs to perform. I remember thinking long and hard on this one—just why do I want to pick a certain piece for a choir to learn? After considerable effort, I came up with a list and turned the paper in. With some minor changes and revisions, this list I prepared more than thirty years ago still helps me make decisions about the music I place in front of my choirs. Perhaps it will inspire you to make your own list.

1. **Does the work have a worthwhile text?** Sometimes the most beautiful music has the most horrible text, and vice versa. Are there any "taboo" words or subjects? Do the words inspire or in any way make us feel there is value in repeating them?
2. **Is the piece well written?** Does it stand up to musical analysis (harmonies, rhythms, etc.)? Some music is poorly written. We only have

time to do so much music—therefore, shouldn't that time be spent on something good, rather than something trite or "junky" or which is musically insulting?

3. **Is the piece within the realistic grasp of the group?** While it is not a good idea to look for the easiest music, constant attention must be paid to the level of difficulty. All groups need to be "stretched" occasionally, but most ensembles will respond better to music which they sense will be attainable. Just what do I want to teach by using this selection? Another factor in this area concerns the amount of rehearsal time available to prepare the work.

4. **Will the piece be received well—does it fit the needs and expectations of the listeners as well as the singers?** This area is the most subjective of all. Some "purists" do not feel that this is a valid criteria because it comes close to evaluating a piece on its "entertainment" quotient. But I use this in two ways. Will the choir be able to sustain its enthusiasm for the piece over the length of time necessary to learn it and perform it? (I have had some pieces fail in performance because, after all the work it took to learn them, the choir felt "yeah, so what!") Hopefully, I have learned to avoid this type of work! Also, I use this criteria in helping me remember that, ideally, those who listen (the audience) should enjoy the work as much as the choir does. Any group must remember for whom it performs. Remember that a complete performance has three parts: the composer who creates the music; the performer who interprets and presents the music; and the audience who listens to the music. If any one of these three factors is missing from the equation, then we do not have a complete musical experience. And, if along the way, the listeners (audience) get some pleasure while providing their part of this equation so much the better!

5. **Other factors.** This is the "miscellaneous" category which includes such varied items as: Is the work accompanied or not? Does it need piano, organ, or some other instrument? Are there soloists? What about the variety of styles, keys, historical periods, etc. in program building—how does this piece fit into this puzzle? Is the piece worth spending the money on? We all know how music costs have gone crazy, so we must be sure that every piece we buy will be used. All things considered, is this a piece I want to add to my choral library? And finally, is this one of those pieces which just reaches out and grabs you and says, "Sing me!"? Some of my best selections have been based on a completely "gut" reaction such as this. So much for a logical checklist!

All of these factors enter my mind when I study new music, or revisit old music, for that matter. The music publishing industry sends out sample scores and score books and demo recordings (very often sung quite poorly) for hundreds of new publications each year. Many of these are of questionable musical value. Whenever I go to ACDA or CMEA or MENC conferences or talk with other choral directors, a topic of much interest is new literature for our groups. Hopefully, we will make our choices wisely. We owe it to our choirs, ourselves, and our profession to select the best possible material with which to work. My own checklist of criteria helps me in this process. If you haven't already done so, won't you consider making your own list? Your choirs will thank you sincerely. Good luck!

Willard Minton is retired from public school teaching, but still remains active in choral music as the senior choir director at the Church of Christ, Baptist and Congregational, in Winsted, Connecticut. This article is reprinted from the Fall 1997 issue of Connecticut's CMEA News. *It originally appeared in the Connecticut ACDA newsletter* Cantabile. *Reprinted by permission.*

Who's Afraid of Contemporary Music? Educational Strategies for Coping and Conquering

Melanie A. Mitrano

One of the ways that today's young music students can begin to demonstrate their keen musicianship is by allying themselves with contemporary music. Many students have found that modern music provides a venue, a niche, where they can finally assert their competence. There is no doubt that being part of a chamber ensemble is a fine way to assert one's independence while still being part of a group effort. Musicians who not only produce a beautiful tone, but are accurate, are those who will work. Modern music is no doubt the best possible training ground for honing one's musical precision. Those who are consistently able to walk into rehearsals with their parts "down" have the best chance of making a living in this most difficult and highly competitive field. As educators, we have a responsibility to develop these kinds of musicians, especially as we prepare to enter the twenty-first century. But how exactly can we meet this challenge? The following ten techniques offer specific steps we can take to guide our students (and ourselves) through this often thorny repertoire, thereby minimizing the discomfort and fear that accompanies the plunge into the uncharted waters of contemporary music.

The Two R's: Resources and Research

When it comes to modern music, ignorance is not bliss. The most successful performers of this repertoire are those who take direct and immediate steps to find out as much as possible about the music they are learning. This includes researching the history of the piece, the composer, the compositional style, the text—in short, anything that makes the piece more present and helps to clarify its message. Students should use all the varied resources at their disposal: books, scores, recordings and their liner notes, dictionaries and encyclopedias of music, journal articles, program notes, etc. Organizations that cater to composers, like the American Music Center, can also be a wealth of information, especially when it comes to unpublished or hard-to-find materials such as old concert programs, press kits, photographs, and performance reviews. Don't forget that people can be resources too! Find out who the local "new music makers" are in your area. Is there a contemporary ensemble at your local college or conservatory?

Seek out the director and ask for his or her suggestions. Best of all, begin to attend more concerts of modern music. A tremendous amount can be learned by watching and listening to how others tackle this repertoire. Make a point of speaking to the conductors, performers, and composers after a concert. This is an excellent way to make contacts and also to establish yourself as someone who promotes the advancement of new music.

Navigate the Score

Just as one would not think of traveling to an unfamiliar place without a map or directions, performers should never think of going into uncharted musical territory without first taking time to "navigate" the score. What does this mean? Contemporary scores are often difficult to read, which accounts for much of the immediate fear and anxiety this repertoire provokes. If students are to get past their initial trepidation, they must demystify the visual complexities of the score as soon as possible. First, performers should always read from the full score—never a part. Then, armed with colored pencils or highlighters, certain key concerns must be addressed immediately, such as entrance cues, meter changes, etc. Singers should indicate how to get their starting pitches, which instruments to listen for and where, specific places where the voice must line up rhythmically with other instruments, and all conducting patterns that will be used. With this kind of navigating, the performer transforms an intimidating score into a user-friendly personal road map.

Get Your Hands Dirty

When it comes to contemporary music, performers are often called upon to execute "extended techniques," which are usually strange and unusual ways of using one's instrument. This can mean anything from playing harmonics to speaking into one's instrument. Singers may be asked to make odd sounds (growls, coughs, gasps, laughs, tongue clicks, whispers, etc.) or sing on microtones. Other extended techniques may involve incorporating stage movement or props into the performance and using electronic media. Needless to say, students often experience a certain amount of embarrassment when asked to do things that go beyond the ordinary. Yet those who are able to dig in and get their hands dirty, rather than shy away from that which seems odd, will find the most success in the end. Strangely enough, when performers throw themselves into extended techniques, and even overdo them, they will find their discomfort quickly disappears. The more natural one can make these oddities seem, the more genuine, accessible, and truly fascinating they will be to the audience.

Meet the Composer

The very idea of contemporary music is appealing to many young performers simply because it is immediate, an artistic expression that speaks directly to the present. Nothing drives that fact home faster than actually meeting and working with composers. Most composers are more than happy to help with the preparation of their pieces, as this translates into performances that more accurately realize their own artistic goals. Students should attempt to coach modern pieces with their creators and ask questions pertaining to aesthetic inspiration and intentions, interpretation, technical execution, etc. The appeal of working with composers is that these issues can be definitively addressed. For performers, it is empowering and exciting to be so well informed, rather than having to guess or hope that one is being true to the composer's vision. The result is that each performance becomes collaborative, an amalgam of compositional accomplishment and artistic interpretation. No other repertoire allows for this kind of teamwork, that which truly elevates the performer to cocreator.

Beg, Borrow, and Steal

There are very few skills in life that can be acquired without some kind of help or instruction from someone else. Because contemporary music is so specialized and much of it is highly academic, students should seek out teachers, conductors, and more experienced performers who can help them uncover the secrets of this repertoire. In short, they must find mentors. A mentor is someone who will spend time listening, offering suggestions, and raising important questions. "Mentorship" can also come in the form of an inspiring concert, a helpful recording, or an informative article. It is important to realize that the path to originality necessarily begins with imitation. Young composition students learn how to write music by copying the styles and techniques of the great composers. The concept of apprenticeship is based upon the same "beg, borrow, and steal" mentality. Performers should not feel guilty then, for making good use of whatever resources are available to them. Observing and responding to the machinations of the ever-changing art world is not cheating. In fact, it is a surefire recipe for progress and at the very core of musical evolution.

Develop Pitch Perfection

Many students mistakenly believe that perfect pitch is required to perform contemporary music. Actually, a skill far more useful than perfect pitch is something that may be called "pitch perfection." Pitch perfection is a combination of several factors. First, it is honing one's technique to be able to sing or play in the center of every pitch. Modern music is not the place to struggle with intonation, although working with this repertoire will most certainly help to improve one's ear and pitch accuracy. Secondly, it is learning to hear intervalically. Executing a difficult melodic line with much chromaticism is nearly impossible to do by listening note to note and attempting to "connect the musical dots." Hearing intervalic relationships will bring the big picture into focus, enabling performers to hear and sing complete phrases that sound musical. For singers there is also a third factor: being able to use "throat memory," a kinesthetic sense of where pitches lie in the voice. This is especially helpful if one is performing a piece for solo voice, or in situations when starting pitches are unavailable or obscured. Generally, singers should apply the "a cappella rule" when learning new music: given a starting pitch, one should be able to accurately sing the entire piece, or at least a large section of it, completely a cappella. If one is unable to do so, then the piece is not truly prepared, and cannot be properly rehearsed with an ensemble, let alone performed! Those who develop "pitch perfection" will find that they are often asked if they have perfect pitch. While there is much debate over whether or not the latter can be learned, there is no question that pitch perfection is a skill that, with some work, is within any performer's grasp.

Go for the Gesture

During the height of the avant-garde movement, many composers were writing pieces marked by academic inaccessibility, and retreating to what is often referred to as "the ivory tower." The inaccessibility of their work extended not only to audiences, but also to performers, which perhaps contributed to the rise of computer music and heightened reliance upon electronic media during this time. While the current compositional trend has shifted toward building audiences and programming pieces with more immediate appeal, performers of contemporary music should expect at times to be faced with demands that seem impossible to meet. It is not uncommon to find examples of overstatement in modern music, exaggerated compositional requests aimed at creating a specific mood or sound. For example, the composer may indicate *fffff* or *ppppp* in an area of an instrument's range that does not lend itself to such a dynamic. Or, one might be asked to execute a difficult melodic passage at an unrealistic metronome marking. Whatever the case may be, in these kinds of situations, students should understand and embrace the concept of gesture. While one may not always be capable of executing exactly what is notated with perfect accuracy, he or she can make the desired musical gesture in a way that is both honest and convincing. This is not to say that performers should not strive for complete precision, but rather that they should not lose sight of larger compositional objectives by immersing themselves in notational minutiae. By going for the gesture, the true artist-performer brings life to the notes on the page without being a slave to them and ultimately transforms mere symbols into active expression.

Don't Count … Listen!

Young music students are often taught that accompanists will follow them, even if they count incorrectly, come in wrong, or have a memory slip. Unfortunately, because this assumption simply cannot extend beyond the ordinary piano duo, it does little to teach the art of collaboration. As a result, students are often sadly lacking in ensemble skills. Those who think of themselves as soloists are doomed to failure. Those who think of themselves as belonging to an ensemble, on the other hand, understand that they are part of a group effort and function both musically and interpersonally as such. One of the key aspects of successful musical teamwork, especially with respect to contemporary repertoire, is a sense of shared rhythmic acuity. A surefire way for performers to achieve this goal is to embrace the aphorism, "Don't count … listen!" Too often when working with a conductor, performers do not actually listen to one another. (I am reminded of one student who, when cautioned that he was not exactly with the ensemble, insisted, "But I was counting.") There is even more at stake with ensemble pieces that are unconducted. Here is where the careful score navigation that was discussed earlier pays off. A score with clearly marked cues will guide a performer better than any conductor. One simply needs to know what to listen for and then open up the ears! By itself, counting is passive and solitary. It is only through truly listening, a learned skill which is both active and collective, that performers can participate fully in the pursuit of music making.

Be Definitive

One of the most fulfilling aspects of dealing with contemporary music is that it offers performers the rare opportunity to be interpretively unique. This is especially true if one is premiering a new work, but even if not, chances are there will not be hundreds of recordings that will dictate how the piece is supposed to be performed. This, therefore, requires students to set their own standards and find their own ways of striving for excellence. Perhaps that means memorizing a piece that was not intended to be performed from memory or deeply exploring an underlying subtext, for example. However they can, performers must strive to be definitive in their execution of new pieces. The old adage "you reap what you sow" is applicable here. The efforts expended may be tremendous, but so will be the rewards.

Let It Go

As performance time nears, students must find a way to settle into a feeling of trust. They should be reminded that sometimes, despite the hardest work, there may still be areas of imperfection, or "patches-in-progress," so to speak. The "patch" must be assessed as objectively as possible, taking into account the texture and balance of the ensemble—exactly how exposed will the performer be at that particular spot? Many times students agonize over minutiae—things that no one will ever know are wrong! They must be given permission to be slightly imperfect. This is not to suggest that accuracy may fall by the wayside, but just that a sense of perspective is maintained. If the "patch" does not represent an all-important musical moment, then let it go. A performance that resonates acceptance and humanity will never fail to reach an audience.

Looking Forward

Unfortunately, students are usually at the college level before they ever begin to grapple with new music. This is disconcerting because, like any new language, the dialect of contemporary music would be best learned and retained at a younger age. The techniques discussed in this article need not be geared solely toward high-school and college-aged students, but can also be used at the grammar-school level, and even by nonmusicians, for the purpose of developing music appreciation. The primary motivation for introducing this repertoire at a young age is to train those professional musicians to come, who will need solid skills to execute the constantly evolving music of the twenty-first century. Yet the larger, even more consequential motive is to build audiences for this repertoire, so that serious music has a future in our society. Armed with strategies for coping and conquering, we can break through the barrier of fear and guide our students to the larger musical landscape that awaits them on the other side.

Melanie A. Mitrano is currently pursuing a performance career and maintains a private voice studio in Nutley, New Jersey. This article originally appeared in the May 1999 issue of New Jersey's Tempo. *Reprinted by permission.*

Political Correctness vs. Artistic Freedom
Jonathan C. Rappaport

As music educators, we are constantly having to justify artistic choices that we make in programming concerts, musical plays, and other presentations. These few paragraphs will outline some pitfalls that many of us would prefer avoiding if at all possible. Hopefully these ideas will spark dialogue amongst music educators throughout the Commonwealth.

A number of years ago I selected Zoltan Kodály's "Ladybird" as a choral piece for an interelementary chorus. In the music, the Ladybird (or ladybug) is symbolic of the weak Hungarians who were dominated throughout much of their history by foreign powers. In the song, the ladybird is told to escape before the Turks come and crush it. This refers to actual historical fact, that of the Ottoman Turkish conquest of Hungary, which was brutal and lasted for nearly 250 years.

However, one of the children in the chorus was of Turkish descent, and as the song was not particularly complementary to Turks of that period, it raised an enormous stink. Unfortunately, the parents did not come to me directly. Instead, they went to a citywide ecumenical religious council, which then called the superintendent of schools, who then called my supervisor, who finally called me. In the end, I was able to reach a compromise and change the words "Turks are" for "soldiers" in order to perform this very worthy twentieth-century masterpiece. However, this was an extremely unpleasant situation, one that left a very bad taste in my mouth.

Part of me remained unhappy with the compromise, because I believe that history, which is often unpleasant and deals with wars and mistreatment of people, needs to be confronted honestly. I also felt that the integrity of Kodály's composition was put into question. And finally, I felt I was unjustly accused of being prejudicial against an ethnic group.

The lessons learned from this experience are many. I now examine music that I program with a much keener sensitivity as to whether someone will take offense. This may include stereotypical views of ethnic groups, racial groups, age, religion, gender, and so forth. However, if I feel a piece is worth performing, I try to program it in a way that there will be an explanation that the piece represents a certain time or place. For example, many folk songs tell of stereotypical male/female roles that we no longer adhere to. However, I do think it valuable for children to know that this kind of bias existed commonly until very recently (and indeed still exists to some extent today). A discussion about these roles can be very valuable for children to experience. Even an explanatory paragraph in the program, or comments immediately preceding the performance, will educate everyone involved.

Another point is regarding religious music. During December, programming such music can be upsetting to various non-Christian groups who don't celebrate Christmas. Yet we know that many of the masterpieces of choral literature through the history of Western music came from this tradition. Therefore, I would program such a piece during another time of year when it does not raise a red flag during an especially sensitive time. We must remember that public schools in particular are open and available for *every* child. If even one student is made to feel uncomfortable, then a teacher must really consider if that piece is more important than the child who will be made to feel unwelcome in her or his own school.

If you foresee that a piece might be controversial, it is much better to discuss it with the principal or supervisor *before* it is even passed out, with a plan in hand for how to deal with any potential fallout. Usually this will align the principal with your point of view before you start. On the other hand, if the principal does not support you at this juncture, it may be prudent not to do the piece, as you will not have the backing you need should a conflict arise.

Because every teaching situation is vastly different from the next, such policies are best handled on a case-by-case basis within each school system. There are certainly many issues involved, including artistic and academic freedom. Because much of our work is performance-based, however, the public views our work much more than almost any other subject area. Thus an increased sensitivity to the needs of the students, the school, the teacher, and the public is necessary.

Some schools address these issues in their arts curriculum, others through policies voted upon by the School Committee. Other schools have no policies and deal with them on a case-by-case basis (and, unfortunately, sometimes in a knee-jerk reactionary manner). If you work in such a situation, you may wish to discuss this with your colleagues (also in theatre, dance, or visual arts) and supervisor, and see if you can recommend some policies that might give a framework to issues of political correctness versus artistic freedom.

Jonathan C. Rappaport is the performing arts liaison with the Worcester Public Schools, Massachusetts, and codirector of the Kodály Music Institute of the New England Conservatory in Boston, Massachusetts. This article originally appeared in the Summer 2000 issue of the Massachusetts Music News. Reprinted by permission.

Choral Music by Women Composers
Edgar Scruggs

Exploring and programming quality choral literature for my women's ensembles is without a doubt my most difficult task as a choral conductor. Even though I spend hundreds of hours combing through potential literature, making the final decision regarding variation in style, tempo, and opportunities for interpretation does not come easily.

It particularly frustrates me when attending concerts programmed for both women's and men's choruses that the audience has a tendency to leave at the end of the evening exchanging comments regarding how "beautifully" the women sang and how they were "excited" by the men's performance. True, the timbre of men's voices and also the rarity of men's ensembles, especially at the high school level, help to spark those comments, but many times the audience is correct. As listeners, we all want and must have those moments in a concert which excite us. One can only listen to so much "beautiful" singing without aching to hear literature that provides both rhythmic interest and dynamic contrast. There is no substitute for energetic singing, but until directors of women's ensembles become passionate and committed to researching literature that offers rhythmic challenges and opportunities to explore both ends of the dynamic spectrum, I'm afraid we may continue to discuss the beauty of the women's performance and how lovely their dresses are.

Following are a few women composers who have written pieces which my women's ensembles have found both challenging to prepare and exhilarating to perform. Some of the works are standards, and some are very new. I hope you will find several that are possibilities for your situation.

Ruth Watson Henderson (b.1932) was born in Toronto and studied piano with Viggo Kihl, Alberto Guerrero, and Hans Neumann and composition with Oskar Morawetz, Richard Johnston, and Samuel Dolin. After completing her Associate of the Royal Conservatory of Toronto (gold medalist) and Licentiate at the same institution, she continued her studies at the Mannes College of Music in New York. Returning to Canada in 1954, she was active for many years as a concert pianist. In 1968, she became the accompanist for the Festival Singers of Canada, where she began writing choral music. Her association in recent years with other choral groups, such as the Ontario Youth Choir and the Toronto Children's Chorus, has led to many compositions for treble voices. Currently on the faculty of the Royal Conservatory of Music in Toronto, Henderson continues a multifaceted career as composer, teacher, pianist, and church organist.

Henderson's settings of both "Creation's Praise" (Toronto Children's Choir Series, Gordon V. Thompson Music, Toronto) and "Gloria" (Boosey & Hawkes) work exceptionally well as opening selections. Beginning a program with either of these pieces will set a high standard for the listener and performer. Both employ brass as accompaniment; "Creation's Praise" is also scored for organ (if using brass), and there is a wonderful four-hand piano score if instruments are not available. "Gloria" includes timpani and percussion. Instead of the 2- to 3-minute pieces which are readily available, "Creation's Praise" pushes the 5-minute mark, and "Gloria" is approximately 5 minutes in length. Both offer exceptional opportunities for exploring dynamics, rhythmic and legato singing, and moments for investigating the conductor's creativity through phrasing. Your toughest task as a director will be determining the divisi in several sections of "Creation's Praise" and establishing balance and tuning on several difficult harmonic passages in the "Gloria." Both are challenging, but your ensembles will enjoy a sense of accomplishment upon mastering them.

Lana Walter (b. 1948) was born in Klamath Falls, Oregon, and attended Oregon public schools. She received her B.Mus. degree in music theory and history from Willamette University in Salem, Oregon, and the M.A. in music history from the University of Oregon, Eugene. She has taught music theory and history at the collegiate level. Walter is the founding director of the Yumpque Youth Choir in Roseburg, Oregon, and teaches elementary school music in Sutherlin, Oregon.

Settings of the Ave Maria text with rhythmic diversity are the exception rather than the rule. Walter's SSA composition of "Elizabeth's Ave" (Treble Clef Music) offers a multimetered, yet accessible piece for your ensemble. The tropes in the 12th-century manuscript are derived from the Office for the Circumcision. As the program notes suggest, the vigorous rhythms "emulate the infant John the Baptist leaping within Elizabeth's womb and Elizabeth's joy which follows," as described in Luke 1:41. The piano accompaniment enhances the feeling of dance throughout the work. Opportunities for creative interpretation are written into its beautiful melody and in Walter's setting of the *pp* Amen.

Katherine Dienes (b. 1970) was born in Wellington, New Zealand. She was educated at the Samuel Marsden School in Karori, Wellington. She earned a double degree in music and modern languages at Victoria University, Wellington, while serving as organ scholar at St. Paul's Cathedral, Wellington, under the tutelage of Peter Godfrey. Subsequently, she was organ scholar at Chichester (U.K.) Cathedral, where she earned her Fellow of the Royal College of Organists certification, and organist and assistant master of music at Liverpool (U.K.) Cathedral. Dienes is now assistant organist and director of the girls' choir at Norwich (U.K.) Cathedral. She is active as an organ recitalist, clinician for the Royal School of Church Music, and conductor. She is bringing the Norwich Cathedral Girls Choir on their first tour to the United States in the summer of 2000.

Melodic line and rhythmic motion go hand in hand in Dienes' setting of "Ave Verum" (Treble Clef) for women's chorus. This SSAA work, when paired with the Walter piece and possibly the "Ave Maria" by David MacIntyre (Intrada Music Group), would provide an interesting section in any program. Though set at a much slower tempo marking than either of the pieces previously mentioned, this multimetered selection offers beautiful harmonies accompanied by opportunities to explore the entire dynamic spectrum. Dienes's writing for the inner voices provides interest for singers, with eighth notes set against a beautiful melody of quarter notes in several phrases. Measures of triplets against duple and duplets paired against a feeling of three provide interest for the listener. This is a short but effective setting of the Ave Verum text.

Gwyneth Walker is a graduate of Brown University and the Hartt School of Music. She holds both the M.M.A. and D.M.A. degrees. A former faculty member of the Hartt School of Music and the Oberlin College Conservatory, Walker resigned from academic employment in 1982 to pursue a full-time career as composer. She currently lives on the Brainstorm Dairy Farm in Braintree, Vermont.

There are numerous settings of the e. e. cummings text "I Thank You God," but Walker's (E. C. Schirmer) is masterful. It was commissioned in 1999 by the American Choral Directors Association in memory of Ray Brock, the ACDA's former director of development and administrative assistant. Walker, very explicit in her markings, develops this text through use of varied tempos, accelerando and ritard, text painting, quasi-recitative, a cappella versus accompanied singing, and diverse opportunities for dynamic contrast. The accompanist must be capable of maintaining strict tempos built around triplet and quintuplet rhythmic passages. This SSAA setting is very accessible for your singers, but if you do not have sopranos with a proficient high C and the ability to sustain it for several measures, you will have to develop a creative ending or wait until next year. Take a look at this setting; you won't be disappointed.

Edgar Scruggs is director of choral activities at Belmont University in Nashville, Tennessee. This article originally appeared in the Spring 2000 issue of the Georgia Music News. *Reprinted by permission.*

Section 3

 # Vocal Technique

Teaching vocal technique requires knowledge not only of vocal technique but also of how voices are different at various age levels. Vocal technique is not just how to use the voice, but how to stand and move and how to make all of your students understand a process largely hidden from view. The articles in this section offer ideas on how to teach students to sing.

 Section 3

Vocal Technique

Alexander Technique as a Method of Body Awareness in Singing
Kathy Enervold

The factors of body alignment, muscle tension, and breathing are interrelated and may have an effect on healthy voice use. Thus, total body awareness may benefit vocal production. The following paragraphs will discuss concepts of total body awareness and the principle of the Alexander Technique.

The Alexander Technique is a field of study involving body awareness which requires the mind and body to work together as a unit. The technique has gained recognition and has been employed along with the study of voice to aid vocalists in producing tones free of tension. Although the Alexander Technique (A.T.) is a growing field, it is one which is still new to or unheard of by many singers, singing teachers, and choral directors. The principles of A.T. may give insight into a way of achieving tension-free and, ultimately, healthy singing.

The development of the Alexander Technique occurred as a result of a ten-year period in which Fredrich Matthias Alexander, a reciter of Shakespeare, conducted an in-depth self-study. The process began when Alexander was unable to find a cure for recurring hoarseness which resulted after or during reciting.

Alexander consulted voice teachers and medical experts and was advised to rest his voice, which alleviated the problem temporarily. He found that no matter how long he rested his voice, the hoarseness would recur when reciting. When specialists were unable to give him a medical reason for his vocal problems, he decided that he must be doing something to cause the vocal distress and he began observing himself to try to find symptoms that could be responsible.

The only equipment Alexander used in his self-examination was a mirror to observe himself while speaking. Unable to notice any physical changes while speaking, he began to recite and noticed three distinct reactions: 1) a pulling back of the head, 2) a depressing of the larynx, and 3) a sucking in of breath with a gasp. Next, he re-evaluated himself in normal speech and noticed the same characteristics but to a lesser degree. He discovered that what he referred to as "manner of doing" greatly affected the functioning of speech. In other words, the process in which his head, neck, and torso moved when he began to speak affected the way his speech was executed. He further discovered that if he allowed his head to move "forward and up" in relation to his torso, he was able to ease the tension prior to speaking or reciting, but when he actually would speak or recite, the old habits that were exhibited prior to his discovery recurred.

Through a great deal of trial and error he realized that he had to give up the idea of the "end result" of speaking before he was able to speak without the old habit taking over the process (Alexander, 1984). Throughout his study, Alexander consulted physicians who, upon examination, corroborated his findings that his vocal organs were becoming healthier and stronger. After nearly ten years of in-depth self-study, Alexander came up with a technique in which a person can learn to control the body through reason and not through feeling, a conscious control of individual self. This process became known as the Alexander Technique.

There are seven operational ideas which are incorporated in the Alexander Technique: 1) use and functioning—the power of choice which determines what action is chosen upon receiving a particular stimulus; 2) the whole person—the treatment of mind and body as one unit that cannot work in isolation from each other; 3) primary control—the relationship of head, neck, and torso; 4) unreliable sensory appreciation—the idea that what feels comfortable is not always right but merely habit, the objective being to explore the unknown sensory territory with reason and not feeling; 5) inhibition—unlike the Freudian definition, the ability to stop or delay a response to stimuli until adequately prepared to make a response; 6) direction—allowing the body to experience something new which may feel awkward; and 7) ends and means—allowing the process itself, not the product, to dominate, whereby the actual goal is more apt to be achieved (Gelb, 1981).

Although the Alexander Technique is a growing field, it is still unfamiliar to many teachers and conductors. It is not something that can be learned by reading a paper or a book, but the present information can be viewed as a preliminary to further study through Alexander workshops and lessons. Even without complete knowledge or understanding of A.T., however, there are techniques and procedures that can be applied in the choral rehearsal if the conductor is sensitive to the entire body: its alignment, its musculature, and the effect it can have on the vocal mechanism.

First, the conductor must study the anatomy and learn the skeletal and musculature structures. If available, a skeleton can be of help in attaining familiarity with the location of various joints and the skeletal relation to the spine. It is important to study the muscular structure to identify what muscles are attached to the larynx.

Second, the conductor needs to become aware of his/her own body. If soreness, stiffness, or aching muscles occur, he/she should make note of the source of strain, what time of day it usually occurs, and what activity may have caused the pain. As movement or body alignment habits are discovered, the conductor should alter the positions freely to feel if there might be other ways of achieving a more comfortable body alignment.

Third, the conductor ought to search for a new vocabulary that encourages freedom from tension. Terms such as "balance," "freedom," "ease," "allow," and "release" are helpful in giving directions without creating rigidity or constriction in the body.

Basics in the choral rehearsal must include a balanced, unrestricted body alignment. Weight should be evenly distributed on both feet, with slightly more weight forward. Knees should be flexed to allow a feeling of buoyancy. Singers should be asked to imagine each vertebra of the spine as being separate from the others with a cushion of space between each one, allowing the spine to rise without stretching (Thurman, 1983).

The head should move slowly forward and back and side to side, resting in a place of balance above the spine. At this stage, singers must be reminded that this position of the head may be different from where they are accustomed to placing it. The rib cage should be free to move if the lungs expand, but only as a reaction rather than a forced expansion. A suggestion was made to the writer of this study to think of the lungs being "breathed" rather than to take a breath. The result was an effortless intake of air. This concept is worth trying with choral singers to give them the idea of freedom and ease in breathing. Encourage the singers to recognize that what is correct does not always feel right at first, but reinforcement and reminders can help bring about good habits and body awareness in choral singers.

The use of natural sounds such as moaning or sighing may help discover the sounds and sensations related to free voice use. By not thinking of a beautiful tone there is more concentration on the process than the result. A good analogy is that of a golfer who is so concerned over ball direction that the eyes leave the ball before the process of the swing is completed, resulting in a bad shot. Too often the result of the desired tone gets in the way of correct, tension-free production.

Healthy singing involves the whole body, and singers and choral directors should know the myriad body parts and how movement and interaction of these parts should feel when singing correctly. The goal is for these feelings to become habitual, but it is unlikely that this will happen automatically. Old habits of incorrect use, either of the body or the voice, occur continually, requiring the choral director to be attuned to the needs of the singers at all times.

References

Alexander, F. M. (1984). *The use of self.* Long Beach, CA: Centerline.

Gelb, M. (1981). *Body learning: How to achieve better health through the world-famous method of mind-body unity.* New York: Henry Holt and Co.

Thurman, L. (1983). Putting horses before carts: A brief on vocal athletics. *The Choral Journal, 23*(7), 15–21.

Kathy Enervold teaches music at Beulah Public School in Beulah, North Dakota. This article originally appeared in the May 1996 issue of the North Dakota Music Educator. *Reprinted by permission.*

The Singing Voice in K–5

JoAnne Greene-Beatty

Six years ago I returned to teaching elementary music after many years of teaching studio voice on the college level. Even though my students were adults, I have always supplemented my income with private teaching, and many of those private students were children. For many years I believed that my teaching voice to children was looked upon with skepticism by my colleagues, who felt the voice should reach a level of maturity (around the 10th grade) before a child should study voice. As I watched my own son sing incorrectly, I came to the conclusion that some children need help to sing correctly. I began to make suggestions to help him sing with a more open, supported tone. I feel that my opinion has been supported by the fact that two students that I began to teach when they were young (one was nine and the other was eleven years old) have recently been awarded the Grace Moore Scholarship, a full opera scholarship to the University of Tennessee, Knoxville. These two students were actively performing in show choirs and community theatre. They needed help because one was not singing in her head tone, and one needed a musical coach because she was performing so much.

A child's singing instruction should not be like an adult's instruction. A child's voice should not be pushed to sound like an adult or to sing at the very top or bottom of his or her range for an extended period of time. However, children can be taught to breathe correctly and to blow out with pressurized air. They can be taught how to open the mouth and how to pronounce words correctly. They can be taught about posture and about how to sing in their head voice.

I feel that teaching good singing techniques in elementary school is extremely important. No longer do children grow up in homes where excellent singers are heard. You can only sing the prettiest note that you can imagine. If you have never heard a lovely singing tone, then how can you possibly sing a lovely singing tone that is supported and free? I challenge all elementary teachers to include singing instruction in their curriculum. This article includes techniques that I use in my teaching, as well as phrases that I use that are geared toward teaching children.

Pitch

One general thing to remember is that not all children get their singing voice early. Many children cannot match pitch until about the fourth grade. When I work with the students, I never say, "You can't sing." I say, "Well, that's not quite right." Or I say, "That's a little over/under the pitch." Sometimes I sing the pitch that they sang back to them and slide my voice up or down to the correct pitch and ask them to try to slide with me. I choose the children who are singing correctly and place children who have not found their singing voice between those who can sing on pitch. I also might pick the best singers of the class and have them sing to the class and then lead the class in singing a song. I use tapes and CDs that have children's voices and I also have the children sing a cappella or with an Autoharp or piano. I have a great story that I tell children (especially boys) who are singing an octave too low. This is what I say:

"I hear some people who are singing too low like grownups. Some of you are trying to sing like adult men, but none of you (K–4) are old enough to be singing this low. A few of you may begin to experience a little voice change in the 5th grade; that will be unusual. I want you to think about baby chicks in the barnyard. All baby chicks say 'peep, peep' in a high pitched voice. You will never hear a baby boy chick crow 'cockadoodle-do' until he becomes a grownup rooster. The girl chicks will always say 'peep, peep' until they grow up. When they grow up into hens, they will say 'cluck, cluck'! So all of you boys and girls should be singing high!!!"

Breathing

Besides being able to hear the correct pitch and repeat the correct pitch with a pleasing tone, breath is the next most important element of singing. Without knowing how to breathe in and how to blow out, the singer breathes too often and sounds weak. If you ask a student, even an adult, to breathe for singing, most of the time that student breathes very high, raising their shoulders and tightening their vocal folds. Then, when they sing, they blow straight out of their mouth as if playing an instrument. This creates a breathy tone. The breath needs to blow in a circular motion up in the soft palate. This creates vibrato and projects the sound and allows the singer to breathe less often. The old masters of bel canto singing had their students sing with a candle in front of them and try to sing without blowing the candle flame. As a teacher, you need to know this, but this information is too much for a young child. Here is how I teach breath to young children:

"OK, boys and girls, let's take a deep breath all the way down to our toes! Some of you are doing turtle shoulders; your shoulders are about to make your head disappear! Let's see if you can pretend to pick up something really heavy and keep your shoulders down when you breathe. Now pretend you have an inner tube all around your middle and let's fill it with air. Now, breathe in and blow out. Good! Mary did it right! Johnny did it right! Suzy, watch Sam, he's doing it right! Good, Suzy, that's better. Now, relax boys and girls and breathe normally. Now we're going to learn how to blow out! You have to blow out with pressurized air when you are singing! The air can not come out like a runaway balloon. The air has to come out with steady pressure like a tire with a slow leak. This time when we breathe in, I want you to blow out with your lips closed tightly so that just a little hole of air comes out between your lips. OK. Breathe in and blow out with your lips tight. OK. Relax. Now what did your stomach feel like? Did it feel tight? No? Well, let's try that again. Did it feel tight that time? Good. Now let's sing a song and try to blow out with a tight stomach. Your lips won't be tight while you are singing, but your stomach will still feel tight."

Sometimes I speak to the children about having a box of air. I have them draw an imaginary box around themselves and ask them to fill the box up with air. Then I ask the students to squeeze with their ribs. You can also have them bend over and breathe into their backs, then straighten up and try to breathe into their backs from a standing position. I also tell the children to breathe through their nose or to pretend to sip through a straw.

As you sing any song, you should speak of how to plan the breathing. Never breathe in the middle of a word. Commas and periods and other punctuation marks are good places to breathe. Breathe at the end of complete thoughts or phrases. Breathe deeply enough to get enough breath to make it to the end of the musical thought or phrase.

Head Voice
As a teacher who has worked with many children, this is the biggest problem you will have to correct. Children today hear so many singers who do not use their head voice and who carry their chest voice up into what I call a holler! Children can usually imitate spoken sounds quicker than singing sounds, so I have the children meow like a cat. Then I have them open that up to a half meow, half singing sound and sing the melody of a song

using the word "meow." (No, I don't have them sing the commercial!) I also use whimpering puppy sounds or sounds of a fire engine.

Speak to the children in a funny open high voice and have them imitate you. Then turn that silly high speaking voice into a singing tone. I use the phrase "Hi, how are you?"

I also sing the following syllables on a scale going down, repeating all of the syllables on a pitch before going to the next pitch: pitch c "me, meh, ma, moh, moo"; pitch b "me, meh, ma, moh, moo"; pitch a "me, meh, ma, moh, moo," etc.

Warming Up the Voice
I think children should learn to warm up their voices. However, they should use warm-ups that are fun and that teach them something about how to sing. My favorite is about an alligator flopping open his big mouth.

This is found in *Vocalise Fun: Warm-ups for Kids* (Barrett/Sanders, 1988). This book is a treasure chest of warm-ups from various teachers. It has lovely illustrations that will thrill the children.

I have another favorite warm-up that one of my private students taught me. A Knox County teacher taught it to them. I'm sorry to say that I do not remember who taught it to me or who their teacher was. It is a 5-note scale going up and down (See Figure 1).

Figure 1. M and Ms
Ma - Ma made me mash my M and Ms.
C   D   E   F   G   A   B   C   D

In the following exercise, you do these sounds with your voice and have them imitate: Have them start high on the fire engine sound and swoop down to their low voice. Then swoop down and turn the low voice into a singing sound. Then start the fire engine sound high and turn it into a singing sound. Then swoop the singing voice down and back up to their head voice. Then sing a scale going down from high to low (*do ti la sol fa mi re do*) on the syllable "ma." Repeat singing the downward scale, singing on the syllable "na."

The M and Ms (see Figure 1) or any humming vocalise puts the voice in the mask and helps with projection and finding your head voice.

Dropping the Jaw
There is something that an elementary teacher who is an instrumentalist rather than a vocalist

might not be aware of. Singing high will be hard to do and squeaky sounding if you don't blow extra air and if you don't open your mouth a little wider on the inside of your mouth. The jaw should be dropped down as the jaw unhinges and the chin will scoot back a little. I have had conductors tell me to put two fingers in my mouth to measure how far to open my mouth. That is wrong. Two fingers are uncomfortable for my mouth. About a finger and a half does it for me. The opening that no one mentions is inside your mouth. With the jaw dropped and the mouth open correctly, it feels about like it does when you are beginning to bite an apple. I tell the children to take a bite out of an imaginary apple. Then I tell them to open their mouth like that to sing high. Biting the apple also raises your soft palate. The soft palate needs to be raised for a good focused tone.

Diction

It is never too early to try to teach good diction and rounded vowels. In order to sing high, the vowels must be adjusted and sung more open. I watched a movie about a silent film star with a squeaky voice. "Talkies" movies had been invented, and because her voice was so irritating no one would cast her. She went to a vocal coach who had her speak with exaggerated rounded open tones. "How, now, brown cow?" was what he had her repeat over and over until her voice became beautiful. Words cannot be sung as you would normally speak them when you are singing them on high notes. (This is also a cure for squeaky adult soprano sections.)

Harmony

It is a little tricky to teach harmony to classes that have children in the group who have not learned to sing on pitch. I recommend the use of echo songs and partner songs. Rounds are extremely difficult. I sometimes sing rounds by assigning each part of the round to a group and letting them repeat that part as we layer the round by letting one group start, then adding group 2, then adding group 3 (no group sings the whole round, only their part). To begin with, I have the strong singers lead the class while I sing part 2. Sometimes I sing with the class and play the round on the piano. If I have enough strong singers in the classroom, I divide the class into two parts while I sing the third part. For fifth graders I put the class into three circles with strong singers in each circle and have them either sing their one part over and over or attempt to sing the entire round. Partner songs are fabulous for teaching harmony. One of the prettiest partner songs that is wonderful for Christmas programs is "Carol of the Angels" by Jill Gallina (Shawnee Press, 1992). Ms. Gallina has written a lovely original melody to partner with "Angels We Have Heard on High." For those of you not yet familiar with partner songs, they have two distinct melodies that create lovely harmony when sung together.

I do hope that those of you who are not incorporating singing instruction into your curriculum will begin to do so. An excellent source for more information on teaching the elementary student to sing is *Teaching Kids to Sing* (K. Phillips. New York: Schirmer Books, 1996). There are too many exercises in the book to use in a music program when you have other skills to teach and only see your students once or twice a week, but it contains a lot of useful information and is well researched.

Good luck and good singing!!!

JoAnne Greene-Beatty teaches music at Hawkins Elementary School in Rogersville, Tennessee. This article originally appeared in the October 2000 issue of The Tennessee Musician. *Reprinted by permission.*

Imagine This … The Use of Imagery in Vocal Production
Debbie Looney

A wise voice teacher once told me, "Good singing is ninety-five percent imagery." The longer I teach chorus, the more I find that her words were infinitely wise. Using the imagination is the basis for teaching good techniques for posture, breath support, and vocal placement. These images, combined with a sense of humor, are invaluable in making students understand how to produce a well-supported, properly placed tone.

In Robert Edwin's article "Do You Practice What You Preach?" he suggests, "Lift [the rib cage] so the sternum is elevated, and everything else falls into line." When practicing good posture, have the students feel for and find the sternum (breast bone). One way to do this is to pretend you are King Kong and beat on your chest while "hollering" at the kids. This will show them where the sternum is located—and how crazy the teacher is! Of course, everyone will want to be a gorilla for a minute, but you will have made your point. Once the students have discovered the location of the sternum, you can simply say, "Raise that sternum," and the posture will improve immediately.

Another technique that has been very successful is to have the students imagine that they are Christmas tree ornaments. Have them reach up and twist a small strand of hair (their own) at the top of the head and pretend that they are hanging from the tree by that strand. Then have them slowly release the hair and lower their arms, while still feeling as though they are suspended. This will put the whole body in line for good singing posture.

When teaching breath support techniques, encourage students to "fill up the balloon in the tummy." They pretend to have swallowed a balloon (now lodged in the diaphragm area) and they must completely fill it up each time they take a breath. This encourages deep, expansive, diaphragmatic breathing. Another method of teaching use of the proper muscles is to practice "the hiss" (like a snake). This can be done in two ways: long, sustained hissing after a deep breath and short hisses produced by pulsing the diaphragm muscle for each hiss. Students may become lightheaded the first few times they practice this exercise, but eventually they will form the habit of deep breathing. As suggested in "The Use of Analogy in the Rehearsal" by Mary Alice Stollak and Lois Alexander, "Pretend you have a 'Slinky' in your hand. Imagine the slinky going from one hand to the other. Follow through the phrase with the same motion." To encourage students to support the voice through a long phrase, have them pretend to "pull the rope." They grab hold of a rope with the right hand and pull the rope slowly and steadily from the beginning of the phrase to the end. Of course, this necessitates a "big belly breath" at the start of the phrase.

Students become much more sensitive to phrasing when they correlate it to breathing. Have the students imagine that they have a large plastic pipe inside their bodies which goes from the lips to the belly button. The pipe contains an elbow which is located in the throat. (Draw this on the board!) They should take in enough air to fill up the pipe. Not only does this encourage proper breathing technique, but students get that "hollow" feeling in the back of the throat which leads to proper placement of the voice.

That same wise voice teacher also said to me, "Placement is everything." No matter how well the students have mastered posture and breathing techniques, if the voice is not correctly placed, the sound will not be lovely. Sometimes a little imagination goes a long way in teaching this concept. Have the students look at a light bulb. They should think about placing it in the mouth with the large end at the back of the throat. Once they have the feeling in their minds, all you need to do is hold up the light bulb as a reminder to place the voice properly.

Judith Civitano suggests that "for younger singers, it's more fun to refer to crocodiles and alligators. Crocodiles have evolved to swallow larger prey; their jaw is hinged so that both bottom and top can swing open. Alligators prey on much smaller food. Therefore, only the bottom part of the jaw moves. Singers are actually alligators, but we should open our mouths like crocodiles! Additional benefits from this idea are usually a higher soft palate, more open throat, and a more expressive face." Other images are an inner smile, the beginning of a yawn, raised back molars, or that feeling of "pleasant surprise" when you find out you've won the lottery. Whatever it takes to produce the open sound, you should be willing to try!

The use of imagery has been proven to be effective in teaching techniques of posture, breath control, and voice placement. If you find it difficult to communicate the concepts of good vocal technique, I suggest implementing the use of imagery in your teaching. It is a way of getting the students' attention and initiating the thought process. It may be the only way to communicate such abstract ideas to inexperienced singers.

References

Civitano, J. (1988). Turning your human musical instrument into a Stradivarius means understanding how it really works. *VocalEase, 1*(2).

Daniel, M. (1993). Balancing space and energy in choral voices. *Music Educators Journal, 80*(1), 29–31.

Edwin, R. (1996). Do you practice what you preach? In "Techniquely Speaking," *VocalEase, 1*(6).

Stollak, M. A., and Alexander, L. (1998). The use of analogy in the rehearsal. *Music Educators Journal, 84*(10), 17–21.

Debbie Looney is choral director at West Hall Middle School in Oakwood, Georgia. This article originally appeared in the Fall 1998 issue of Georgia Music News. *Reprinted by permission.*

Section 4

 # Program Development

All teachers face challenges in keeping students involved in music and finding new ways to help their programs grow. Whether it's starting a new chorus or finding new recruits for your existing groups, these articles give a broad spectrum of ideas to try or to adapt for yourself.

 Section 4

Program Development

Establishing an Out-of-the-School-Day Elementary Choir: Getting Started and Beyond
Karen Baldwin

Nearly fifteen years ago, the Riverside School District set a goal of establishing a select choir composed of fourth-, fifth-, and sixth-grade students. Just how to go about this was a complicated task. In meeting with the district administration, we agreed that the main goal was to focus on those students who wanted to learn more choral techniques than they could in a regular classroom setting. The technicalities of time, location, audition skills, activities/performances during and outside of the school day, and repertoire all needed to be discussed and decided before this could become a feasible part of the school program. This article addresses how we developed the Riverside Select Choir in 1984 and also some of the changes that have been made since its conception.

Time
There were several options available for the time to meet with the choir. We chose to meet one day a week before school. I chose Wednesday, looking at future programming needs and also programs that were already in existence on Tuesday and Thursday. At the time we started the choir, we were on a staggered schedule. The high school began the day about an hour before the elementary and middle schools. This enabled the students to ride the high school bus to school and a shuttle bus to their various schools after choir practice. We currently have a simultaneous start time, and so riding on the high school bus is no longer a valid option. Fortunately, the program is so strong and the community support so great that the parents carpool the children to practice. The choir meets from 7:00–7:50 a.m. once a week. They then either walk or are bussed to their various

schools. We have examined other options for meeting with this choir, such as an after-school or lunchtime program, but have found the before-school time works best for us. Meeting after school would mean students would need to have a shuttle service provided and would not leave until 5:00 p.m. on the activity bus. Lunchtime would not work because the choir has students from Riverside Elementary, Chattaroy Elementary, and Riverside Middle School. These schools are approximately five miles apart and have different operating schedules.

Location
My main school is Riverside Elementary. Although I do direct a fifth-grade choir three days a week at another school, meeting at my main place of work seemed to be the logical choice for storage of materials and setting up for performances. This school is also centrally located in the school district, making it the most convenient for transportation purposes. We meet in the music room. This is not a large space, approximately 1,200 feet, but it serves our purpose well. I do not have chairs or risers to accommodate the choir for practice, so we stand in four rows for most of the rehearsal. Ideally, we would have room to have risers available all the time, but in our situation we only use risers on the day of concerts.

Audition
Right from the beginning, we decided to have the members chosen by audition only. I wanted 55–65 students to be in the choir. By having a larger number of students, you can produce good volume and yet still work on developing each child's voice without overstraining it. This also helps when preparing for an outside performance. In working with a larger group, if several students must miss the concert, you are not worried about who will cover the parts. I must admit that the children are wonderful about attending outside

performances, even when it means being gone for an entire Saturday. So having missing performers has never been an issue with our choir.

We usually hold auditions for the Riverside Select Choir on the second or third week of September. By this time students have been in their regular music classroom at least five times. In the music classrooms, all students are told about tryouts and what will be required of them. The children are given a permission slip which tells about the history of the choir, expected rehearsal schedule, performances, expenses, and the stipulation that they are expected to participate for the entire year. By signing it, the student and parent/guardian are signifying their willingness to support this venture for the entire year. This signed slip must be returned in order for the student to audition.

I feel it is very important for the welfare of the group that the students take pride in the fact that they are members of an elite group. One year I took every child who auditioned for the choir. It was also the year that I fought apathy the most. They did not feel that they had earned a special place in the group. I had more students miss practice and drop out that year than ever before. Since that year, even if I have to reduce the overall size of the choir, I make sure that only the very best students are chosen.

The actual tryout is done on the first Wednesday morning of practice. This gives me only fifty minutes to audition everyone. The goal is for them to know if they are members of the choir by the end of this first session. As the students arrive, I make sure they have turned in their signed permission slip. On this slip I mark their current grade level and if they are a past member of the group. Everyone must audition each year. This is because I want new members to gain courage from those who have already been through the process. If I felt that a choir member was not deserving of being in the group again, either because of absenteeism or behavior problems, I would have discussed my concerns with them in private before the tryouts.

The audition process is divided into three parts:

1. Echo and match pitch on three simple *so-mi* patterns. This analyzes for correct pitch and also for vocal placement of the voice (alto or soprano).
2. Sight-read several rhythm patterns. We use Kodály notation for this step (e.g., *ta, ti-ti, ta-a, ti-ka-ti-ka,* and silence of equal length for the corresponding rests). I use patterns that gradu-

ally get more difficult. They are made up of quarter, eighth, half, and sixteenth notes and quarter, eighth, and half rests. We read sometimes in large and small groups and sometimes as individuals, especially if I spot someone who is very talented in sight-reading.
3. Sing part of a song that we will be preparing for the holiday season, first with the large group and then in small groups to analyze their blend.

During all of these steps, I am not only making notes about how they are matching pitch, clapping rhythms, and singing melody and harmony, but also examining the children's behavior, energy level, and response to directions. This is no easy task, as it is not unusual to have 100 students try for the 55–65 positions.

At the end of the audition, I add up their scores and announce the winners by calling their names and giving them a letter of congratulations. This is personally the hardest part of the audition for me. There are always shouts of joy and tears during this process. No preference to grade level, gender, or participating school is ever used; however, we usually end up with the members being equally divided by thirds for grade level and school, and about one-quarter of the group is male.

Several years ago, I instigated dismissing the new members as soon as they received their letters. After they leave I meet with the children who were not chosen. This gives me the opportunity to thank them for their willingness to audition, explain the things that need to be improved, and encourage them to try again either in January or next year. I explain how we sometimes have students that must leave the group for a variety of reasons and that I will possibly be inviting two to four of them to join us in January. Taking that break after the audition gives them a chance to ask questions and relieve some of their anxiety before returning to their classes.

Activities and Performances During and Outside of the School Day

We have several activities that are annual events, and I try to schedule one special event each year. These events vary according to the behavior and skill levels of the choir. The yearly events are:

1. An Around-the-Town Tour during the Christmas season. This is a full-day activity on a Saturday. We visit several nursing homes to sing Christmas carols, and we also sing three full-length concerts at

area shopping malls and a retirement center. The caroling involves singing about eight well-known Christmas carols. In the full concert, we sing carols and about six to seven two-part songs. We usually add choreography and instrumental parts to some of these selections.

2. The EWMEA Large Group Choral Festival in the spring. The students perform three or four songs and sight-read for adjudication. This usually involves their missing a half day from school. As part of this event, we stay to listen to several other groups perform. Each student has a copy of the adjudication form being used. They mark scores as if they were judging the group. On the bus ride back to the school, we discuss these scores and their own. This process helps teach them acceptable audience behavior, clarifies the evaluation process, and develops analytical thinking skills.

3. A mini-musical involving not only their choral skills, but also playing barred and rhythm instruments, recorders, movement, and drama. This is performed during the school day for their respective schools and also as part of a nighttime concert for the community.

4. Two concerts—one in the winter involving all of the Christmas tour selections and one in the spring, in which they perform their selections from the festival and their mini-musical.

Special events have included a tour to Washington State University, working with a choral director from an area college or high school, and performing concerts for community events. I try to keep the days missed from regular school time to under three. The teachers, parents, district administrators, and I understand the fact that these students are talented, but they are needed in their regular classroom environment to learn the required grade-level materials and also to act as leaders for the rest of the students.

Repertoire

The materials this group currently sings are far different from when we began fifteen years ago. At that time I was working towards singing unison and two-part songs while trying to teach them the ten skill levels utilized as part of the adjudication process for festival. We now work on two- and three-part music and they are self-evaluating for pitch, rhythm, blend, dynamics, performance skills, etc. I try to select a variety in the six songs for the Christmas concert, which include songs about winter and related holidays of the season and those that are complimentary stylistically to each other. In aiming for this, I choose pieces containing foreign language, instruments, choreography, unison/two-part/three-part singing, and various tempos and styles.

We sometimes reuse a selection from the year before. I usually try to choose one piece that can be used as a festival piece in the spring. *Dona Nobis Pacem, Jubilate Deo,* and *Gloria!* are pieces we have used which work well for both concerts.

In choosing the spring pieces, I look for selections that will highlight the skills of the choir. I try to use pieces that contain clear examples of the ten areas in which they are being adjudicated. Usually one of the songs is in a foreign language and one is a cappella.

Choosing the songs for our first festival was difficult. Through this experience I learned about a variety of resources that were available. I relied greatly on the recommended festival selection lists available from WMEA and local music dealers. Today, I try to select one of our pieces from that list and then the other two from our music files or new publications.

The *Henry Leck, Doreen Rao,* and *Heritage* series have a lot of quality music for elementary choirs. I usually preview about ten pieces with the choir and then teach them the art of choosing complimentary concert music. We discuss tempo variations, styles of music, themes that could be created, and also the adjudication procedure. I find they are more willing to work hard on the music when they are given an integral part in selecting it.

There are many excellent mini-musicals on the market for choirs that involve singing, instruments, movement, and drama. Usually, I choose our piece for the year after attending the American Orff-Schulwerk National Conference. At this conference there are groups performing and focusing on musicals. These examples help give me a foundation to create my own musicals.

The actual ability to create these has come through my obtaining Levels Training in the Orff-Schulwerk. I would recommend taking a levels course. It helps to build on your own creativity and also gives a clear process that can be shared with students to help them grow musically.

If you don't feel comfortable writing your own works, then contact your local music dealer for samples. Randy DeLelles and Jeff Kriske are authors/composers of several very fine ready-made musicals. They have an excellent variety of programs that are either based on folk tales from various countries or stories with morals.

Conclusion

Starting the Riverside Select Choir was one of the most challenging but gratifying decisions I have ever made. Every week is a wonderful new experience. The most exciting moments happen years after students have graduated from choir. The other day a former choir member saw me at the high school solo and ensemble festival. She came running up and said, "Mrs. Baldwin, thanks for making me work so hard in Select Choir. The things you taught us are the reason I love singing so much today. You have inspired me to sing for the rest of my life." That's reason enough to make any teacher run out and start an elementary choir as soon as possible!

Karen Baldwin is an elementary music specialist at Riverside Elementary School in Chattaroy, Washington. She is also an adjunct faculty member at Whitworth College in Spokane, Washington, and Eastern Washington University in Cheney. This article originally appeared in the May 1999 issue of Washington's Voice. *Reprinted by permission.*

Ten Steps for Creating or Adding Vitality and Improving the Quality of Your Choir
Tina Bull

This article is meant to provide a little boost to your choral music program. Whether you are an experienced music teacher looking for that something extra to spark some energy in your group or just beginning your choral music career, here are some suggestions that may help you think in new ways. Feel free to brainstorm and come up with your own ideas for expanding upon this list. These are simple ideas and suggestions that I hope may be of benefit to you, and there is no reason why these must relate exclusively to the choral classroom. Share them with your other music colleagues and let me know what else you would add!

Here are my ten basic suggestions for improving the quality of your choral music program:

1. Begin warm-ups one minute before the period begins. There are studies showing that most music teachers lose five to ten minutes of every class period at the onset, and some lose many more. Although you must manage those details such as attendance, notes from the office, and announcements, put those off for just a few minutes. By getting started ahead of time, students enter the room and join right in while they get settled. You should find that there is less talk and more time to meet those goals set for the day. And what a mood setter! The students will learn that in music class we make music right away!

2. In order to move forward, *retreat!* Nothing builds cohesiveness and unity like spending time together away from the normal routines of life. Although it may be expensive and time-consuming to plan, take your choir on a retreat, and do so early in the school year. Find a beautiful spot to get away to overnight. Work together, play together, and make music together. Be sure to give students interactive games and activities to encourage the building of relationships among those who might not otherwise be friends. By the end of the retreat, your students will feel more like they belong to a special group, and, hopefully, they will have made several new friends in the meantime. I found parents very willing to come along to enjoy the atmosphere and provide a few inexpensive meals!

3. Create a council with real jobs and genuine responsibilities. Student leadership provides vital energy for the choir and relieves you of some of those overwhelming details that always need attention. Take a day to nominate and elect officers who have specific responsibilities. Consider going beyond the typical offices of president and secretary by choosing a person to handle publicity, social activities, and concert logistics. Students find it very satisfying to be needed, appreciated, and complimented for a job well done.

4. Let the choir members be decision makers whenever possible. The role of the conductor may traditionally be somewhat like a dictatorship. But when a singer feels merely like the instrument the conductor is playing, it can be a less than satisfying experience. Why not occasionally ask the choir to make some of the musical decisions? I enjoy having the altos listen to the sopranos and give a bit of feedback, and vice versa. They start to take on a role that responds more to the whole sound, rather than their own individual parts. Try different

approaches to tempo and dynamics and ask the singers what they think. Occasionally rotate a few students out front and allow them the privilege of listening outside of the group. Sometimes we forget how different the total sound is from that on the risers.

5. Know your music very thoroughly. Make sure you can personally sing every part throughout each piece. Nothing is as discouraging to a student as working with a teacher who is pretending to be prepared when the bluff is not working. If you usually learn the music along with the students, you're learning the music too late. When you know every part thoroughly, it becomes much easier to anticipate the difficult passages and prepare means through which the singers can approach those problems. It is also much easier to conduct when you have internalized the piece. Some conductors recommend sleeping with the score under the pillow, but I prefer a more active approach—practice!

6. Select music that is of lasting value. The "cutsie" songs get old quickly. Bring out some of those favorites from years past. Ask other directors for standard pieces that work well with young voices. Pay attention to the text as well as the music itself. Those words may whirl around in the students' heads for a very long time. Meaningful music with a strong text will stay with them for years to come.

7. Invite students you recognize as school leaders to join the choir. You may be surprised by how many will be willing to participate if you show an interest. Whenever you successfully recruit one leader, several students will follow. Do you supervise a study hall? What a great time to encourage students to come talk with you about choir. Speak individually to several students a day, and your numbers will grow. Help your job become what you would like it to be by growing your own music program.

8. Show students the respect you would like them to show to you. Sarcasm, humiliation, and embarrassment are tactics that are best left out-

side of the classroom. Never put the students in an embarrassing situation. Make sure that before they perform in front of an audience they are fully prepared. Demonstrate professionalism through all of your actions, and students will notice and respond. This is not the solution to all problems, but this should be the foundation of your classroom management strategies.

9. Model a strong work ethic. Demonstrate the fact that you expect a lot out of yourself and therefore, you also expect a lot out of the students. Teachers lose respect when they are under-prepared or disorganized. When you stay on top of all of your responsibilities, the students will feel more of an obligation to hold up their end of the bargain. Give them dates by which to have their music learned. Offer regular opportunities for individual assessment. Set goals and let the students help you accomplish them.

10. Interact with other choir directors and music teachers. Share your ideas and listen for new ones. Invite a guest conductor to your school for a day and set him or her loose while you observe. It is never too late to keep learning, and one of the best ways to improve is to stay involved with others in the profession. Guard against the trap of confining yourself to your own room in your own school. Get outside of that comfort zone, take a chance, and expose yourself to new and different opportunities. There are many other conductors in the state who would welcome an invitation to come work with your students. And there are many festivals to experience with your singers. Don't forget that OMEA and ACDA offer several opportunities each year for interaction, finding new music, and learning new skills.

Tina Bull is associate professor of music and coordinator of music education at Oregon State University in Corvallis. This article originally appeared in the Spring 2001 issue of the Oregon Music Educator. *Reprinted by permission.*

Using a Cultural "Broker" to Enhance Your Concert Program

Regina Carlow

Choral directors constantly seek ways to expand their repertoire of programming ideas. One of the ways to do this is to include music from a variety of cultures in our concert programs. This takes work. Not only is it difficult to find accessible world music arranged for chorus, it is also a challenge to know how to go about performing the music authentically.

Several issues come to the fore immediately. Probably the first barrier we encounter is the language. Many languages have spoken nuances that are traditionally ignored when sung, and in some cases, the reverse is true. In addition, many arrangements offer translations emphasizing the English text as poetry, which sometimes changes the original meaning of the text. This brings up the issue of the context of music, which is often contrived or convoluted by inaccurate or invented translations. Another problem is phrasing or musical subtleties that are not printed in the score. While we can always turn to a number of printed resources for pronunciation and interpretation, and recordings to help us get a feel for tempo and instrumentation, it helps to have a cultural "broker" or consultant who can give us more contextual information about the music.

Last fall I found an arrangement of "Alla en el Rancho Grande," written for two-part treble choir, that I wanted to program with one of my children's choirs in the spring. All I knew about the piece was that the tempo was lively, it was in two, and the text was Spanish. I did a little research and found that it was a *ranchera,* a type of Mexican music often accompanied by a *mariachi,* an ensemble of itinerant folk musicians. I found a recording of the piece and decided that I wanted my students to perform the songs accompanied by authentic instruments.

I got in touch with a colleague who conducts a choir that performs mostly Spanish music and told her that I wanted to perform a *ranchera* with a children's choir and authentic instrumentation. We spoke over the phone a number of times with her coaching me on style, phrasing, and text. She eventually put me in contact with several musicians who lived in my area who agreed to work with me and my choir. The musicians were not only willing, but very excited about sharing this music with children in their community.

The musicians met with me and the choir's accompanist, helping us get the feel of the music. Needless to say, we let them lead us and learned a great deal from the experience. The musicians came to rehearsal, spoke to the choir about the song, and told the children how the *ranchera* often romanticized farm life and work. The leader told the children that he sang this particular song at birthday parties and on the way to and from school. He also told the children about his native Andean music and explained how the music of the Andes was somewhat different than that of Mexico. On the night of the concert, the men added much to our performance, not only adding richness to the choir's musical experience, but enhancing the audience's enjoyment as well.

Things to consider when using a musical consultant:

- Find a coach or mentor to help get you started. Listen to recordings and use the Internet to find resources and musicians in your area.
- Plan ahead. Make sure you communicate rehearsal/concert dates, times, honoraria, etc. clearly with your guest. If you do not share a common language, use an interpreter to help with details and logistics.
- Attend a rehearsal or meeting with your consultants to watch them on their own turf. Watch how they communicate. Take note of rehearsal dynamics and synergies.
- Ask the guests to wear native clothing to the performance. If there are students in your group from the same culture, invite them to dress in native costume or give them an opportunity to introduce the group (perhaps in their own language).
- Include information about the group or performer in your program notes along with the context of the particular piece.
- Make sure your conducting style reflects the music being performed. Better yet, "give up your choir," and let the artist take over for that particular piece.

Regina Carlow teaches choral and general music in Montgomery County, Maryland, and is currently a doctoral student in music education at the University of Maryland. This article first appeared in the January/February 1999 issue of Maryland Music Educator. *Reprinted by permsision.*

Student Conductors: A Tool for In-depth Teaching and Student Empowerment
Lucy E. Carroll

"Take the rehearsal, Lucy, I'll be back in a few minutes." So saying, my high school choir director left to get some music from the closet, leaving me in charge of rehearsal. This was, of course, more years ago than I would readily admit, but the opportunities I had from such experiences led me to my first conducting job (at age fifteen) and college conducting courses while I was still in high school.

Today, my own students are delving into the inner secrets of musical scores as they learn to conduct. Last spring, one of my students conducted the concert choir in the district's Fine Arts Festival; this year, the number of students in our student conductors chapter has risen dramatically, as more students seek to discover what happens "beyond the beat pattern." For student empowerment and for in-depth teaching of a musical score, there's nothing like student conducting!

Student conductors may be the great untapped resource in most high school music programs. While many teachers may think that student conductors are possible only in college situations, the truth is that high school students are capable of entry-level conducting, and, often, of more advanced techniques as well.

All students in school performance groups can benefit from learning the basic skills of conducting. It is wildly fun to have a whole group trying to sing and beat a pattern at the same time. But it also gives students a tool to develop an internal feel for the rhythm and the structure, and it is so much quieter than tapping or stomping! A few minutes out of a rehearsal here and there having everyone beat a pattern, hold a fermata, or indicate a consonant can reap rewards at performance time as students internalize the elements of the music they perform.

At William Tennent High School in Warminster, Pennsylvania, we are in the third year of a student conducting chapter. We received a charter from the American Choral Directors Association (we were the third high school in the country to be so honored) to have a student ACDA chapter. The students meet together only once or twice a month. They practice the beat patterns and take turns con-ducting each other. They analyze the score and are led to asking integral questions about the music. How can you indicate this entrance? How can you control the accelerando? How can you show legato, marcato, tenuto? All the students sing along, careful to do only what the student conductor shows in the conducting. These sessions are relaxed. There is no stigma attached to bad cueing, erratic pattern-beating, a wandering ictus, or unclear directions. Student conductors are encouraged to "try whatever you like." This usually results in unusual musical interpretations, vast changes of meter, and other surprises. The discussion then leads into "which interpretation was musical and which wouldn't work in public?" which then leads to the in-depth discussion of "how do you know how to interpret a score?"

The amount of music history, literature, theory, and harmony that can come from one of these sessions is remarkable. Many of the students in the group do not want to conduct in public, but many others do. Students are not given a conduct-ing task unless they are truly conducting, not just beating time. Student reaction to student conduct-ors is quite remarkable. The members of our group have tried to follow the student conductor and do the interpretation asked. It is easier here at WTHS because the students are so accustomed to student teachers. They expect to see different con-ducting styles and interpretations. One of my stu-dents told me the most valuable thing she learned through all this was that there's more than one right answer in music, and there are many degrees of good and better!

Students can take sectional rehearsals, take over when the teacher is called to the door or phone, or even conduct on days the teacher is absent and there is a nonmusic substitute teacher.

What is true of the choral program is equally true for students in instrumental groups, although there is no comparable student organization to the ACDA for instrumental students. Any school can institute its own after-school club for student con-ductors!

This past December, the president of our stu-dent ACDA chapter saw himself on television, KYW TV 3 in Philadelphia. He was conducting one of the pieces our Madrigal Singers performed at the Ronald McDonald House for the Share-a-Night House Lighting, and the news camera came right up to him and recorded. The singers truly did their best for him. Now I am flooded with requests from students who want to learn more and to conduct a piece with one of our groups in one of our spring events. What a happy turn of events!

Retired after thirty years of teaching music, most recently as director of choral and theatre activities and coordinator of music at William Tennent High School and K–12 music coordinator for the Centennial Schools, both in Warminster, Pennsylvania, Lucy E. Carroll is currently a Humanities Council Commonwealth speaker and a scholar-in-residence for the Pennsylvania Historic and Museum Commission as well as organist/music director for the Carmelite monastery in Philadelphia. This article originally appeared in the March 1996 issue of Pennsylvania's PMEA News. *Reprinted by permission.*

Using Student Evaluations to Help Improve Teaching and Learning
Jeff Doebler

You'll Always Learn Something

Asking students for their opinions on class procedures—everything from grading to social activities—can be an excellent way for them to increase their level of interest in your class or ensemble. Even though I constantly tell students that my door is always open for them to make suggestions (and many do) and regardless of how well I think I know their opinions, I have found that I *always* learn something.

Providing time for anonymous student evaluations on a regular basis gives pupils the opportunity to be constantly thinking about their next round of suggestions. Evaluations once per term or once per year serve this purpose. Short evaluations on a specific topic can also be used as needed. For example, perhaps your school just hosted a district music festival. While the event is fresh in their minds, the students' suggestions can be solicited. Similarly, after a trip or a new project that impacted the whole school, it might be well to ask the opinions of faculty, administrators, and/or parents, in addition to students.

Implementation and Follow-up: Don't Ask If You Don't Want to Know

People will give opinions if they think you will sincerely consider their responses. It can be a great way to garner suggestions from those directly involved with your teaching. Be honest with yourself, though, before administering such an evaluation, or it will not be successful. Think about these two statements: (1) Don't ask if you don't want to know, and (2) Don't ask if you won't consider student opinions. In the first case, you'll be frustrated, and in the second case, your students will be frustrated.

Administering the evaluation can take place during class time, ensuring 100 percent response.

Upon distributing the evaluation, always emphasize that students should state *their* views, not what their friends might say. Ask that instead of just listing complaints ("I hate this class"), students always offer a solution when they state a concern ("I hate this class, but here's what could be done to help make it better …"). It's amazing how quiet the classroom becomes when students are writing their opinions.

Implementation can take the form of further class discussion ("Several people commented they would like to modify some of our classroom procedures …"), or another brief evaluation on a specific topic ("Please give your opinion on these three student suggestions …") or simply tacit personal awareness of a situation ("You seem to show favoritism toward …").

Write Questions: Specific and Open-Ended

As implied above, some evaluation items might be specific questions about a particular issue—perhaps one that has appeared to be a concern for the group. Other questions might be open-ended, allowing students to say what's on their minds. This is where I frequently learn the most—both positive and negative.

Sample Evaluation Introduction and Questions

On a separate sheet of paper, give *your* anonymous responses to the following questions. Your opinions are valuable in helping me to plan class procedures. Whenever you state a criticism, please offer a solution. (Feel free to make suggestions, ask questions, voice concerns, etc., at any time.)

1. How did you feel about the Parents' Day Concert?
2. How do you feel about the upcoming Holiday Concert?
3. What is your opinion on the level of the music for the Parents' Day and Holiday Concerts: too easy, too hard, about right?

4. Which of these pieces, if any, have you played before? (list selections)
5. Do you feel that you get enough, too much, or too little personal attention from me? If too little, how could I give you more?
6. What social events should we try to sponsor for ensemble members to get to know each other better?
7. What can we do to make the classroom more attractive?
8. What was your opinion about and do you have any suggestions regarding the audition procedure?
9. What were your favorite and least favorite pieces of music that we performed this year? Why?
10. I think it would be a nice tradition to combine ensembles for at least a couple of selections during the December Concert. What is your opinion on this matter *and* on sharing fall and spring concerts with (another ensemble)?
11. Next term, I am considering implementing the following ideas for this class. Please give your opinion on any or all of these suggestions. (list of ideas)
12. I am very pleased with the volunteer response for commencement. How do you feel about having a volunteer ensemble for commencement?
13. What do you like most about this class?
14. What do you like least about this class?
15. Any other comments, suggestions, or concerns?

Jeff Doebler is director of music education and bands at Valparaiso University in Valparaiso, Indiana. This article originally appeared in the May 1999 issue of the Indiana Musicator. *Reprinted by permission.*

Obtaining and Organizing Your Choral Library
Patrick K. Freer

Ask any choral educator what is the most arduous task they face, and the answer will almost surely be "choosing repertoire." Choral literature is the textbook of our profession. It is through repertoire that we explore developing vocal technique, make relationships between aural sounds and written notation, and discover the meaning of musicianship.

The task of choosing music appropriate for the developing adolescent is not an easy one. Compared to the vast quantities of literature written for treble choirs or high school ensembles, very little music has been specifically composed for the middle school singer's vocal needs. Various music publishers and composers have recently embarked on ambitious projects to remedy this situation, but it is still difficult to sort out the pieces which are not simply watered-down versions of repertoire originally written for other ensembles.

Your School's Choral Library
Before you decide you need to purchase new music for your school choruses, make certain that you have fully explored the choral libraries of the schools in your district. This will not only save money and research time, but you will know exactly what materials you will be using on the first day.

When you arrive at your new school and begin to prepare the room for the new year, inquire about the existing choral library:

- Where is it?
- Is there any other music hidden in another location within the school building (which hasn't seen light since King Tut lived)?
- Can arrangements be made to share repertoire from other schools in the district?

Organizing the Library
OK. Let's imagine that you have unearthed and dusted off the choral library. If you're lucky, the teacher before you left everything sorted, marked, and cataloged. When you find chaos instead, that's the perfect moment to stop and survey the situation, because now you have a big decision: how do you want things organized?

Many directors spend exhaustive amounts of time arranging their libraries. It isn't necessary. All you need to do is assign each title a number. Sure, it might be helpful if you did some presorting and put things in alphabetical order by title or composer. Sooner or later, though, you will be adding pieces to the library, and you will be forever shuffling stacks of music around to make them fit. By simply assigning a number to each title and then keeping your music in filing cabinets or closets in number order, you will always know exactly where each piece is located. You can then use a computer database or index card file to keep track of:

- title
- composer/arranger
- text author
- musical style (art song, jazz, American folk, holiday, etc.)
- level of difficulty
- number of copies in the library
- when and where the piece was performed.

The beauty of this system is that you can put your index card file or database into a thousand configurations—and you'll never misplace anything because each piece has just one number in your catalog. Let's say that you accidentally lose cards 1–10 of your index file. Your backup is to open your closet door and see what pieces of literature belong to numbers 1–10. Simple.

If you ever want to discard a piece of music from the library, then you have simply opened up a space (and number) for the next piece of music you buy. And think of the teacher who will someday inherit your library. Were you happy with how you were greeted the first time you opened those closets? If yes, then you were lucky. If no, you now have a chance to remedy the situation!

About Discarding Music

Once you know what is in your school's choral library, you get to decide what is tossed and what is kept in the files. Some "Do's and Don'ts" before you throw a party and use mountains of sheet music as a bonfire:

1. Don't throw away music which might be valuable for another teacher.
2. Don't discard music when there is extra storage room. Until you are certain that you will be teaching in your school for many years to come, it will be best to keep as much music as practical in your library.
3. Do throw away photocopied music. It's illegal.
4. Do discard music which is so tied to a particular time or event that it will never be performed again (e.g., "Disco: The Tender Moments" or "Kermit Salutes President Ford").
5. Do check with your administration before throwing away music. There may be a reason that the music has remained in your classroom for all of those years!

Finding New Music

There are many ways to locate literature for you to consider purchasing for your curriculum and concerts. The quickest, most reliable way is to obtain recommended pieces from teachers. Beyond that, the quest for finding quality repertoire is similar to a hunt for hidden treasure. Some areas to search include:

Experienced Teachers. These will be your best resources. Asking for help from experienced colleagues accomplishes several objectives: it gives you an excuse to call and introduce yourself, it shows your willingness to cooperate with others, and it will give you a wealth of knowledge about current and standard repertoire.

Don't limit yourself to teachers in your district. Call teachers in neighboring districts, talk to your former college classmates, and use the resource people identified by your professional organizations. To obtain telephone numbers of teachers you only know by reputation, try calling the various Boards of Education offices. If they won't release phone numbers, then try networking from teachers you can reach. You can always leave phone messages at the schools you wish to contact.

Music Stores and Distributors. Most larger music stores and university bookstores regularly receive single copies of recent releases. Call ahead to be certain that the resources exist, then plan on spending an afternoon browsing through repertoire.

Some larger distributors make available packets of recommended literature for you to peruse. Make certain that you only spend what you can afford to when purchasing these packets—or, better yet, ask to see the packets on approval (meaning that you can return what you don't want to keep).

Professional Organizations. MENC: The National Association for Music Education and the American Choral Directors Association (ACDA) provide numerous resources. First, their journals periodically publish lists of appropriate repertoire and resource materials. Keep these lists in a file folder for easy referencing. Secondly, both organizations sponsor numerous reading sessions of both new and recommended repertoire. Over time, these will be great resources.

Perhaps the best resources of the professional organizations are the middle school/junior high state chairpersons. These folks are selected because of their knowledge of the repertoire and adolescent vocal development. Call anyone on your organization's state Board of Directors to get in contact with these people.

Reading Sessions. These are often organized by professional organizations or colleges, and they include a tested repertory recommended by an experienced teacher.

Hint #1: Immediately discard what you will never use (unless you have unlimited closet space).

Hint #2: Write a brief note at the top of each octavo with the date and name of the session where you received the piece. If, at some future point, you find that a piece you obtained five years prior in a reading session has gone out of print, then you may be able to contact the original clinician and borrow the copies.

Publishers. Being a new teacher (or a veteran teacher in a new position) gives you a perfect excuse to call up publishers directly and ask to be sent copies of music they would recommend. Not all publishers will be able to fulfill your request, but some others will be extraordinarily generous and helpful. When you find a salesperson or company representative who is eager to offer assistance, be certain to remember the name of the person and send a thank-you note. Some of your best contact people for new and innovative repertoire can be from within the music industry. Don't overlook this possibility!

Updated Lists. Lists of repertoire are published at varying intervals by some organizations. For example, the New York State School Music Association (NYSSMA) publishes a triennial exhaustive list of repertoire for almost every imaginable ensemble, complete with publisher information and level of difficulty ratings. Call MENC's national headquarters for the current NYSSMA contact person. Various other states are in the process of developing their own lists as well.

Many books about adolescent choirs contain repertoire lists. Be sure to check about availability with the music publishers or a distributor before you decide to use a piece which is more than two or three years old.

Festival Repertoire and Tapes. There are growing numbers of festivals and All-State choruses for junior high students. If you have a teaching acquaintance in another state or region, ask for the repertoire lists of the festivals in their areas. Also, obtain as many recordings of festivals and All-States as possible. These will provide outstanding repertoire selections, and they will enable you to hear what exemplary adolescent choirs can sound like.

Computer Access. The technologies available to music teachers continue to expand. Many publishers, state organizations, and knowledgeable individuals exchange repertoire lists through e-mail and other on-line services. Numerous message boards exist through the Internet and the World Wide Web.

Ordering New Music

Be certain to check with your school's administration before purchasing any repertoire for your school's library. Most schools have strict procedures which must be followed regarding the purchase of any materials.

Shop around for the best price. Many large distributors offer substantial discounts from the listed price of music octavos. You might even check for ideas with the choir director at the college you attended. Alumni working in the music industry will often provide discounts to graduates of their alma mater. It doesn't hurt to ask!

Plan ahead! It will probably take your district's central office at least several weeks to process, send, and receive shipment of the pieces you select. Remember that your budget is for an entire year—always leave some funds in your account for unexpected situations at the end of the year.

Most districts will "freeze" budgets at some point during the year, meaning that you will no longer have access to any funds remaining in your account. Stay informed about this date, and then place a final music order to empty your account before the budget freeze. If you find yourself with extra funds, begin to purchase for the following year. Best of all, order some repertoire which you feel is essential to a quality library.

When You Cannot Order New Music

You may find yourself without funds during the first year of your teaching. Perhaps the previous teacher had placed music orders before leaving, or the budget simply doesn't allow for new music purchase. Be creative and resourceful in this situation.

- Use your school's library to the fullest extent possible.
- Use other libraries in your district.
- Call the local college and ask to borrow repertoire in exchange for using one of your ensembles as a demonstration choir for future music education methods classes.
- Arrange your favorite folk song for your sixth-grade chorus.
- Invent a unit about "choral arranging" for your choruses and then use the results in a concert (with a student conductor).
- Introduce the "theme and variations" form to your students, then compose several variations on a familiar tune ("Brother John" works well)— language, tempo, accompaniment, mode, text, etc.

- Work with the local college's composition class. A possible composition project would be to write for the specific requirements of your choir!
- Check with your local high school director to see if there is any appropriate literature in that library.

Patrick K. Freer is the education director of Young Audiences of New Jersey. This article originally appeared in the May 1996 issue of New Jersey's Tempo. *Reprinted by permission.*

Starting an Elementary-School Choir
Martha Hohweiler

One of the most rewarding things that I have ever done is to start a choir at my elementary school. It has provided me an opportunity to grow musically as well as improve my school's music program and the musical skills of my students. The following ideas were developed from information gained in a year of reading, observation, and visits with teachers of other elementary school choirs.

Before the Start of Auditions

1. *Recruit your administration, staff, and parent supporters.* Plan the kind of group you would like to have. Go in with a list of advantages in having a choir; a plan for the age levels involved, numbers of students in the group, audition procedures, rehearsal times, and concerts; and a general vision of what you want your outcomes to be. Discuss funds that might be available and other funding resources. I decided to try funding our choir through fund-raisers and sources outside my general music budget. The money we raised was put into a music PSA account in my building so I would have easy access to purchase things the choir would need. I was also able to carry over the balance from this account from year to year for the purchase of large items such as sound and recording equipment for the group.

Fund-raising techniques we have used are:
- A farmer's market
- A chili supper and concert with the parents' organization
- Punch and refreshment sales at field days
- Hosting parties at our roller-skating rink where proceeds are shared with the choir.

Be creative in your fund-raising planning. If you have a ways-and-means committee in a parents' organization, they might have some good ideas.

2. *Plan and select music for your first concert.* Because of the cost of new music, it is unlikely that you will be able to purchase enough for a large library soon. Purchase a few selections that will be standard pieces in years to come, and borrow selections from fellow teachers in your district or surrounding area. A great resource for music can be found from programs used by elementary choirs at the CMEA Clinic/ Conference. Many times the publishers and catalogue numbers are included on the programs. This also gives you an opportunity to listen to the selections being performed. For a beginning choir it is effective to use unison songs, echo songs, ostinato songs (repeated patterns), rounds, partner songs, and easy two-part songs where much of the music is in unison with a few two-part sections to develop part singing. This will build confidence and success in your group and prepare it for more difficult part singing.

When selecting music make sure to use a variety of styles that will appeal to all audiences and give your group experience with contrasting literature.

3. *Plan when to rehearse your group and determine the length of rehearsals.* I tried lunch and recess rehearsals for a couple of years and found them to be too rushed and hard on the kids and myself, especially during the spring when the students wanted to be outside. We now rehearse before school for forty minutes twice per week and have had great success with this plan. It is a plan that helps bring in dedicated students who want a choir of high quality.

4. *Plan your concerts and outings for the year and place them on your master calendar.* You can then give dates to students while recruiting so that they can see the opportunities ahead for them. Advance planning also gives parents time to clear dates, plan family events, and coordinate other schedules so they will not conflict with that of the choir.

5. *Recruit students for your choir by talking to your classes and describing plans for the group.* To help

eliminate the fear of auditions, teach your classes an audition piece so that they are all prepared and reassure them that they can audition by themselves or in groups of two or three.

6. *Put up a bulletin board for recruiting.* Have separate sections for audition times, expectations, and dates of concerts and outings.

7. *Decide on how you want to set up parts and sections in your group.* I have tried several ways, and I am still experimenting. I have found that three-fifths of my group on melody and two-fifths on harmony help to keep a fairly nice blend. I place a section of students in the middle of the choir whom I call swing singers. These students have strong voices that can be placed on either harmony or melody, depending on where I determine there is a need for more strength. It is also good to select a group of high and accurate voices for obbligato parts when music calls for it.

8. *Set up a three-ring notebook with dividers for sections devoted to aspects of the program.* There should be sections for the following:
   • Music and narrations (to keep a record of selections used at each concert and to plan for upcoming programs)
   • Seating chart and attendance
   • Calendar and concerts
   • Forms and letters
   • Budget and expenditures
   • Warm-ups
   • Any other areas that are of importance to you.

I keep such a notebook, which is separate from my music folder, so that it can be used for attendance.

Auditions, Permission Slips, and Contracts

I send a letter home with all my fifth- and sixth-grade students inviting them to audition for the choir at my school, known as the Linton Pride Choir. Included in the letter is information about the following:

1. Starting date and rehearsal days and times
2. Audition dates and times
3. The size of the choir as influenced by music-room size and busing limitations
4. Attendance requirements
5. Excused absences and tardies
6. Expectations and behavior standards
7. Performances
8. The choir uniform
9. Skating-party dates and fund-raising activities.

Included in the information letter is a choir contract which must be signed by the student and a parent, a bus permission slip for performances during the school day, a phone-tree permission slip that I use for emergency communication, and a parent volunteer information form. It is much easier to have all the forms returned together than at separate times.

Auditions

I audition all interested students so as to know the strengths and weaknesses of each voice. This helps me to determine which parts to place them on and how to seat the students. Some may have weaker voices and need the support of stronger voices around them. A student's participation in the audition process also indicates to me that he or she has a strong desire to be in the choir. I check range, tonal memory, accuracy of pitch, and blend with other voices. Auditioning is a valuable musical experience and gives the students confidence in their voices.

Attendance Clerk, Librarians, Setup Crew, P.A. Crew, and Narrators

Not all students can be soloists, but many still desire to have a special part in the activity of the choir. The roles of attendance clerk, librarians, setup crew, P.A. crew, and narrators not only give them such special parts, but make my job much easier. I put a list on my door and have the students sign up for jobs they are interested in doing.

Taking Attendance

The attendance clerk for my choir records attendance at each rehearsal and concert. To make this task more manageable, I type the students' names on a tag board, laminate the board, and cut each name apart. When students arrive for rehearsal, they place their names in a coffee can. At 7:30 a.m., we draw two names out to be winners of a small candy bar. Students whose names remain outside of the can are counted tardy or absent. A colleague shared this idea with me, and it is amazing how prompt students can be in the hope of winning a candy bar!

Rehearsals

Rehearsals must be organized so as to proceed smoothly. I write the list of the music to be rehearsed on a chalkboard so that students can have the pieces in order. Some of the things I include during rehearsals are:

1. Warm-up
2. Announcements
3. A song they have been working on
4. A new section or a new piece of music
5. Finishing with choreography or a song they particularly enjoy (so as to end with an especially positive feeling).

I have found that elementary school students are very capable of good diction, phrasing, and musicality. Work these elements into the music while they are learning it. Sometimes it is difficult to change habits that students develop once they have worked on a song for some time.

Decide on how much of the year you want to run your choir. I usually take the month of September to audition and organize the choir. We rehearse during October through December and perform our winter concerts and outings. We take the month of January off and start again in February and perform our spring concerts in April. The choir schedule usually ends by the middle of April.

Uniforms

When we started our choir, we had a contest to determine a name for the group. The school's art teacher helped design a logo to coordinate with the name. We decided to use T-shirts as our uniform and began looking for the best supplier. We found that by using a shirt with a polyester and cotton blend, the color and size stayed true and the shirt lasted for several years. By using this type of shirt, the cost can be kept to a minimum. Members of my group also wear solid black turtlenecks under their shirts during the winter and just the T-shirts during the spring. Along with their T-shirts, the students wear solid black skirts or pants. When they are in uniform, I find that the students identify more with the group and have a greater sense of pride.

Performances and Trip Checklist

I have found that trips go more smoothly with teachers or paraprofessional chaperones along who know the students and how to step in when need-ed. A trip checklist has been very helpful to make sure every detail is completed. When a trip is well organized and expectations of students and chaperones are clearly defined and understood, the outing is highly likely to be enjoyed by everyone involved.

There are a number of places an elementary choir can perform:

1. Nursing homes
2. Choir exchanges with other schools
3. District events
4. Concerts for the student body
5. Concerts for parents
6. Community events.

The most difficult concerts will be those in front of the students' peers. The problems that can develop should be discussed with the choir ahead of time. Concert etiquette by the student body should be reviewed in your general music classes before the performance.

Communication

Effective communication is essential for any choir. Your communication should be clear to the choir, staff, administration, and parents. Do not assume anything. Be sure everyone involved is well informed in a timely manner. Any questions that may arise should be answered prior to a performance. With good communication and a clear understanding, the support you need to ensure a successful choir is sure to follow.

An elementary school choir can enrich your general music program and is a highly audible and visible reminder of the importance of music in our schools. If you start a new choir with good organization and are excited about what you are doing, the results can be very satisfying and rewarding to both you and your students.

Martha Hohweiler teaches music at Linton Elementary School in Fort Collins, Colorado. This article orginally appeared in the Spring 1995 issue of the Colorado Music Educator. *Reprinted by permission.*

High School Male Chorus: Rare Bird, Strange Beast, Definite Challenge

Allan Hoke

Male choruses seem to be rather rare in high schools, although there are a few strong ones. It is effective to schedule the male chorus as an entry-level chorus and start building a tradition (do the same for your females, also). It would be great to have these men in another music class.

Since this class would be viewed as entry level, time should be spent every day on the basics of musical skills. A minimum of ten minutes each day should be spent on sight-singing. In the long haul this effort will pay off. There are many methods out in publications today, but I can strongly recommend *Successful Sight-Singing* by Nancy Telfer, published by Kjos, as a valuable resource.

There is something about working with adolescent males that is quite unlike any other experience. One certainly needs to maintain a sense of humor with a group like this. (A degree of raunchiness is also to be expected!) This chorus presents certain unique problems, especially when it comes to selecting music and working with the group vocally.

Selecting music is one of the most important and difficult tasks and must be approached delicately. Music selection is not only important; it is also a political process. My male chorus does not start out by doing "serious" literature. At the beginning I like to start with a two-part sea chanty or two, or a song like "As Beautiful as She" by Butler in three parts, and then four-part barbershop from "Young Men in Harmony." It is important to get them singing and enjoying a nice rich male chorus sound. The men will really like and enjoy any and all barbershop tunes you sing. The more you sell them on this a cappella style, the easier it will be to introduce a Renaissance Latin "Ave Maria" or motet and hold their interest. Introducing Randall Thompson's "The Pasture" and "Stopping by Woods on a Snowy Evening" helps them to work on a good piece of music and obtain a good sound in a fair amount of time.

I believe that students really would prefer spending their time on literature that has more depth than popular music, though when a group is in its infancy, literature of this type might initially be brought in through the back door. What is needed is music with depth as well as music that is just fun to sing. The music must be challenging, yet accessible.

Male chorus is a strange beast! Getting a good male sound in high school is a tricky process. There are several things which I find useful in accomplishing this feat.

1. The first goal is to get the group to sing. The challenge is to get a good sound, but if they're not singing it's futile to try and improve the sound.

One technique I learned from Don Neuen in a workshop is the following: Each male student is asked to imagine that a girlfriend is walking by the room in the hall and that this is one of the few opportunities he'll have to talk with her, so in a robust voice he says (since she's now several hundred yards away), "Hey—come here and sit down." The sound should be healthy and robust—not screaming—and come from the diaphragm. Inform the students that those who are less than robust will be volunteering themselves to try it in front of the group (a friendly threat you probably won't implement). Pulling this off usually results in a fairly healthy sound that can be translated into a good singing tone.

2. The next step is to get the men to use their head voice frequently and with ease. Try the following procedures:

- Start with a high-pitched hum in a head voice, descending to a low point in the vocal range.
- Next, do the same thing on "oo." Try to make a smooth transition from the higher register to the lower register; avoid cracking.
- Check students at this point to be sure their high pitch is free and taking place in their head voice, not in a forced chest voice. Ask students who are doing it correctly to demonstrate.
- Sing descending five-note scales (5-4-3-2-1) starting on B-flat above middle C. Move down by half steps, all the way to the low point in the range.
- Above all, always warm up the voice starting at a high pitch and work down. Never start with low notes and work up—this tends to create stress. The tone should always be free. We spend most of our rehearsal time during the first term working on a good sound. Some of the things we try have been mentioned above. Simultaneously, we worked on accurate intonation. The process is sometimes laborious. However, I think the time spent on sound and

intonation at the beginning of the year is worth it and critical.

If you have a male chorus, continue the effort; if not—start one. Directing a male chorus can be a true challenge. The exciting part is that adolescent males, always unpredictable, are able to achieve great things when they work together.

Allan Hoke taught music in the Knox County Schools in Tennessee for 25 years. Currently, he is executive secretary and treasurer for the East Tennessee Vocal Association and director of music at Messiah Lutheran Church in Knoxville, Tennessee. This article first appeared in the Winter 1993 issue of The Tennessee Musician. *Reprinted by permission.*

Effectively Involving Band Parents—Tips for Beginning Band Directors (Choir and Orchestra Directors, Too!)
David Maccabee

We are all looking to be more efficient at our jobs. In addition, we want to generate enthusiasm for band in our community. Obviously a band parents' organization can provide substantial help in both areas. As I began my teaching career eighteen years ago, I had no idea how to tap into this resource effectively.

As a young teacher I did not want to ask for help. I felt that I should be self-reliant and simply handle my job! Therefore, I started my teaching career measuring my own students for uniforms, taking the uniforms to the cleaners, collecting cheese and sausage orders, obtaining chaperones for trips, ordering chili for the chili supper, and every now and then—I would teach. Unfortunately I made a lot of mistakes along the way because I foolishly tried to do everything.

We must ask for help for three very important reasons:

1. We cannot handle all the administrative duties in this job. If we try to handle everything, we will inevitably make a lot of mistakes. Giving away work allows us more time to organize and tend to our teaching responsibilities. In addition, we will have more time to be thorough and organized in dealing with the administrative work we alone must do.
2. More importantly, by giving our parents work to do in support of the band, they feel a much stronger sense of ownership of the band program. We want our parents to be partners with us in the development of a quality instrumental music program.
3. There are people in every community eager to contribute to the band program. In fact, the vast majority of people will be flattered that you asked for their help! Seek out those great volunteers in your community—they'll be thrilled to chip in.

How should a new band director go about obtaining band parent help? First of all, make a list of nonteaching responsibilities you have. This will take a long time to do. (You might be rather overwhelmed when you are finished!) Go through the list and decide which tasks you personally do not have to do. These are the things you are going to try and delegate to your band parents.

Next, set up a meeting with your band parents' president. Go to this meeting armed with the list of projects you would like the band parents to help with or contribute to. Ask for the president's help in finding people to fulfill these tasks. Encourage your band parents' president to be frank about what and how much he or she can realistically handle. In other words, don't overdo it. In your discussion with your band parents' president, ask the president to assess personalities as well as skills in recommending people for different jobs. In other words, you don't want an abrasive parent working public relations. Maybe that parent could collect cheese and sausage orders!

Your band parents' president can contact individuals who might consider helping out. Or, you can wait for a band parent club meeting to obtain interested volunteers. I actually recommend calling people first. It gives you a little more control of who is working in specific areas.

Here are some ways that parents can meaningfully and significantly contribute:

- Chaperones for trips
- Ushers for concerts
- Band newsletter (This is a *must!*)
- Publicity
- Fund-raising needs
- Band awards night
- Equipment moving and transportation
- Flag sewers

- Band trips
- Uniform maintenance.

There are literally hundreds of other opportunities for parents to make meaningful contributions to the band program. If you cannot think of any tasks your parents can do, try harder! *Create* something for them to do. You need their involvement in the band!

Once you have parents engaged in an activity or project, insist that they contact you with any and every question. ("Mr. Smith, should I get the cotton or nylon thread?") When you begin to utilize band parent help, you may be busy for a little while as they learn their jobs and ask lots of questions. Do not be afraid to get their thoughts and opinions regarding the logistics of the project they are working on. Over time, they will become more self-sufficient and rely on you less.

I feel very strongly that a band parent group must never have the power to decide where fund-raised dollars are spent. Every school district should have some sort of policy related to this matter. In terms of fund-raising, a band parent club can decide how much money to raise, but not how to spend it. This should be a matter of board policy. Your administration hired you to make the decisions. Your parents don't know you need a bass clarinet more than a new band trailer—you must make those decisions, and you were hired to do so.

Protect your professionalism and control of the band program. If you have not spoken to your administration regarding this matter, do so soon.

Finally, thank your parents at every opportunity. You will be surprised at the generosity of some people—it is easy to take their kindness for granted. Your constant enthusiastic gratitude will make a big difference in maintaining their support.

David Maccabee is band director at United Township High School in East Moline, Illinois. This article first appeared in the Winter 1999 issue of the Illinois Music Educator. *Reprinted by permission.*

Concert Etiquette, or How Does Your Audience Measure Up?
Deborah A. Mello

As the frenzy of December concerts has subsided and my students and I have had time to reflect upon our musical endeavors, I find my thoughts turning to the ever-present concern of the audience and its role in the concert.

As music educators, we have a responsibility to educate the public concerning music education and the performing arts. This is a never-ending and oftentimes frustrating charge. As conductors, performers, and audience members, we've all witnessed the demise of proper concert etiquette. While attending an All-County High School Band and Choral Concert last season, I observed a gentleman who, in the middle of a piece, decided to leave. He was sitting in the middle of the fifth row of the auditorium and proceeded to disturb nearly the entire audience to get out. Of course, he let the door bang as he left, adding insult to injury. After intermission, he and his wife returned during the first selection, and the process occurred in reverse! This man and his wife clearly had no idea that their actions caused such a disturbance during that concert. They did not feel connected to the performers on stage, even though they probably had a child in the band or chorus.

Each concert situation has unique physical characteristics and needs to be looked at carefully in those terms. For instance, few elementary schools have auditoriums, and groups must perform in the cafeteria or gymnasium. The audience needs to be able to focus in on the purpose of their presence for that evening. There are some general rules they must be made aware of in terms of their role in the concert as a whole. We might even use the word "inclusion." These are ideas and rules that I teach in the music classroom to provide the next generation with the knowledge and understanding of their role as performers as well as members of an audience. Concert etiquette is something that students need to internalize, so they can draw upon it throughout their lifetime.

The art of listening is an active rather than a passive ability. In terms of getting these ideas across to students, there are many ways. First, active listening must be an integral part of every child's musical experience and education. Throughout each year, active listening must be included in what is taught in the music classroom. Music educators do this all the time by playing recordings or providing live music and directing their students' attention to different components of the music and appropriate responses to it.

A concert encompasses several components: the music, the performers, and the audience and their importance in the performance medium. Role playing is a wonderful means to teach students the importance of their role as a performer or audience member. Informal performances by small groups of students for their class, with the remaining students as audience, will allow students to experience firsthand what their responsibility is as a performer and a member of the audience. With younger children, who need some guidance, take time to discuss expectations and follow up with how each group performed its role and perhaps how each might improve.

Concertizing is a means of communication for both the performers as well as the audience. Be aware of what you are communicating. Again, role playing can be an invaluable teaching tool. In chorus rehearsal or in music class, you can ask the student performers to perform a song several ways to express different ideas. The use of tempo, dynamics, posture, blank looks, animated faces, energetic singing, and diction are some of the ways a song could be performed and then evaluated by the audience with applause and a follow-up discussion. The performers must be aware that they have the power to set the tone and open the lines of communication. The audience must be aware that they must be willing to receive the communication and respond to it.

Hopefully, your students have the knowledge to enable them to be aware of proper concert etiquette. How do we impart that awareness to our audiences? The following are some suggestions that I have used and have observed in use:

- A music newsletter discussing lessons taught on concert etiquette with specific examples
- Administrators encouraging parents to leave infants and very young children home with a baby-sitter or providing a baby-sitting service at the school
- A written paragraph in the program addressing some general rules
- A reception following the concert for "socializing"
- An announcement to the audience inviting them to be active listeners and reviewing concert etiquette. This can be made by your administrator, yourself or a teaching colleague, or a student.

How difficult are these rules to remember? Which ones apply to your situation?

- Please do not talk during the performing of the music.
- Please do not come in or leave during the performing of the music, but between selections.
- Please do not take flash pictures during the performing of the music, but between selections.
- Please do take a child out who cannot sit quietly.

As music educators, we must continue to strive for ideal concert situations. Learning is a lifelong endeavor, and as educators we have a responsibility to our students and their parents to continue that process, particularly in an area that is greatly neglected. Setting guidelines for the performers and listeners in a concert situation can only enrich the musical experience for everyone.

Deborah A. Mello teaches general and choral music at McKeown Elementary School in Hampton Township, New Jersey. She is also the founder and artistic director of the Children's Chorus of Sussex County, New Jersey. This article first appeared in the January 1997 issue of New Jersey's Tempo. *Reprinted by permission.*

Keeping Junior High School Boys Singing

Mark Munson

It is no secret among choral music educators that junior high school represents a turning point in student participation in school choral programs. In many districts, one would find a large number of students singing in the elementary school, many entering but dropping out of the junior high choruses, and even fewer participating at the senior high level. Especially apparent in many cases is the limited number of boys participating in the junior and senior high programs. For teachers experiencing this situation, it may be time to focus again on the root of the problem: the attrition of male singers at the junior high school level. Unfortunately it is often true that once a student drops out of the choral program, he (or she) will not return. Therefore, while it is possible to recruit boys at the senior high level, it is desirable to maintain a large number of them in the junior high choruses.

Junior high school boys go through many changes. Dealing successfully with the emotions and personality of the junior high boy is as important as dealing with his changing voice. It is important for this young adolescent to feel successful, and he would like very much to be part of a winning team. He is very concerned about what his peers think, possibly quite self-conscious about his voice change, and, although he may not admit it, he wants to please and be accepted by his teachers.

Scheduling voice tests for every junior high school boy a few times each year can be a most valuable investment of time. Tests could be given every four months for boys in seventh, eighth, and ninth grades. To make sure that each is in the appropriate section of the chorus at the beginning of the school year, the first test should be given in September. The second test might be given in January after the busyness of the holiday season, and the third test after the spring concert in May.

Prior to the initial testing of the seventh graders, the boys are called together to have explained to them the basics of the voice change and the procedures that will be used to record the growth of their voices. A simple chart for each boy consists of two staves divided into measures. While boys may come individually for the voice tests, it is more expedient to test several at a time who have similar vocal ranges, one right after another. During each test, the vocal range and age of each boy is recorded. The choral music teacher also may want to record height so that correlations can be drawn. From their charts, the boys can easily see how much their voices have grown between tests. What a pleasure it is to monitor this aspect of each boy's development and watch each stand a little taller when he is told that he has gained two or three new low notes since his last voice test. It is also amazing how much loyalty can be earned by the choral music teacher who will take this time to encourage each boy as he is going through his voice change. With the good news which follows so many of the voice tests, it is not surprising that the boys actually look forward to being tested.

Examples A, B, and C are some samples of completed charts. It is easy to see that some voices, such as Kurt's (example A), change gradually, while others, such as Kevin's (example B), have a more sudden change.

One of my favorite charts is Jeff's (example C). At the beginning of the seventh grade, Jeff's range was limited to a major third! How easily he could have been discouraged. As can be seen on the chart, his range grew in both directions. Encouraged partially by this visual representation of his progress, Jeff became an enthusiastic leader of the chorus.

After determining voice ranges, it is important

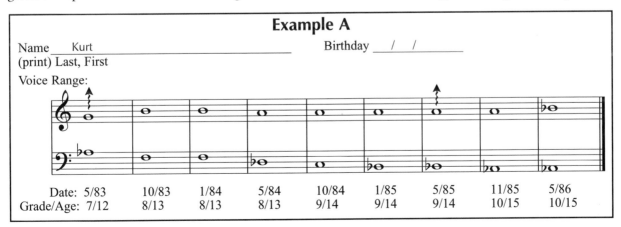

Example A

Name ___Kurt___ Birthday __/__/__
(print) Last, First

Voice Range:

Date:	5/83	10/83	1/84	5/84	10/84	1/85	5/85	11/85	5/86
Grade/Age:	7/12	8/13	8/13	8/13	9/14	9/14	9/14	10/15	10/15

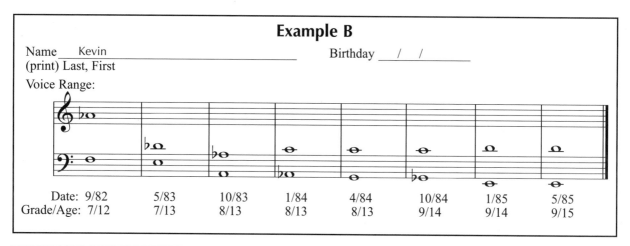

Example B

Name Kevin

(print) Last, First

Birthday / /

Voice Range:

Date:	9/82	5/83	10/83	1/84	4/84	10/84	1/85	5/85
Grade/Age:	7/12	7/13	8/13	8/13	8/13	9/14	9/14	9/15

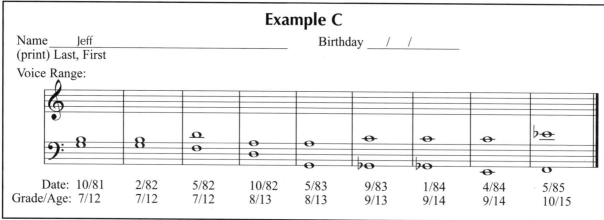

Example C

Name Jeff

(print) Last, First

Birthday / /

Voice Range:

Date:	10/81	2/82	5/82	10/82	5/83	9/83	1/84	4/84	5/85
Grade/Age:	7/12	7/12	7/12	8/13	8/13	9/13	9/14	9/14	10/15

to put each boy into a section where he can realize success as a singer. Many boys drop out of junior high choral programs because they are asked to sing parts that they are not able to sing well or able to sing at all. One can only speculate on the number of men in our society who could enjoy singing as adults, but do not simply because of some frustrating experiences at the time of their voice change. How many came to the conclusion that they could not sing, when really they were being asked to do the impossible?

Much of the currently published music written for three-part mixed choruses works well with the seventh-grade mixed chorus. Not to be confused with the more traditional SAB arrangements where the "B" is a baritone part, these three-part mixed compositions and arrangements consist of two parts for treble voices and one part for the changing (cambiata) voice. The range of this cambiata part is typically from the F or G below middle C to the D above. Example D shows the voice ranges of thirty-six boys in the fall of their seventh grade year. As can be deduced from the chart, nearly all of the boys would be able to sing at least one of the parts of the three-part music. It should also be noted that most of these seventh graders would not be able to sing typical unison or two-part treble arrangements.

By the time the boys enter the eighth grade, there are several whose voices have changed enough that even the lowest part of the three-part mixed voicing is too high for them to sing without straining. Asking these new baritones to sing this cambiata part will surely cause frustration.

Remember that frustrated choristers are not likely to continue singing. Example E shows the vocal ranges of the same thirty-six boys at the beginning of their eighth-grade year. Note that about one third of the boys in this sample will have problems singing the cambiata part of the three-part mixed arrangements.

Because a number of new baritones will emerge during the eighth-grade year, there needs to be at least one additional part to accommodate their voices. For the benefits of these new eighth grade baritones, I advocate combining eighth-grade singers with ninth graders rather than with seventh graders.

Example F shows the same thirty-six boys as they entered the ninth grade. With a substantially greater number of baritone voices in the ninth grade, combining the eighth and ninth grade singers will put the eighth-grade baritones in a section with enough peers to confidently sing a

Example D

A Random Sampling of Voice Ranges of Boys
in the Autumn of their Seventh Grade Year

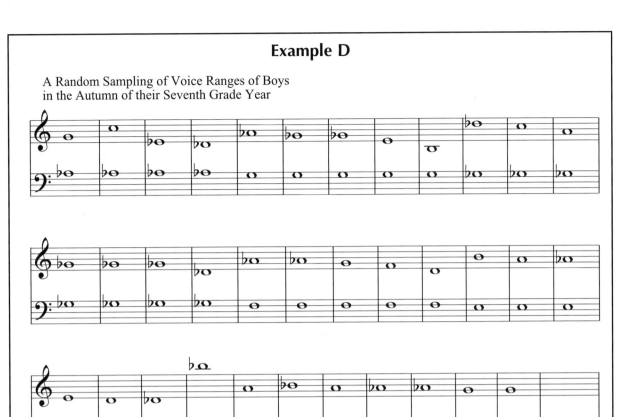

Example E

Ranges of the Same Boys in the Autumn of their Eighth Grade Year

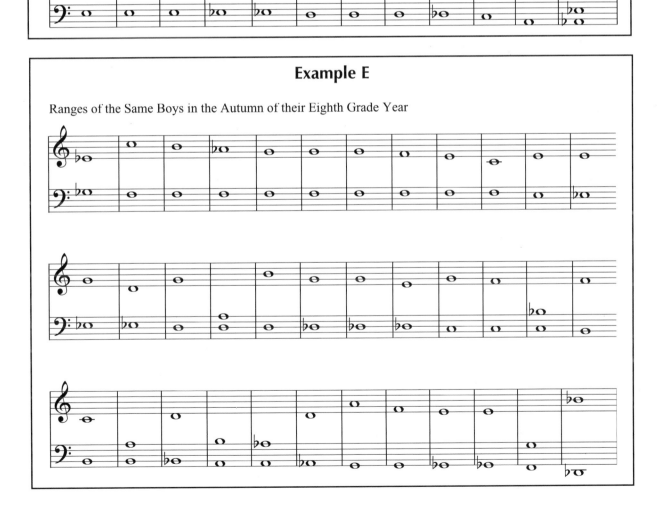

Example F

Ranges of the Same Boys in the Autumn of their Ninth Grade Year

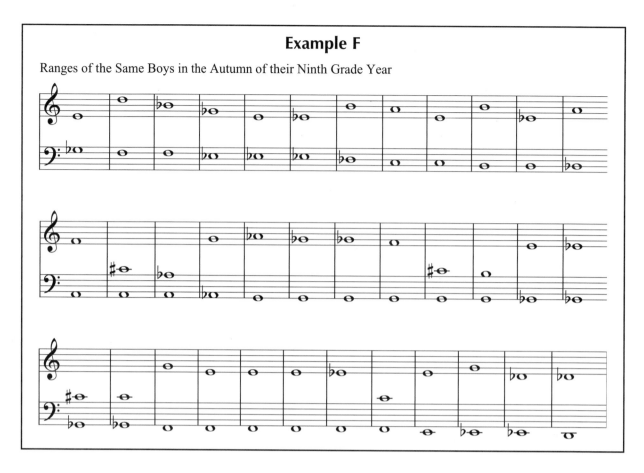

bass-baritone part. Being part of this successful team, the eighth-grade baritones are more likely to continue in the choral program and become leaders as freshmen the following year.

Having been helped through the most radical part of their voice change, these young men are more likely to participate in choral music at the senior high school, and throughout their adult lives. What a mistake it is not to have a place for these eighth graders who are the new baritones. Many of these early bloomers are the boys of the greatest physical stature and athletic ability and, consequently, the social leaders of the class. What music teacher does not want at least a few of the student leaders participating in his or her program?

In addition to the eighth- and ninth-grade grouping, this author advocates separate male and female choruses for this age group. Experiencing a less radical voice change, the females' needs in the choral rehearsal differ from those of the males. With the boys out of the room, the girls can make remarkable progress in developing skills in music reading, part-singing, and vocal technique. Likewise, with the boys in their own chorus, the teacher can focus on the challenges of the changing voice. Further, in a separate junior high boys chorus, TTB repertoire can be introduced, which

will further accommodate the needs of these young singers. The top tenor part can be sung by boys who still have at least a perfect fifth above middle C in their range; the second tenor will normally work for those who have the smaller five or six-note range of the F below middle C to the D above; and the bass part (provided that it is not too low) will work for the baritones of the chorus. Besides working better vocally, the successful, all-male junior high chorus has the potential of being very popular in the school community.

It is unfortunate that the eighth- and ninth-grade grouping will be difficult if not impossible to schedule in school districts where those grades are housed in different buildings. It is advisable in those situations to give as much attention and care to the changing voices as possible. While we cannot expect every adolescent to enjoy singing, our junior high school choral directors can play a crucial role in encouraging boys through this time of transition.

Mark Munson is director of choral activities and an associate professor of music education at Bowling Green State University in Bowling Green, Ohio. This article originally appeared in the May/June 1995 issue of Ohio's TRIAD. *Reprinted by permission.*

A Choir Retreat in Your Classroom

Michael Ross

Have you tried a choir retreat? Rebecca Winnie (Homestead High School, Mequon, Wisconsin) wrote an article several years ago for this column that contained great information and suggestions about having a choir retreat. I got interested in the idea from another colleague, Randy Swiggum, when I attended two of his school's retreats as a chaperone. I witnessed firsthand the amazing experiences choral students can have at this type of event. Two years ago I held my first choir retreat. I brought in several clinicians to lead rehearsals and sectionals. The musical growth and focus that resulted from those experiences were remarkable. But it was the "other" experiences, the small-group discussions, the large-group games, the art projects, and the team-building experiences that students (and I) remember most.

This year we were not able to schedule a retreat. My students and I were disappointed, so we decided to bring some of those "retreat" experiences into our daily rehearsals more often. In fact, the entire music department at Madison West High School has set a departmental goal for the next two years: to increase our use of team-building activities in our large-ensemble rehearsals. Here are a few of the games/activities that have worked for us. Some are from friends or are my own invention; others are from other sources (which I have given credit where necessary).

Sing-Down

Can be played with any size class. (I learned this at a camp where I used to work.)

Divide the students into groups of 5–8. Students need to work within their groups to come up with songs that fit the theme (either using the title of the song or lyrics from it). They should come up with as many songs (that fit the theme) as they can in five minutes, writing them down.

After five minutes, stop them and review the rules for the next part of the game. Pick a group to start and then continue from group to group around the room and have them share one of the songs on their list. *Everyone* in the group needs to sing the song, just a short excerpt which shows the connection to the theme, or at least fake it. Continue around the room. Groups get out either by repeating a song that has already been sung (you'll have to take fast notes to keep track), by

not having a song ready fast enough when it's their turn, or by not having everyone in their group singing.

Possible Themes: (you pick)

- Colors (or choose one color)
- Emotions (or choose one emotion)
- Weather (or choose rain or snow)
- Numbers (or choose a particular number)
- Cars
- Magic

Section Commercials

(My own invention)

Have each section in your choir meet as a group. Give them a set amount of time to come up with some type of "commercial" that (1) introduces *everyone* in the section and (2) introduces the name of the section and something unique about it. There are no more rules; students can sing/dance/act/whatever they want. My students love this; the tenor section still uses some parts of their commercial as a rallying cry.

People Machine

(From many sources including *Tribes* by Jeanne Gibbs.)

Put students into groups (by section?). Each person thinks of a sound and a motion. The group "assembles" these sounds/motions in some way (usually the people physically connect, but they don't have to) to make a "machine." Groups can present their machines to the class. A variant on this game is to choose one student as a conductor for each group and present a "people-machine symphony" complete with dynamics and tempo changes.

Two Truths and a Lie

(Also from many sources, including *Tribes*)

This game can be played in large or small groups. Everyone thinks of two "truths" and one "lie" about themselves. Then, one at a time, students share all three of these facts. The other students vote to decide which was the "lie."

Pen Pals

(From *Tribes* also)

Have students all write some interesting fact about themselves (that most people don't know) on a 3 x 5 card. Collect all the cards, shuffle them, and pass them back to the students. If a student gets his/her own card again, they should trade it for another until everyone has a card that is not their own. Next, students move around the room asking each other questions about the information on the card, trying to figure out who the card belongs to. When a student finds the owner of their card, the writer of the card signs the card and the cards are displayed somewhere (chalkboard, etc.). When all students have finished getting their cards "signed," read the cards aloud to the class. Keep them displayed somewhere and refer to them from time to time!

Use these activities throughout the year. Don't be afraid to "take away" from your busy rehearsal schedules. The time spent on these and other similar activities can help create a group bonding experience that will only lead to more successful music making.

References

Gibbs, J. (2000). *Tribes: A new way of learning and being together.* Sausalito, CA: CenterSource Systems.

Michael Ross is the music department chair and vocal music teacher at Madison West High School in Madison, Wisconsin. This article originally appeared in the April 2001 issue of The Wisconsin School Musician. *Reprinted by permission.*

Teaching Music in the Urban Setting: Point of View
Annice M. Schear

As I reflect on my five years as vocal music director at Nathan Hale Middle School, I think especially about the challenges and rewards of teaching in an urban school. I focus on the idea that every child is entitled to a music education taught by a qualified, certified teacher, and I reflect on my personal mission to use music to fix the world.

Throughout my music education course work, nothing in particular was mentioned about working in an urban environment. As a matter of fact, it appeared that the only difference in teaching music to children was the grade level of the children. My field work prior to student teaching was focused in the middle school, working with adolescents in both general music and choral classes. The behaviors and attitudes of those students were talkative, obstinate, energetic, and challenging.

After teaching part-time general music K–8 for two years in private schools, I finally landed a full-time teaching position with the Cleveland Public School District (now the Cleveland Municipal School District). Out of twelve new teachers hired that year, I was one of only two teachers with middle school experience. And so in 1995, I began my teaching career at Nathan Hale Middle School, one of twenty-three middle schools in the district.

When I arrived at the school, the now former principal was eager to rebuild the music program that had been stagnant after the death of the previous music teacher. No replacement was hired due to budget constraints. Band and orchestra instruments were stored away somewhere in the building, choir robes were scattered in various storage closets, and the music room was used for other purposes. The principal informed me that it was my assignment to rebuild the music program as I saw fit. The principal was in full support of any idea or decision I had about the music program. The first thought that came to mind was "I wasn't taught how to start a music program!"

The challenges I faced were overwhelming. To begin with, there were no performing ensembles in the school. I chose to focus on vocal music because of the lack of well-maintained instruments available. Recruiting from my seventh-grade general music classes, I created a choir of twelve students. Once I had a choir in place, I tried to find places for them to perform. I discovered that performances outside the school day were impossible because many students could not get to the school in the evenings. Students were bussed from all over the district to the school, and parents/guardians were unable to get to the school after school hours. So I limited their performances to during school hours.

My students might have problems that suburban students may never experience, but adolescents are the same everywhere—children trying to act mature without losing their childlike qualities. I was also overwhelmed by the outside problems with which my students had to contend. Many came from broken homes. Many had witnessed violence and drug use in their families. Several experienced sexual situations before they were ready. These problems gave my students very little hope and very little reason to be happy. I spent many days in the guidance office learning about the students I was assigned to teach to appreciate music. I admit I did not fully understand their problems, but I tried to help in any way I could. I had no previous experience or knowledge from which I could base my answers. I relied on my colleagues for guidance.

An additional challenge was that there was no music supervisor or district music department. I was extremely fortunate to be the last class of new teachers to experience peer mentoring. Without my peer mentor, I would not have survived my first year in the district. I probably would have left the first week. What I learned my first year teaching was not taught in my college music education classes for various reasons. The main reason, I believe, is because one has to experience the first year. It cannot be taught. My seventh- and eighth-grade students that first year were testing me to see if I would stay. They knew the status of the music program up until I arrived.

I survived physical and emotional distress that year with the help of my peer mentor. I remember the late night calls and the emergency day calls, begging for help. I also remember her visits with supplemental music resources for me to use. I did not know how to help these students. I decided to become personally involved in fixing the world through these children. And I would use my music program as the means.

Five years later, I am humbled as observers remark about our music program. The challenges that I faced were overwhelming. However, I set realistic goals for myself and for my students. I am proud of what we have accomplished. Though not all of the goals I set in 1995 have been realized to their full potential, I know we are on the right track in creating an outstanding music program for our students The rewards definitely outweigh the challenges.

My choral program grew from a humble beginning of one choir of twelve students to two choirs of thirty-five students each. Both choirs are scheduled into the regular school day, and students receive grades for their work in the ensembles. The seventh and eighth grade choir schedules 12–15 performances each year for the school and Cleveland community. This year we were extremely honored to perform at the OMEA Conference in Cleveland. We also participate in OMEA adjudicated events and other non-OMEA-sponsored adjudicated events by conduct-

ing two fund-raisers each year. The students are capable of performing quality choral literature and are expected to maintain and achieve high standards to remain in the choir. There is now a waiting list for students to join this choir. The sixth-grade choir is remarkable. Their behavior and attitude is refreshing. They are willing to try anything new. Their classroom teachers are motivating and offer continued guidance in shaping these young people. They will be a welcomed addition to seventh- and eighth-grade choir next year.

Although the rewards have been slower with the seventh grade general music classes, some goals have been reached. I have incorporated the National Standards for Music Education as a guide, as well as assessment strategies from MENC. More students are enjoying the class. Activities have been more hands-on, although there are no melody instruments for general music students to use. Students understand the relationships between music and the other disciplines outside of the arts. When they complete their required semester of general music, they must demonstrate in one way or another that they know something about music. I have more to accomplish with general music, but I know I am on the right track for continued improvement. With the newly created Department of Arts Education and newly appointed music supervisor, the arts education program at Nathan Hale Middle School will continue to grow and prosper.

I have come to the conclusion that my urban students are just like those I worked with in my field experiences and early teaching—talkative, obstinate, energetic, and challenging. My students might have problems that suburban students may never experience, but adolescents are the same everywhere—children trying to act mature without losing their childlike qualities.

Keeping that in mind will help me and others understand urban children and the urban school environment.

Annice M. Schear is department chairperson of fine arts and vocal music director at Nathan Hale Middle School in Cleveland, Ohio. This article first appeared in the February–March 2000 issue of Ohio's TRIAD. *Reprinted by permission.*

More Room at the Top

Christopher Shay

It is common for high schools to feature one top choir, usually for mixed voices. One objection to this format is that singers who are not in the top choir identify themselves as second best. Once identified as second best, it is difficult for these singers to generate the kind of effort and concentration that they would have generated if they were in the top choir. It is equally difficult for a conductor to expect 100 percent from "lower level" groups.

It is possible to offer more than one top ensemble by featuring a top men's chorus, a top women's chorus, and a top mixed chorus. This will allow at least three times more room at the top. Separating the boys and girls in the ninth and tenth grades and putting them back together in eleventh and twelfth grades has many advantages. The best feature of this arrangement is that the ninth-grade cambiata voices are celebrated for the contribution that their light, high voices make to a perfectly balanced ensemble. TTBB repertoire is frequently written in a range that fits these voices beautifully. Many ninth-grade cambiata tenors cannot sing lower than the F or E below middle C, but they can float up to a high B-flat with no problem. It would be a dreadful mistake to tell them to sing with the girls until they can sound like real men! These voices are the solution to TTBB music. This same music is out of reach for most eleventh- and twelfth-grade boys. This is one of the few opportunities for less physically developed ninth-graders to celebrate their present condition. Much of society promises them that everything will be all right, just as soon as they become men.

There is also a wealth of superior repertoire for women's voices. The learning curve is somewhat more kind to ninth-grade girls. While the boys are fussing around finding their voices, their pitch, their choir folder, and their head, and after they have finished roughhousing and jumping up and down on one another, the girls have already mastered twice the repertoire and have moved on to Brahms and Bach. Ninth-grade boys can appear like discipline problems in a mixed chorus. Add this to their inferior numbers and they might conclude, "Who needs this?" We would prefer not to discourage the boys any more than necessary. For every boy in ninth grade, there are probably four girls. A boys' chorus of twelve to twenty-eight members seems luxuriously abundant. A girls' chorus of forty to fifty seems equally comfortable. But surround twelve boys with forty or fifty girls and they are likely to start questioning which class they will take in place of chorus.

The voices of ninth- and tenth-grade boys do not blend with those of girls as well as they will in eleventh- and twelfth-grade. The boys' voices tend to be quite brassy just after their voices change. The girls seem to have smaller voices at this age. I happen to be particularly fond of this sound. By eleventh- and twelfth-grade, girls start investing heavily in their natural vibrato and are reluctant to relinquish it for high art or threat of punishment. A three- and four-part ninth- and tenth-grade women's chorus can be simply exquisite. Put them together with the boys and the sound is simply adequate.

By eleventh grade, the range, the dynamic balance, and the class participation/behavior seem to work themselves out. The development of the high school choral program is not served well by asking ninth- and tenth-grade singers to wait for a few years to sing with the best. The time is now.

Christopher Shay teaches music at Shepaug Valley High School in Washington, Connecticut. This article first appeared in the Spring 2000 issue of Connecticut's CMEA News. Reprinted by permission.

Where Have All the Accompanists Gone?

Donald Speer

Have you experienced difficulty in finding pianists who are both able and willing to accompany? It seems that the days when good accompanists were readily available for any event are long gone. The problem is not only with accompanists; the number of students studying piano into the intermediate and advanced levels appears to diminish with each passing year. Why has this become a problem? And what, if anything, can we do about it?

One important factor related to the diminishing number of pianists and accompanists can be found in the nature of piano study itself. The traditional approach to piano study is a rather isolated experience. It consists primarily of a one-on-one relationship between a student and an adult, quite unlike the ensemble experience among a group of peers. Unlike music activities like band or choir, where a group interacts regularly to rehearse and make music, a pianist will spend many hours alone perfecting his or her skills. This sense of isolation may become more acute during the middle and high school years, when the student is not only developing social skills with peers, but also progressing to more difficult piano literature, which ultimately requires more practice and time alone. This tends to result in students dropping out of piano lessons just as they are becoming ready to develop the skills necessary to accompany.

A related reason contributing to the short supply of pianists/accompanists can be found in the fact that our students now face an ever-increasing number of extracurricular options. This is nothing new—all music educators are confronted with the challenge of student choices and priorities. Unfortunately, these activities often compete directly with the number of hours available for private music study (and the practice time that must go into it).

Because most other extracurricular options involve groups of peers (team sports, school plays, academic team, etc.), they seem to have a particularly profound effect on long-term commitments to piano study, a necessary element in the development of competent accompanists.

Can anything be done to remedy this short-circuiting of piano study? Is it possible to regenerate an interest in long-term piano lessons and accompanying? Of course, the problem is a complex one, but I believe that at least part of the solution is found in facing the isolation of advanced study with additional peer-related activities. In other words, healthy student experiences in accompanying may keep pianists interested enough to develop into accompanists! This will most certainly have to involve the cooperation of private teachers, band and choral directors, and church musicians. Here are five suggestions for moving in that direction:

1. *Get to know each other.* Can you identify the students in your classes and ensembles who currently study piano? Do you know their piano teachers? Do the piano teachers know you? A piano teacher can be an excellent source for identifying potential accompanists.

2. *Enlist the help of the private piano teacher in developing potential accompanists.* Of course, suggestion #1 above is a prerequisite! Private teachers are often willing to help their students with warm-up routines or choral accompaniments during lesson time *if* they are given plenty of advance notice to work it into the lesson. (A semester is not too long for the beginning accompanist!) Consequently, piano teachers must train their students in areas other than repertoire alone. The successful accompanist must possess a variety of skills, including a solid foundation in keyboard technique and sight-reading, following a conductor, and playing with continuity.

3. *Get pianists involved* early *with accompanying experiences.* We often make the mistake of waiting too late to introduce a student to accompanying. Most of the accompanists I know became involved relatively early in their piano study. This generally happened after a few years of lessons, when they were in the sixth or seventh grade. (However, it is important to consider each student's ability individually—see suggestion #2.)

4. *Provide plenty of learning experiences for the developing accompanist.* Early accompanying experiences could include warming up a choir, playing one or two vocal parts in rehearsal, playing for a children's church service, and eventually working up to selected easier choral accompaniments (in rehearsal only, then possibly in concert) and easy solo/ensemble literature. Events such as hymn-playing festivals are also great opportunities to give students more experience. There has been even some discussion among a few KMTA and KMEA members about reinstating some type of accompanying festival, allowing pianists to further develop their skills.

5. *Ensure that accompanying experiences are "safe" and fun for the student.* (Don't forget, we are *playing the piano!*) The creation of a safe accompanying environment *must* include plenty of advance notice for the pianist, specific directions, and careful supervision for less experienced performers. Be realistic with what you expect out of an inexperienced accompanist. View this as a teacher/student relationship, not as a conductor/accompanist relationship.

So where have all the accompanists gone? I believe they're still among us but we may need to work harder and a bit smarter to identify them, then give them the opportunities to develop and succeed!

Donald Speer is associate professor of piano and accompanying at Western Kentucky University in Bowling Green. This article originally appeared in the May 1999 issue of Kentucky's Bluegrass News. *Reprinted by permission.*

Survival of a Music Program: Six Steps to a Successful Program
Barry Talley

When you take a close look at your program and question what you have done to establish a successful tradition in your school, the answers are not easily apparent. A successful music program is built over an extended period of time, and the building process involves the work and efforts of many students, teachers, and parents. I want to share some insight into what has been successful at Deer Park High School over the last fifteen years.

Deer Park is located 20 miles southeast of Houston. While viewed by the state of Texas as a wealthy district, most of our students come from middle and lower-middle income families. There are around 3,200 students in grades 9–12. When I began teaching here in 1981, the high school choral program had an enrollment of 85. Today, we have 270 students involved in four performing choirs.

Deer Park offers a traditional six-period day to all students. We also offer students the chance to take an AM Flex Class or a PM Flex Class. The AM Flex Class starts at 6:30 in the morning, while the PM Flex Class runs after school from 2:30 until 3:30 p.m. There are nearly 300 students taking at least one Flex Class. The biggest drawback to the Flex Classes is that the PM Flex Class is not available to athletes, band members, the drill team, or cheerleaders due to after-school practice.

I believe there are six basic components that make a music program successful. They include a quality student, a high performance standard, strong public relations, on-campus support, a central administrative endorsement, and the individual personality of the director. While the order of impact may vary from school to school, they are each very important in the overall development of a music program.

Step 1: Recruit Top Students
The first step in building and maintaining a successful program lies in the strength of the students. The first action I took at Deer Park was to recruit the best kids in the school. I actively recruited athletes, band and orchestra members, student council members, cheerleaders, and any other smart-looking student I saw. I went to every football game and chaperoned every dance. I befriended the coaches and landed the announcing job at our home football games. This gave me even more credence with the coaches and the athletes. In 1986 I convinced our starting quarterback to join choir. He was one of the best student leaders our school has ever had. That student did more individually for our program than any other student over the last fifteen years. He spoke at the junior high schools of the similarities between choir and athletics. He talked about working hard, about teamwork, and about competition. He told them that he regretted not joining choir until his senior year. That next fall ninety freshmen enrolled in choir, the largest number we had ever had enroll. One of our other senior recruits, Andy Pettite, recently pitched for the New York Yankees in the 1996 World Series. Andy was a good singer and had a great attitude; he added respect to our program. Another of our alumni who joined choir as a junior was Chelsi Smith, who just completed her reign as Miss Universe. Seek out the best kids in school, recruit them into your organization, and you will soon have a respected program.

Step 2: Develop High Performance Standards
Offer your students a good product. Students want to be a part of a successful organization. This does

not necessarily mean First Division ratings at UIL contests. We stress to our choirs that every performance is like a competition. I believe that most students like to compete if they feel they have a chance to succeed. The challenge for us as directors is to see that all of our students reach 100 percent success. The quality of a program is determined by parents, students, administrators, community members, and most importantly, ourselves. Too many music educators only program music for themselves, refusing to include music that is entertaining to their audiences. We perform over thirty times each year. None is more important than the District Convocation that is held each year before school starts. All administrators, teachers, and school board members attend. We perform selections that will be received in a favorable way by that audience. It does not diminish the positive benefits that come from the performance. Establish a high standard of quality for your group, then use that standard for success, and work diligently to achieve the goals you have set.

Step 3: Establish Strong Public Relations

Every prospective music director should be required to attend classes in public relations. Too many music teachers seem unable to be a PR person for their own program. I think of my parents and students as "customers," and I try to treat them the way I would want to be treated as a valued customer in my favorite store.

We also need to be more positive in our rehearsals. For every negative comment we make it takes three positive comments to have equal impact. Always try to accent the positive and eliminate negative comments from your rehearsals, building a better classroom climate. If your students are happier, you will be happier.

Every performance provides the opportunity for more public relations for your program. If you are not proud of your group, no one else will be either. It is important to be a part of the community in which you work. People need to recognize you as the music director or you are falling short in your public relations.

If you are the high school director, you must be readily available to attend events at the feeder schools. I have known some successful high school directors who never attended junior high concerts, but I think they were just lucky to have a successful ongoing program. Kids look up to the high school director. A dramatic impact on their continuance in music can be made by simply being visible at the middle schools. Our middle

schools come to the high school for a precontest concert each spring. It provides the students a chance to perform on the high school stage. I try to clinic every middle school choir before contest so the students get a chance to see what I am like as a director.

Step 4: Build On-Campus Support

One of the most important ingredients of a successful program is support in your school from teachers, counselors, and principals. The teachers have gained more power through site-based management teams, and we must work to win the support of our peers. Be a friendly person around school. People should rarely see us in the lounge, but when they do, be sure to smile and greet them. The counselors are perhaps the most important people on campus. They can easily deemphasize your program, or just as easily they can make it a good choice for students. It is the counselor who recommends a correspondence course that allows a junior or senior to stay in music. Whoever makes out your master schedule should be your best friend. They can virtually make or break your program. You must use your creative skills to present your program's needs to the schedule makers. The building principal holds tremendous power over us. Do you personally invite him to your concerts? I invite our principal on every trip we take. Luckily, he is a former band director and enjoys our music trips. Keep the principal informed about what is going on in your program. Tell him when you have had successes and do not be afraid to share the frustrations of defeat. Make him one of your satisfied customers.

Step 5: Work for Administrative Endorsement

The fifth component of a successful program is endorsement by central administration. That support comes through budget, staffing, and recognition. Before the administrative support comes, the previous four components must be in place. Many times a director wants to be handed the world's best program, and he isn't willing to work to establish a quality product before being rewarded with support. The support will come if the director has been willing to serve his students, parents, and community. It is important to stress student success and not individual directors' successes. Work through the building principal or music supervisor to reach administrators. Involve administrators in your program. There is much to gain when they feel a part of your program. Do you list your administration and school board in your programs? Learn to effectively verbalize your needs to your administrators. No one likes to deal with a whiner; be a professional and keep your emotions in control.

Step 6: Cultivate Personal Relationships
One final factor that is a strong influence on successful programs is the personality of the director. Our personal contact makes or breaks us as teachers. Take the time to speak to every student in your program on a daily basis. Take time to speak to each student outside rehearsal. Greet them at the door as they enter, and be there to shake their hands when they leave. No matter how badly the rehearsal has gone, create a feeling of success before they leave for the day. Let them know that you care about their lives outside the classroom. If you are not willing to build strong personal rela-

tionships with your peers, students, and parents, you will never be successful in the long run.

We have enjoyed great success in our music program at Deer Park over the last fifteen years. Still, every year is a new challenge. Recruiting new students is ongoing. I believe the six components for success are readily present in our music program. While the impact of any one component may be stronger from one school to the next, they are all important. The order in which they occur will vary from school to school, but until all six factors are part of a program, it will not reach its full potential.

Barry Talley is the director of fine arts for the Deer Park Independent School District and choral director at Deer Park High School, both in Deer Park, Texas. This article originally appeared in the Winter 1996/97 issue of Texas' TMEC Connection. Reprinted by permission.

A Recipe for Successful Recruitment and Retention
William H. Yoh, Jr.

The issue of recruitment and retention of students to elementary and secondary music programs is of paramount importance to all music educators. It is no longer solely the concern of the novice music educator beginning his or her first job in a new school. During a time of deep budget cuts and the persistent criticism of so-called experts who question the importance of the arts, each of us must have a well-thought-out strategy for establishing, building, and maintaining significant numbers in our ensembles. Without some type of formula, our programs will gradually starve and cease to exist.

In thinking about an article on the topic of recruitment and retention, I found myself searching for my own particular formula. After much reflection, I have realized that there is a recipe that I use to cook up a hearty and tasteful music department. Some of the ingredients are essential to the mix, while others are personal favorites that add some additional spice. The following are a few of the items which have proven successful in the past.

The attitude and general demeanor of the music educator is of utmost importance when building any program. You must demonstrate that you are in it for the students and the school. Time and time again I have seen educators in the profes-

sion with their own personal agenda. This works to a point, but your students will sense your indifference and apathy and will eventually drop out.

Take a genuine interest in the likes and dislikes of your young musicians. Regardless of the age level, find out what's in and what's out, what cartoons are "cool," which *Star Trek* series is better, and what happened on your favorite soap opera yesterday. When you discuss these pressing issues with your young people, they will begin to realize that you are as human as they are. You are no longer seen as the omnipotent teacher who is out to make their lives miserable and unbearable. When you begin to relate to the students at their age level, the word spreads quickly that you're okay. Within a year, the students will begin to seek you out to join the program and your recruiting becomes easier.

The myth that you should not smile or laugh until the second semester is a falsehood and should be dismissed. Surely you can reflect on your past education and you will most likely remember those educators who could smile and joke on a regular basis. In my experience, those who did are remembered vividly and brought out the best in my education. We as music educators deal with emotions at all times in our repertoire. Allow some emotion to filter through in your interaction with the students during a lesson plan. This may be difficult at first, but your young musicians will respect you for it and will remember it when they pass it on to their friends. Nine chances out of ten, it will most likely improve the performance of your ensembles.

When building any ensemble, be sure to take advantage of any performance opportunity that comes your way. If your local shopping mall presents a holiday concert series, make plans to have your groups perform there. Call up your local nursing homes and AARP organizations to schedule a performance for monthly meetings and activities. If at all possible, perform for your local school board, school retirement parties, faculty meetings, and pep rallies. Pursuing these activities will aid in a number of ways. First and foremost, they will make your group highly visible in the community. In turn, all citizens, including your prospective musicians, will see the group and want to be a part of the action. Your numbers will undoubtedly improve. In addition, these activities will give your young musicians performance experience, confidence, and wonderful memories which they will talk about throughout their lifetimes.

Take pride in the performance of your ensemble, regardless of the level of experience. You spend more time with your musicians than any other individual in the field. You must be a cheerleader and a positive voice for everything they do. If your ensembles are not performing at a level with which you feel comfortable, do not shy away from the performance opportunities mentioned previously. You will find that their quality improves with each and every concert. Make every effort to set up a performance/field trip for your music ensembles towards the end of the school year. This will provide an incentive for being in your program well after the holiday programs are finished. If you have access to local theme parks and amusements, take the time to complete an audition tape and application. Provided that funds are available and your groups are accepted, this will assist you in the retention of your musicians. Let's face it, fellow educators, in today's society everyone wants to know, "What's in it for me?" Well, with a concert/field trip of this magnitude, you can offer your students the three p's: performance, prestige, and play.

Once in a while, you will come across an administrator who appreciates the arts. You will find that he or she has been influenced by the arts in some manner during his or her life. I have been fortunate to have such an individual during the past six years. Administrators who support the arts curriculum give you a great deal of latitude and leeway in your musical undertakings. They tend to understand the importance of numbers when developing quality ensembles. The flexibility of an "artistic administrator" will allow you to pursue all of the ideas mentioned. Their support will give merit, significance, and stability to your program, which will be evident to your future musicians.

If you do not have the luxury of a supportive administration, your job will be made more difficult. Not to fear, however. You are the music educator, and it is your job to get these members of the group in tune with what you do every single day. Going out of your way to present programs for every possible event will bring your administration around to your way of thinking. This process may take some time, but with patience, it will benefit everyone involved in the music program.

If at all possible, take all of your performing groups to the elementary and middle schools to perform mini-concerts. You may want to begin this process as early as December so that your ensembles will be comfortable with the concert setting prior to winter performances. This will also plant the seed in the minds of your prospective musicians to inquire prior to the preregistration assembly, which always seems to be scheduled earlier each year. Have your groups perform again in April or May to refresh their memories. The more familiar a group is to individuals, the more likely they will be to participate in and identify with it.

Make an effort to offer a music camp during the months of June and July. Perhaps the administration will allow your school to sponsor the program. If this is not possible, you may want to seek out a parks and recreation service or a local college to assist you in establishing some sort of summer workshop. Such a program is an excellent opportunity for you to start your young musicians prior to the first day of school. In addition, these young musicians are probably changing to a different educational level for the upcoming school year. They will find comfort in knowing who at least one of their teachers will be and where one of their many classes will be held. Most importantly, they will get a big head start on the instrument of their choice. If your camp is successful, meaning fun but educational, you will have students knocking on your door in August wanting to join your program.

The techniques mentioned above are just a few of the many that music educators have at their disposal. There are many other methods out there waiting to be discovered by all of us. The issue of recruitment and retention is one that takes a bit of creativity on your part. More importantly, a great deal of time is needed to make the operation a successful one. When students have so many electives to choose from and when funding for the general arts is dwindling, we as music educators must take whatever time is needed to create effective methods to attract students to our music programs.

William H. Yoh, Jr., teaches music at Robert Louis Stevenson Elementary School of the Arts in Merritt Island, Florida. This article originally appeared in the May 1996 issue of the Florida Music Director. *Reprinted by permission.*

Adopt an Audience Member
Catherine J. Young

I have utilized the following idea to promote attendance of board members, administration, faculty, staff, and prominent community members at our concerts and music department functions. Not only do these target audience members often attend the performances, but they also often communicate with each student afterwards with a personal note, phone call, or one-on-one conversation. Students and audience members share the musical performance and discuss the individual pieces (history, composer, performance, requirements, etc.) afterwards. This has increased support of our music department's activities, made choir members responsible and accountable, and has improved communication skills.

Step 1. Students brainstorm a list of potential audience members who are identified as influential in the community and school.

Step 2. Each student sends a personal written invitation to the upcoming concert/event to his or her "adopted audience member." This invitation would include a specific explanation of either a piece being performed or information that might be pertinent to the interests of that individual audience member.

Step 3. Follow up: Students must contact "their" audience member to express their appreciation for attending. This could be done before the concert, at the reception afterwards, or by any form of personal communication.

Catherine J. Young is director of choral activities at the Tyrone Area High School in Tyrone, Pennsylvania. This article originally appeared in the Fall 1998 issue of Pennsylvania's PMEA News. *Reprinted by permission.*

Section 5

Conducting and Score Study

While your students may not notice, what you have done to prepare yourself before the first rehearsal and how you wave the baton are critical to successful rehearsals. In this section, you will find helpful ideas to improve yourself as a conductor.

 Section 5

Conducting and Score Study

The Choral Conductor: Reflections of a Singer
Peggy D. Dettwiler

Most choral conductors would agree that we strive for a choral sound that is warm, buoyant, and freely produced. As we regularly rehearse our ensembles, we coach our singers in the proper use of vocal techniques: a deep, expansive breath; good posture; vertical vowel formation; and the healthy use of head voice. Perhaps we don't realize that some of this teaching could take place without words, simply by the way we present ourselves as conductors. Our posture and conducting gestures can have a direct influence on the sound produced by our choirs. They mirror us! If we assume the physical and mental image of a singer, it is easier for the singers watching us to respond in kind.

As I work with my choral conducting students at Mansfield University, I encourage them to utilize gestures that influence good singing techniques. Specifically, we strive for the following goals:

1. Good posture with an elevated rib cage.
2. Placement of the elbows at 4 and 8 o'clock positions.
3. Positioning the forearm horizontally to the floor with a curved palm.
4. A facial expression with lifted cheeks, slightly open mouth, and widely open eyes.

Let us examine each goal and its effect on choral tone. First, what do we mean by "good posture"? Good posture manifests itself in an elongated spine, the feeling of being tall with the head well-balanced on the top of the spine, and feet slightly separated with the greater portion of weight on the balls of the feet. Placing the body in proper alignment relays a sense of energy and readiness for singing. Combining this with an elevated rib cage without shoulder tension produces the foundation for a deep and expansive breath.

Our second goal, placing the elbows at four and eight o'clock positions, works in tandem with elevating the rib cage. Both encourage the singers to breathe deeply and refrain from collapsing as they sing through a phrase. Of course, these positions are only a point of departure from which one digresses for the sake of flexibility. Maintaining fluidity in the right-hand beat pattern and left-hand gestures is paramount.

Third, positioning the forearm horizontally to the floor places the ictus of each beat at the level of the diaphragm and lower ribs. Through this approach, we encourage our singers to inhale deeply and support the choral tone. We should follow through with conducting gestures that move back and forth across the front of our body along a horizontal plane to help singers sustain the vocal line. If the points of each ictus are too high, singers may breathe from the clavicle and produce a sound that is shallow and unsupported.

In addition to the placement of the forearm, the position of the hand must be observed. Straight, tense fingers or a baton held at an angle can inhibit breath flow and produce jaw tension. A curved palm, flat to the floor, encourages singers to produce a sound with a lifted soft palate, thus incorporating more head tone into the vocal production. This concept, introduced to me by Rodney Eichenberger, is particularly helpful in conducting slow, lyrical works.

Finally, our facial expression can have a dramatic effect on the ease with which our singers produce the sound we want. Lifting our cheeks and widely opening our eyes generates a raised soft palate, producing a more buoyant tone quality. Combining this with a slightly open mouth, particularly on the preparation for singing, will encourage our singers to open their throats and form vowels more vertically as they release the sound.

Because the choral tone reflects the conducting gesture, we must strive to show physically what we mean. In the end, if we not only pres-ent the image of a singer, but also feel ourselves as singers, our body language will occur quite naturally.

Peggy D. Dettwiler is director of choral activities and associate professor of music education at Mansfield University in Mansfield, Pennsylvania. This article first appeared in the Winter 1997 issue of Pennsylvania's PMEA News. Reprinted by permission.

Better Preparation Equals Better Performance: Score Study and the Choral Conductor
Leslie Guelker-Cone

I was thinking recently about two phenomenally successful choral conductors I know. Though extemely different in personality, temperament, and style, both are people who have the ability to make truly beautiful music. While little else is the same about them, from the way they dress to the way they approach life, I believe that the one unifying factor they share is their exceptionally thorough knowledge of the music they conduct. Both are tangible proof that a choral conductor's level of success is directly proportional to his/her knowledge of the score. This means we must commit to the never-ending task of score study in order to be the best that we can be. Listed below are a few ideas that can serve as a basic score study checklist.

Collecting Background Information
Gather information about the composer: Who was he (she)? When and where did he live? What did he write? What/who were his influences? Research the specific piece. When/why was it written? Who performed it? How does it fit into the rest of the composer's output? Who wrote the text? Is it part of a larger text source (as the Kyrie is part of the Mass, for example)? What language is it in? If in a language other than English, what does it mean and how is it pronounced?

Try to find interesting stories about the composer or the work that make the music come alive for your students.

Understanding Stylistic Considerations
Related to the above is the development of an understanding of style and performance practice issues. How is a Renaissance motet performed differently than a Romantic part-song, for example? Explore issues of pitch, tempo, and dynamics. Know who would have sung the music: Was the soprano part sung by little boys or by women? How many singers on a part? What about vocal tone? Vibrato? What are the rules governing articulation, use of instruments, ornamentation?

Listen to recordings of choirs/conductors considered experts on style. Read all you can. A good basic source book on style issues as they affect the choral conductor is Robert Garretson's *Choral Music: History, Style, and Performance Practice,* published by Prentice Hall.

Analyzing the Score
I like to begin with a textual analysis. We should already know the source and language of the text, as well as its pronunciation and translation. The next step is to dig in to the words to find out what they really mean. How is the text structured? Does the poet use imagery or other literary devices? How does the composer express the text musically?

Then dig into the music. Do a thorough analysis of the musical elements: What is the formal structure? How are melody and rhythm organized? What is the important thematic/rhythmic material? In which voices does it appear? Where are the high points of the phrases? What is the harmonic structure? Which notes are consonant and which are dissonant? How are the cadences approached? How is modulation accomplished?

Only when we thoroughly understand both text and music can we make intelligent decisions regarding phrasing, balance, word stress, and myriad other issues that will affect our performance.

Marking the Score
Score analysis will determine a great deal of score marking. Mark important musical concepts discovered in your analysis: form, important melodic/rhythmic ideas, harmonic structures/disso-

nances, textually stressed syllables. Write in the translation and pronunciation of the text where applicable. Circle the composer's indications of dynamics, expressive marks, tempos.

In conjunction with effectively marking the score in preparation for rehearsal, we need to thoroughly learn it. Sing through all the parts; play through parts in different combinations (don't forget the accompaniment). Circle problem spots. (If they're problems for you, they will most likely be problems for your choir.) Decide on and mark phrase shaping, balance issues, breathing. Mark important cues and cutoffs as well as anything else you will want your choir to know.

Make whatever marks will help you remember the important elements in the score. Your method of score marking is not as important as your consistent use of markings that will immediately tell you what it is you're trying to say.

Determining Conducting and Rehearsal Issues

Locate problem spots in the score (much of this will happen during score learning): Where are the difficult melodic leaps and rhythms? Where are the harmonies difficult or hard to tune? Are there problems of range/tessitura or breathing? Plan ways to deal with these in rehearsal.

Develop a concept of the piece as a whole;

make choices relating to mood, tone color, and vowel shaping.

Spend time in front of a mirror practicing conducting gestures until they become second nature. Rehearse cues and cutoffs (which should be marked in your score). Identify and mark other potential conducting problems: changing meter, dynamic contrasts, and changes in articulation.

Develop both a short-range (daily, weekly) and a long-range (from the first rehearsal to the concert) rehearsal plan that will allow you to successfully prepare the piece in the time you have.

Does this seem like a lot to do for every piece we conduct? Yes!

Does it still need to be done? Yes! Remember, nobody ever said this profession was going to be easy! In our already hectic lives, it's hard to imagine finding more time for study and preparation, but choosing to make score study a priority will allow us and our singers to reap rich musical rewards in both our daily rehearsals and our choral performances.

Leslie Guelker-Cone is director of choral activities and coordinator of vocal studies at Western Washington University in Bellingham. This article first appeared in the March 2000 issue of Washington's Voice. *Reprinted by permission.*

Negation: Try It. You'll Like It!
Clarence Miller

"Don't conduct notes and time signatures, but rather measures and phrases," said the conducting teacher. These words of advice have perhaps meant more to me than any others I received during my forty-eight years of conducting. When everything in choral singing is in place, i.e., diction, harmony, tone, pitch, dynamics, etc., etc., etc., it's the measures and phrases that separate the best from the rest.

How often at the postconcert gathering pub do conductors come to agreement on good ensembles heard at a convention? Whatever their differences, they generally come to closure on one aspect of the singing: either the group was musical or it wasn't.

I have been most fortunate to conduct the college Concert Choir at several national and divisional conventions of ACDA, MENC, and NATS. The comments I cherished the most were from

those who said, "it was a beautiful performance, very musical, and moving." I'm always amused at comments from those who stand in the back, exit after one or two songs, then criticize what little they heard of the total program. Regardless, their comments can't all be negative if what they heard was musical. If you have ever performed with Robert Shaw, you know what it means to sing measures and phrases plus pay strict attention to rhythm.

What part then does negation play in all that we do in choral conducting and the results we accomplish? I suggest that negating (doing away with or making ineffective) unshackles the director from beating air, imitating a pump handle, or sticking to that "damnable" time signature. Try the following exercise:

Conduct the first four measures of "All Through the Night" (quarter note = 66–72) using the 4/4 time signature. Next conduct the same four measures, same speed, but in two measures of 4/4. Next, conduct all four measures in one large measure of 4/4 keeping the same tempo. Lastly, conduct all sixteen measures in four measures. If you have done this correctly, you have freed your chest, face, and entire body to portray dynamics, cuing, etc. In other words, by negating the beat, beat, beat, beat, one starts to think phrase, phrase, phrase, phrase, and musical singing is the result. It's much like the bulletin board in early September when important announcements are clear, but by the second week the board is cluttered to the extent that the important messages are lost in a maze of unimportant debris. Conducting gestures are similar: less is better. Don't pollute your conducting atmosphere.

We as directors are rather hypocritical at times. How often we yell at our choir to "sing with feeling, sing legato," then wave our arms and hands as though aboard a ship leaving shore saying good-bye to a thousand friends on land. The title of the video "What They See Is What You Get," produced by Hinshaw Music, Inc., featuring Rodney Eichenberger and Andre Thomas, really says it all.

One last point I would make concerning negation. Why would/should anyone conduct beats at the end of a piece that ends on a whole note—why beat air? All an ensemble needs is a clear cut-off. If there is a crescendo or decrescendo at the final note in such a piece, it makes sense to allow the chest and face to take over and keep the arms out of the way. It is my opinion that we spoon-feed our choirs too much with our active arms and hands. Allow the singers to do more thinking for themselves. Suggest to them that measures and phrases are the routes to beautiful singing. I think less is better; therefore, less is more.

Try negating, and I hope you like it.

Clarence Miller is professor emeritus at Glassboro State College/Rowan University in Glassboro, New Jersey. This article first appeared in the November 1998 issue of New Jersey's Tempo. *Reprinted by permission.*

Section 6

Performance

Now that you and your students have learned all this music, it's time to share it with others. Here are a couple of articles to help you improve your performances and make performance day easier.

 Section 6

Performance

Checklist for a Successful Elementary Music Program or Concert
Lori Kipfer

After twelve years of teaching and doing over fifty music programs, I have come up with an all-inclusive list of things to do for a successful show. It helps me to be more organized and reduces my stress level. My administrators really like it too, because I can show them exactly where I am in the process. I believe that this would be especially useful for new teachers.

- *Set the date.* Beware of conflicts on the school or district calendar and your personal calendar.
- *Choose a show and plan enough rehearsal time!* Consider asking the grade-level teachers what themes they are studying.
- *Make sure you have all of the materials you need to begin rehearsals.* Student scores or a typed copy of the words and tape-recorded music will be helpful.
- *Notify the parents as soon as possible through a letter.* Do you need their help? They are busy and will need to mark their calendars or prepare a costume.
- *Send a memo to the teachers or have a brief meeting.* They can be your best resource if they have the information.
- *What kind of set decorations will you need?* I usually ask the grade-level teachers or parents for ideas and help.
- *Fill out any paperwork regarding the facilities you plan to use.* Contact the custodians to make sure they know about your show, too.
- *Contact the newspapers and TV stations.* If you have a public relations director, drop her a note as well.
- *Meet with your principal and department head to go over the details.* This is especially important if you are in a new situation.

- *Assign special parts.* These may be singing, speaking, or dancing.
- *Decide whether or not you want to use costumes.* Be sure to practice with them.
- *Plan a dress rehearsal as an assembly for the school.* Invite parents who may have other commitments in the evening.
- *Send invitations as reminder notices to parents and staff.* Just a half sheet is fine. Send one to the superintendent and board members, too!
- *Invite the PTA to make announcements.* They will appreciate the opportunity to speak to such a large and captive audience.
- *Make arrangements to have your program videotaped (this could be done during a dress rehearsal).* The students will enjoy seeing themselves on TV.
- *Type the program and copy it.* Check with administrators to see how many you will need to run off. This is a good time to use your computer skills.
- *Find a few volunteers to pass out the programs.* A brother or sister of a performer would consider it a big honor.
- *Write thank-you notes to the people who helped to make the evening possible.* A list of "Special Thanks" should also be included in the program.
- *Think about what you are going to wear.* It is important to feel confident because lots of eyes will be on you.
- *Write down what you want to say.* You will probably be nervous, so plan ahead.
- *After the show, greet as many parents as possible.* Imagine that you are running for public office.

Lori Kipfer teaches music at Wyandot Run Elementary School in Powell, Ohio. This article originally appeared in the November 1998 issue of Ohio's Triad. *Reprinted by permission.*

So You Can't Hear Your Show Choir … So What's New?

Rick Whitney

Does your sound system make your show choir sound as if they're from the Twilight Zone? Have you been heard to say, "Kids, something tells me we're not in Kansas anymore?" So … what can you do?

Here is a list of problems I have encountered and some possible solutions.

Problem 1: Your singers are not singing with maximum projection.

Solution 1: While you don't want your students to sound like opera singers trying to sing rock and roll, the basics for all singing still apply. Your students will need to support the sound with correct breath control and *must* make good use of the same projection techniques used in choir and solo work.

Problem 2: The band is too loud for the singers.

Solution(s) 2: This is not an easy problem to fix, but it can be done. (a) Determine if the whole band is too loud or just certain instruments. Usually the bass is the main problem. This is due in part to the fact that low pitches do not easily get absorbed and, therefore, project longer and louder. Simply turn the bass amp down and make a written note as to the levels that are appropriate to the mix. (b) Also, the drummer tends to get carried away. While the medium is pop, it still needs to be controlled. If controlled playing is difficult for your drummer, then pad the bass drum with a pillow and/or put baffles around the drums. (c) Equally a problem is the brass section playing too loudly. Usually, the parts are too hard for high school students to play with the correct dynamic control. You could try damping the horns with a baffle. However, a solution I stole from the group "Steely Dan" was to rewrite the parts for a sax quartet. This is particularly effective with the first trumpet part; a soprano sax can wail on it and never get too loud. In fact, you may need to amplify the sax section, but that will give you greater control over the balance. A PCC or PZM mike on a Plexiglas sheet will work very well in this instance.

Problem 3: The choreography is too hard for the singers to be able to dance and sing effectively. This is a real dilemma. Of course, you want your group to sound and look good. You've even hired a choreographer to create an outstanding visual presentation. And, of course, the climaxes in the music should be accented with the singers, band, and the choreography.

Solution(s) 3: The first thing you need to check out again is whether or not your singers are giving you 100 percent on stage; they will have to be physically fit to dance and sing well at the same time. Another obvious solution is to compromise the dancing, but to what degree? Later in this article, I will give you some other solutions I used with my show choir.

Problem 4: The sound system is not meeting the needs of the singers.

Solution(s) 4: The simple answer is you need a better sound system, but let's not throw the baby out with the bath water. Start with some very basic checks. (a) Play some recorded music through your system, sit back, and listen. You be the judge. Do you like what you hear or not? Pick a variety of styles of music with which you are familiar, making sure you have equalized the system properly before you start (adjusted the bass and treble controls). If you are not pleased, try replacing the speakers with better quality ones and re-listen. (b) If this still does not fix the problem, it's possibly the mixer. Many mixers will give you an affected sound; you want it to sound natural. If you need to affect the sound, you want to be in charge of that, not the mixer. (c) If the recorded sound is good, next test your mikes. Have your students gather around the mikes and sing. Just as with affected mixer sounds, mikes can greatly change the quality of the sound. You may need to upgrade to a more natural-sounding mike. In addition, the pick-up pattern of the mike may be affecting the balance of the group. A super-cardiod pattern may be too narrow for the number of singers at the mike considering how close the students are to the mike. (d) If all of this still sounds great but when you do a performance with the band you still can't get enough sound out of the system, further adjustments need to be made. First, make sure the speaker cabinets are closer to the audience than to the mikes. In other words, keep the mikes away from the speaker cabinets. Also, try to aim the speaker cabinets at the audience. Try to keep the sound from hitting anything but the audience, especially walls; aim the speakers at the audience. This problem will adversely affect gain before feedback. Make sure the speaker cabinets are positioned high enough to permit the speaker(s) high pitches to be unobstructed. (e) With regard to tone quality, you can fix this with the equalizer. Use your ears. Always preset your quality with a very simple recorded sound; a Windham Hill piano recording is great. Then, compromise these settings to get more volume by cutting back or boosting frequencies that need adjusting to make the ensemble sound like you like them to sound. (6) Finally, the number of microphones you have turned on at the same time is critical. This is the NOM (number of microphones) and is calculated as follows: Every time you double the number of mikes opened, you have to decrease the volume of the system by 3 dB to avoid feedback. In simple terms, "more is *not* better." I realize that sometimes you have to bring up several mikes at the same time. This is especially true if your singers are not mixed (SATB) all over the stage and you want to get a better balance of all the parts. Try to do it with fewer mikes; the fewer the mikes, the greater the gain and the cleaner the sound!

Problem 5: The performance site is not conducive to great sound. The types of floor and wall surfaces are too reflective and create too much reverberation and poor balance, or the surfaces are extremely absorbent and the sound is too dry.

Solution(s) 5: If I have just described your home performance site, you are in luck. It will take some work, but you can change the way your auditorium sounds. (a) Concerning too much reflective surface, here are a couple of quick fixes. Locate the band on an absorbent area or create an area with carpeted floor (put padding under it), and use padded movable baffles (thick foam is the best). Unfortunately, there is not enough space and time here to go into detail, but there are probably sound engineering companies in your area that can give you some other permanent fixes for this problem. (b) On the other hand, if the problem is too much absorption, this is good. Just add some electronic reverb to your sound. (c) If you are going to perform in a new place, first and foremost, go and check out the site in advance. This will enable you to rationally pick out the best location for the singers and the band. Also, you can bring some carpeting and portable baffles to enhance the sound.

Problem 6: The music is inappropriate for the style of ensemble.

Solution 6: (a) Either the music is too difficult for the band to play, or it's not written well (it interferes with the singers). The solution is simple.

Take the time to really peruse the band parts and don't be afraid to change the music. (b) Also, be careful with the music you choose for your group to sing; if the group moves, keep the music simple. If you're talking about your "stand-at-the-mikes-and-groove" type jazz or swing choir, then, by all means, bring on the hard material, but keep the show choir music relatively simple.

Problem 7: Where to place the band in relationship to the singers and their mikes.

Solution 7: While it is vital for the singers to hear the band, putting them upstage from the singers will only add to your sound problems. The sound of the band will be amplified by the singers' mikes, and if you have monitor speakers for the singers, there will be a greater chance of feedback. Set the band up, stage left or right, or better still in the pit. You may need to put the band into the monitor system for the singers to hear, but you don't have to put them into the audience mix.

Problem 8: The monitor sound for the band is inaccurate.

Solution 8: Make sure the volume level for the band monitors gives you and the band a fairly accurate aural image of what the singers sound like (their volume and quality).

While the content in this article, to this point, may have been helpful, it also may not have fully addressed your problems. The following solutions, while somewhat controversial, will work wonders with your sound problems.

1. Scrap the band for a prerecorded tape/CD. While this may step on the toes of the band people, it certainly makes balancing the band and the singers a lot easier. One additional drawback to this method is the fact that the program has no room for musical changes (such as tempo), but the show will always be consistent. This is a great way to take a group like this to difficult locations such as malls and/or nursing homes.
2. Don't be afraid to have the choir just stand in a fixed position (poise) for a whole song. This is especially good if you want people to hear how well your students really can sing. It will also add variety to the texture of the show.
3. Why not feature certain groups or singers? (a) Some schools tend to avoid using too many soloists, but this is very appropriate for this

medium. Also, why not have a soloist with backup singers and a featured dance duet? This is an effective way to highlight your star singer(s) and dancers. (b) Have different students sing different songs. This will give your dancers more room to move and be seen by all. In addition, you may just find the sound is better.

4. Turn the choreographer loose on a song, which the students just dance. It doesn't even have to be an instrumental. This will work fine if you've covered yourself by singing the rest of your show, and this will create excitement for your students and the audience.

5. Have some students sing in the pit with the band. This will ensure the vocal sound is always heard. These singers can be a separate group, maybe even your jazz singers. Alternatively, you could either use members of the show choir as permanent pit singers or rotate this assignment. Make sure your singers on stage are also singing, and feature soloists from the stage and the pit. I used this format exclusively with my high school show choir and found it to be an outstanding solution. We took top honors everywhere we performed, including the very tough "Music Maestro Festivals."

6. This last suggestion will be very difficult for most of you to even consider. Prerecord your singers and have them sing along with the prerecorded version of themselves. (Now that you have just re-read that statement, let me explain.) (a) Keep in mind it is their voices the audience will hear from the tape and live on the stage. (b) Let's again consider the show choir medium. It is pop music, created in studios or stages with lots of electronics. Unless you have an incredible sound system with all of your singers wearing wireless microphones, the

sound is never going to approach the medium you are trying to duplicate. Trying to emulate other styles with your singers is quite possible. (Your madrigal group sounds like a madrigal group.) However, copying the pop medium is a monumental task. Why do you think all of the musical groups in the Macy's Thanksgiving Day Parade lip-synch? Because the circumstances require it. You're putting your students in a no-win situation. It's not you or your students; it is the medium. You can still keep your solos live, but just prerecord the chorus parts. (c) This would also give you the ability to teach your kids how to do a recording session. Seize the teaching moment; give your students the ability and tools to become studio musicians. While I think this is the ideal way to teach and perform this medium, I understand how unacceptable this might be. Keep in mind this solution would only work with a group such as your show choir. You would still have your outstanding a cappella chamber ensemble and a great-sounding show choir.

So there you have it … "the good, the bad, and the ugly" of show choir sound. And, with some creative problem-solving and hard work, your show choir will be the hit of the town. A show choir the students, parents, and you will be very proud of! A show choir from your hometown, not from another planet!

Rick Whitney is a choral director in the Pittsford Schools outside of Rochester, New York. This article originally appeared in the January/February 1999 issue of New York's The School Music News. *Reprinted by permission.*

Section 7

Copyright and Recording

With the easy availability of copy machines and recording devices, knowledge of basic copyright law is more important than ever. Also, if you want good quality recordings for your own use or to sell, you need to know what you are doing. These articles offer tips and resources to lead you further.

 Section 7

Copyright and Recording

An Educator's Guide to Recording for CD Release
Jerome Bunke

In this article, we will discuss some of the special procedures and tips that can help improve the quality of your group's tape for CD manufacture. First, we will take a look at "the paper chase"—the written materials your CD replicator will need from you to expedite your project through the production process.

The Paper Chase
To turn your tape into a CD, you'll need to supply the production service with a number of carefully compiled, accurately written materials.

Most importantly, be sure to include an accurate cue sheet with your master tape. This cue sheet should include the titles of the songs and their running times in the form of a continuous digital time log. This starts at the beginning of the tape (pp:00:00) and runs to the end of the program.

Also, check to make sure that your sequencing and timing information, as well as your side breaks for the cassette format, matches all of your print work and label information. This will eliminate the cost of reprinting your cassette J-card or CD booklet, unnecessary tape editing, or changing the order of your musical program at a later date and incurring additional production charges.

In addition, be sure to note on your cue sheet any noise reduction used or any special or unusual situations, like a particularly loud passage or a number of very short musical selections on your tape. This will help facilitate matching levels on the finished cassette or CD.

Finally, double-check to make sure that your project's written information accurately reflects either the cassette or the CD format. Some mis-takes are as simple as forgetting that there's no "Side 2" on a CD!

You Can Save Time, Money
It is possible to keep costs to a minimum during the production process if your written documentation is reliable and accurate. Here are a few suggestions that can add to large savings.

If you alter your master tape in any way, like changing the order of the songs, it will affect your label information, the J-card, and the CD booklet. This may sound obvious, but you'd be surprised at the number of tapes that are "almost" finished and that wind up having to be worked on after the fact, causing myriad revisions cascading from the tape to the printed material.

For example, if you change the order of the songs or extend a fadeout for a few seconds, make sure that your cue sheet reflects those changes.

The CD Label
Also, it is important to remember that the CD label is part of the manufacturing process. This is dramatically different from the vinyl LP. A CD label cannot be reprinted without re-replicating the entire CD at great cost, whereas the label on a vinyl LP is printed separately and is then affixed to the finished LP. If a correction to the LP label is necessary, you can intercede before the final production and have it reprinted. The vinyl LP itself would have remained unchanged, with the music remaining unaltered.

Finally, to help you prepare better for your next release, always get feedback and a report on how your tape shapes up with other clients. This feedback should include not only audio quality concerns, but paperwork issues that might have saved time at the production service.

By focusing on proper planning and scheduling, you can help guide your project painlessly through the production process.

Mastering: Five Easy Pieces (x2)

1. Before sending your master anywhere, make a safety copy.
2. Always supply the production service with a digital audio tape (DAT) copy of your master tape.
3. Record your DAT at the 44.1 KHZ sampling frequency, the same rate at which all CDs are recorded.
4. Listen to the DAT copy of your master tape to make sure it's accurate and sounds the way you want it to sound.
5. Make sure all your songs are in the right order to avoid editing charges.
6. Check that your print order matches the order of your CD and cassette labels as well as your liner notes.
7. Make sure you have the proper spacing between songs (three to five seconds of silence between each cut).
8. Always include an accurate cue sheet, with the titles and lengths of the songs in the form of a continuous digital time log.
9. Make sure your levels don't peak above 0. On the Sony PCM-1630, a level above 0 results in a mute.
10. Always get feedback from your production service on how your tape compares with other clients' tapes.

Jerome Bunke is president of Digital Force, former chairman of the National Endowment for the Arts Music Panel, president of Boosey & Hawkes, and executive director of the Concert Artists Guild. This article originally appeared in the August 1995 issue of the Nebraska Music Educator. *Reprinted by permission.*

School Concerts, Cable TV, and Music Licenses
Corey Field

For music educators, the future has arrived. Not very long ago it would have seemed like some sort of futuristic fantasy for families to enjoy their children's performances in local school concerts on television, but cable television transmissions and VCRs have forever altered this landscape. Some cable systems include educational access channels that transmit content produced by the local elementary, middle, and high schools. Family, friends, and other cable TV subscribers can tune in to see the local children on television as part of a sports contest, school news broadcast, book review, or musical event.

Consider then this question, recently posed by a high school band director about to present a concert which was going to be videotaped and later shown on local cable television: What sort of licenses, if any, are required?

From the educator's point of view, there may be room for confusion for several reasons, among them the practice that the performing rights societies ASCAP, BMI, and SESAC generally have not required performance licenses for live concerts at the high school level and lower. Educators who are not aware of the several different rights included in a music copyright may mistakenly believe that this situation also applies to videotaping of the concert for cable transmission. Still other educators may have heard discussion of fair use for instructional purposes and educational exemptions in U.S. copy-right law and believe that these apply to making and transmitting a videotape of a school concert. The educator may also believe that if a local cable television company is transmitting the concert video, then the cable company will handle any issues of rights or royalties. To add to the potential confusion, there are different issues for grand-right works (operas, ballets, musicals, and other theatrical presentations) and small-right concert performances because the performing rights societies do not license dramatic performances.

The short answer for the educator is that videotaping the concert may require a license to record the work as part of an audiovisual program, known as a synchronization license. The educator should contact the publisher of each work to determine the policy of each copyright holder. If the local cable station has licenses from the performing rights societies and the transmission of the concert is then picked up by the societies' survey of local cable programming, then the performing rights society will pay the publisher and author(s) a royalty for the transmission. If the cable station does not have licenses from the societies, the publisher may grant performance rights as part of the synchronization license. An educator who wants to facilitate the process should ascertain the status of the local cable television company before contacting the publisher.

For grand-rights (staged/dramatic) performances which are not covered by performing rights societies, both the performing organization and the cable television station will need to contact the publisher or other licensing agent for licenses covering performance and synchronization rights.

To assist the music educator, the Music Publishers Association publishes the *Sales Agency List,* which also includes information on the copyright contact person at each company. This publication is available from the MPA or online at http://www.mpa.org/agency/pal.html.

Corey Field is currently an intellectual property attorney with Ballard, Spahr, Andres, and Ingersoll, LLP. When this article was written he was vice president of European American Music Distributors Corporation. This article originally appeared in the September-October 1998 issue of Ohio's TRIAD. *Reprinted by permission.*

How to Record Your Performing Ensemble
Lee Walkup

Making a high-quality recording of your performing ensembles is easier than you think if you follow a few simple guidelines. The equipment that you will need is not overly expensive and is easy to operate. There are many reasons to make a recording, but the main reason is that both you and your students will learn from listening back to the performance. The following is a short discussion of the equipment you will need and some guidelines to follow to make better recordings.

The recording equipment does not have to be expensive to make a good recording. Here is a discussion of affordable items that every music department should own.

Cassette Deck
The cassette deck you choose should have "Line In" and "Line Out" connectors in the rear of the machine. When choosing a cassette deck, the most important thing to look for is the specification for "frequency response." Frequency response refers to the frequencies that a particular recorder is capable of recording. Humans with perfect hearing are capable of detecting frequencies between 20–20,000 Hz. Therefore, try to find a deck in your price range that has a frequency response as close to 20–20,000 Hz as possible. A deck rated at 30–18,000 Hz would make an excellent recording. Be sure to ask your salesperson about frequency response. This is much more important than any other feature on the deck. Another feature you should check is the recording level meters on the machine (sometimes called VU meters). They should be marked off in stages and give you a clear indication of how much signal is going in and out of the machine. Also, make sure that you can adjust the input levels (record levels) of the machine

manually. Features like auto-level, auto-locate, and auto-mute are frills that will not necessarily make your recording better. Your machine will probably have an option for using Dolby B or maybe even Dolby C. These are good features, but not absolutely necessary to make a good recording.

You should be able to find a good cassette deck for $300 or less. Some good brands are Tascam, Teac, and Sony. I recommend the Tascam 102 for around $300 dollars, since I have used it.

Mixer
Since most high-quality cassette decks do not have built-in microphones or inputs for external microphones, you will need a mixer. You will plug your microphones into the mixer. Then come out of the mixer into the "Line In" inputs of the cassette deck.

The mixer you choose should be unpowered. This means that it will not have an amplifier built in. Do not use a "PA" head. Powered mixers will generate noise. There are several good, small unpowered mixers from which to choose that are not expensive. I recommend the Mackie 1202. It is a small, rock-solid mixer that is quiet and versatile and costs around $300 dollars (street price). It has 12 inputs all total, 4 of which are standard microphone inputs (XLR-type). (Note: Just in case you have an opportunity to use upscale condenser microphones, the Mackie has "phantom-power" included.) The headphone monitor is excellent.

Microphones
There are more microphones from which to choose than any other item in the recording chain. First of all, you will need two "low-impedance" microphones in order to make a stereo recording. Low impedance means that you can run long cables (if needed) without losing any strength in the signal. A low-impedance microphone will be rated at 600 Ohms (Ω) or less.

(Note: The symbol, Ω, stands for Ohms. You might also see the phrase "Low-Z," which means low impedance.)

Any good PA microphone will probably be fine for your recording. Again, check the frequency response specifications for a particular mike. The closer you can get to a rating of 20–20,000 Hz, the better the microphone will be for recording. You will find some good dynamic, cardioid mikes made by Electro-Voice, Shure, and Audio-Technica in the $100–200 price range. (Note: "Dynamic" means that the mike does not have to be powered as condenser microphones do. "Cardioid" is the shape of the pattern of sound the mike can hear from the front and sides.) You will also need two 20-foot standard mike cables with "XLR" connectors.

Microphone Stands

You will need two microphone stands for your mikes. Make sure they are sturdy and preferably come with boom arms. Boom arms will give you additional height and help you to get into some tight places if needed. You will want to be able to get the stands up as high as possible to record a large ensemble. Qwik-Lok and Atlas are two good brands. (Note: Some dealers have been known to throw in the mike stands for free when you buy mikes. It's worth asking.)

Cassette Tape

When recording anything important, always use the best quality tape you can find. Use a good chrome or metal tape from a reputable manufacturer such as Maxell or TDK. Always use factory-fresh tape for important recordings. If you re-use a previously recorded tape, you run the risk of getting ghost sounds from the other recording. Also, an old tape might tend to lose some of the oxide coating, which would cause drop-outs. Do not skimp on tape. It is better to be safe than sorry.

Also, I would recommend that you use cassettes no longer than C-60 (30 minutes per side), if you can. Tape lengths of C-90 (45 minutes/side) and longer are thinner in width and can stretch or even break when shuttled back and forth. It would be better to use two C-60s instead of one C-120, if that is possible. You will have to consider the length of the music you are recording—and whether or not you will have time to change tapes.

Headphones

You will need a good set of headphones to monitor the music while recording. It is important to

know what is coming in through your microphones. You should choose the closed-ear type, since they will give you better isolation from the live sound. Get the best you can afford. Again, check the frequency response specifications. AKG, Audio-Technica, Sony, and Koss are good brands.

Here are some recording tips:

Setting the Record Levels

When setting the record levels, have the ensemble perform the loudest part of the piece. While they are playing/singing, set the master level on the mixer to peak around 0 VU on its meters. Then set the record level on the cassette deck to peak no higher than +3 W on its meters. Make a short test recording and play it back if you can. (If recording live, you will not have this luxury.) If the recording sounds clean and there is no distortion, you are ready to record the entire piece. If there is distortion, try attenuating the mikes a little. The attenuator pots are located at the top of the mixer. They should usually be set around the 12- or 1-o'clock position. Turning the attenuators to the left will decrease the signal, and vice versa to the right.

In general, when recording you will want to get the hottest signal possible without distortion. This will take some experimenting, but you will soon learn the settings for your own applications.

Using EQ

Personally, I do not use any equalization when doing live recording. I prefer to set the equalization pots on the mixer to the 12-o'clock position (referred to as flat), so that they do not color the real sound of the ensemble. You can always change it later. This is a matter of preference.

Microphone Placement

When recording a large ensemble, I would recommend placing the mikes between 20–30 feet in front of the ensemble—and as high as possible. You will have to experiment with the distance to suit your personal preference. The closer the mikes, the more presence and less room acoustics. The farther away, the more room, and less presence. Reflected sound can be good or bad, depending on your room. (e.g., Gregorian chant in a Cathedral would require more room sound.)

Place the mikes side by side, approximately 12–14 inches apart. Think of the mikes as two ears on a normal-sized head. If you place the mikes too far apart, there will be a large hole in the middle of the stereo image. You will hear extreme left and extreme right, with nothing in the middle. To avoid this, keep the mikes rather close together.

Using Dolby or No Dolby

If your cassette deck has Dolby noise reduction, you will have to decide whether or not to use it. Dolby is a compression scheme that is designed to reduce tape hiss that is inherent in all tape recorders. If the program material is quiet and sensitive (pianissimo or piano) throughout, you might consider using Dolby. If the average program material is not particularly quiet throughout, you might not choose to use Dolby.

Dolby B will reduce tape hiss, but it will also tend to reduce the crispness and high-end frequencies of the music. If you have set the record levels properly and are getting a good amount of signal into the recorder, you probably do not need to use noise reduction.

Break the Tabs!

After the recording session, break the tabs at the top of the master cassette with a ballpoint pen! This will prevent your precious recording from being erased.

Duplication

You can get copies of your master cassette duplicated for your students by almost any local recording studio. Real-time copies are better than high-speed copies. They should cost around $3–4 each or less. You can even get CD-ROM duplicates made now at a reasonable price.

I hope this recording primer is useful to you. I am passing on this information from my own experience. Through your own experience, you will find techniques that work for you. Listening back to a performance is not only fun, but a valuable learning experience.

Lee Walkup is the music technology resource person for the Connecticut Music Educators Association. He teaches music technology at Shelton Intermediate School in Shelton, Connecticut and is co-owner of Grace Recording Studio, Inc. in Hamden, Connecticut. This article originally appeared in the Spring 2000 issue of Connecticut's CMEA News. *Reprinted by permission.*

Section 8

Adjudication and Competition

Though you can't control what actually happens at a competition, you can make sure that your students are prepared for what faces them. Two authors share their ideas about getting ready.

 Section 8

Adjudication and Competition

Preparing Students for All-State Choir Auditions
Steve Meininger

After this year's All-State Choir events are completed, I will become the chair of All-State Choir for the next two years, which is probably why several people have asked me for some ideas to help in preparing students more thoroughly for the tryout. I have picked up several ideas from others who are successful with their preparations with students, so if you see something here that is your idea, that is why.

The first thing that I do is probably more for me than for my students. That is, I develop a schedule that will allow me to meet all deadlines easily. First, if by September 5 or so, I haven't received the packet containing all of the tryout information, I make a call to someone on the All-State Choir governing board to see if I missed it. I do this so that I don't miss the deadlines for getting everything in on schedule. I also let the students know from the first day of school that this material is coming soon, so they can begin to think about a solo to sing, conflicts with the tryout schedule so they can petition for another site if necessary, and so on. Once I get the materials, I post a schedule that includes everything that has to happen prior to my getting the forms sent off by the deadline. I am sure to have the students get application sheets and checks to me two days before the deadline. This allows me to have the activities person in my school check on the students, sign the forms, and get them back to me in time. I also must know at this time if the students have some conflict problems, such as not being able to try out on a Saturday morning.

As far as the actual tryout is concerned, here are a few things that I hope prove helpful.

In my opinion, there are two considerations for preparation. Part of the tryout is in the category of "things you can directly control," that is, things that can be directly prepared with no surprises or guesswork. The solo, scales, and triads fall into this category. All of this preparation can be thoroughly done prior to the tryout. The other part of the tryout includes those "things that you cannot directly control." This would include the aural recall and the melodic and rhythmic sight-reading. To be sure, one can improve these skills through preparation, but one doesn't know exactly what is going to be on the tryout.

The solo selection is the largest point factor in the tryout, so it deserves considerable attention. Choosing the right solo is critical. Some of my students study privately and therefore get help from their voice teachers when choosing a song, but the vast majority of students who try out need help from me. I start by trying to determine with the singer what is the best quality of his or her voice that we want to show off in a solo. That is, what is a strength with a student's voice that would make him or her a more desirable singer to have in the All-State Choir? Sometimes I ask students what it is that they feel that they do well, and sometimes I hear them sing. It may be characteristics like an ability to sing rapid passages very accurately, an ability to accurately sing unusual intervals in a song, an ability to take a highly animated text with music and look the part, or perhaps it is a warm, beautiful tone that is the student's strongest attribute. Once this determination is made, choosing a solo is easier. I also have the student determine the best range for his or her solo. I don't have students choose solos that go out of the range of pitches that can be hit with quality every day (rather than pitches that can be hit only on good days).

Once students are armed with this information, I send them searching. Sometimes they read through songs with other students, which makes things much more fun. A trip to the music store is also more fun with another student. I suggest collections of songs just because they get more for their money than with a single song. Some directors buy some of these collections each year, developing a solo library that is available to students, and often students go in groups to purchase a book together. Be sure to have students check the table of contents to make sure the book contains the appropriate types of songs and composers. Brahms, Schubert, and Schumann are always dependable, as are some contemporary composers like Copland and Niles. If there is music by people you don't know, you had better have a look at the song to make sure it isn't from a collection such as *The Best of Three Dog Night*. If students are searching for their own music, I ask them each to pick a favorite for preparation, or, if they want me to help, to each bring me two or three selections that they like. I then will hear them and tell them which one I think makes them sound the best. I also make myself available to help individually with such things as phrasing, breathing, foreign-language pronunciation, and so on. By the way, singing in a foreign language is not necessary, nor is it an advantage as far as the judge is concerned.

Approximately one week before the All-State Choir tryout, I hold a recital during my large-choir class time. Typically, most of the students trying out are in that choir, and it also provides the largest possible class audience. It is a requirement of mine that singers present their solos to the Concert Choir from memory. If they do not, I withdraw them from the audition. Prior to this day, I cover with the students how to enter the room, what they can expect to see, how they should introduce their solos, how they should dress for their tryouts, how to relax with a deep breath before a cue to the accompanist to begin, and so on. They then get a chance to try these things out before the real thing. If the students can sing for their peers successfully, then it becomes easy to sing for a judge whom they don't know and who is probably someone that they will never see again. I know there are many directors who employ this procedure.

For solo preparation, I work a great deal with students individually. All other preparation is in groups of some sort. I have had the greatest success teaching the scales and triads to all in the

choir as part of warm-ups. I start out singing patterns that the choir sings back to me. Once the singers can do all of the scales and triads as a group as I call for them by name, I begin to combine patterns. That is, I may give a harmonic minor scale followed by a major triad for them to sing back to me. Silly contests sometimes allow me (and the class) to hear individual singers demonstrate their ability to do these things. I often will ask the class to give a score to the person singing a scale, based on singing the right scale, intonation, and all of the other things that a judge would listen for. I have had the best success teaching triads to students if I teach the triads in pairs. If a student can sing a major triad correctly, it is easy to alter that triad to sing an augmented one, or to alter a minor triad to sing a diminished one. As you can see, this procedure is basically drill. One other advantage to using it with the entire choir is that it illustrates to all singers that anybody can sing scales and triads.

Two weeks before the tryouts, I hold voluntary brushup sessions after school. They last only twenty minutes each day. That way everyone really hits it hard for a short while and leaves before becoming "brain-fried." I also set up a practice room with materials that students can practice reading. These sessions work best with pairs. The students can take advantage of these things or not, as they choose.

Sight-reading is something that we all work on all of the time. In preparing students for the sight-reading in a tryout, I try to have them implement a standard procedure. For instance, when they get something in their hands to read, I tell them first to look at the key signature and try to find a tonal center. We cover relative minor and major in the after-school sessions. Once the students have dealt with the key signature, I have them check out the first note and last note for possible help with key center, and I have them quickly scan the entire piece for accidentals. Often, something in minor uses the harmonic minor with the raised seventh. I then have them take one more quick look for large leaps so as not to be surprised by them later. All of this is enhanced by reading in the large-group rehearsal every day. I keep the melodic sight-reading materials rhythmically very simple, since the same standard is employed for All-State Choir tryouts.

Over the years, I have accumulated many things for use as sight-reading exercises. There are many fine things available from publishers that are effective. Directors often comment to me that they don't know what difficulty level to expect in the tryout sight-reading items. Try writing a few of them. Suppose you were told to write a melodic sight-reading exercise to be used for the tryout that would (1) be about four measures in length; (2) be easy enough for most singers to be successful and difficult enough to find out if a student can read; (3) make sense musically; (4) use only eighth, quarter, and half notes; and (5) stay in a comfortable, central range. I'm sure that all of us could write things that would be in the ball park in terms of difficulty. Have your students read examples in both major and minor, with both duple and triple meter signatures, that use intervals as large as a sixth, and that might involve an accidental (such as would result from going to a secondary dominant).

When reading melodic exercises, it is most helpful to find or write things in two or three parts just because they are more interesting and more fun. One thing that I didn't use very much for years was the process of dictation of short patterns for students to write down. I have found over the last few years that this enhances intervallic, melodic, and rhythmic understanding. It is most important that you design all reading activities from the standpoint of the students being successful. They find out that they really can do this successfully. Confidence is a huge part of jumping in with both feet.

Rhythm reading is drilled in a manner similar to melody reading, except with the obvious differences. If you were told to write a rhythmic exercise for reading that could use any combination of sixteenth notes, eighth notes, quarter notes, half notes, and all corresponding rests as well as triple and duple meters, you could certainly do that. Also keep in mind that the things put down for students to read should make sense musically and not be something designed to trick them into making mistakes and yet should be difficult enough to see if they can read rhythms.

At an ACDA convention, Greg Gentry once presented something that he uses for teaching rhythms. It is a grid consisting of a large number of squares. In each square is the equivalent of one beat of notes and rests. For example, in the 4/4 grid, one square might have two eighth notes, another might have an eighth and two sixteenth notes, another an eighth rest followed by an eighth note, and so on. Similar grids can be designed for other meters, including compound ones such as 6/8. The director could simply point to a square and the choir would do the rhythm. It

follows, of course, that squares could be put together for larger numbers of beats. This is a fun way to drill a large number of rhythms in a very short time. Greg uses this as part of his large-group rehearsal, and it is obvious that his students read successfully. I also use a system like this. Here, as with melody reading, it is helpful to have students write down rhythms given orally by the director. In addition, find ensemble rhythm-reading pieces to use—they are also fun and beneficial.

Aural recall is something that is a little more difficult to do methodically. Each year I find out from students how they do this. There are a few things that students who are successful at this skill consistently describe to me as part of the process they use. One is that they visualize a direction of melodic flow. That is, they could probably draw a picture of the melody, noting that it starts high or low, where it goes from there, and how it ends. They also make themselves get the first pitch for sure, as well as the first interval. An important rule to be applied to this process is that one cannot quit. Once you start, keep going, and if you totally lose precision, at least follow the melodic shape as best you can remember it and end logically.

For the last several years, the aural recall used at the All-State Choir tryouts has made sense musically. Obviously, some students have an easier time of this than others. Some who take to this easily are able to focus on tricky rhythms and odd leaps. I have found that students improve greatly at this skill as they practice it. I use aural recall practice with my large choir, starting with five-note passages. Gradually, the exercises I use become more involved rhythmically and intervallically, and then the length increases as I move back toward more simple intervals and rhythms.

One last guideline that I have found that is important in several areas of the tryout is not to stop once you have started. This is true with melodic and rhythmic reading, as well as with aural recall. If you are reading rhythms, for example, and run into something that stumps you, you are faced with a choice. You can stop, whereupon the judge may think that you can't do this at all, or you can keep going and lose a point or two because of a mistake. The same is true for melody reading and aural recall.

From time to time, in a rehearsal, I will give a student a mock tryout in front of the choir. This does not include presentation of the solo, but just the other skill portions. It is important to choose someone who can do it successfully. I tell the student and the choir the number of points I would probably give for each portion, and sometimes I will ask the choir to award points based on accuracy and so on. I am also sure to tell the students that my tryout may or may not be like the actual one. The All-State Choir tryouts change a little from year to year.

Overall, I tell my students that they must prepare each area of the tryout well enough so that they can muff one area and still have a good score.

I hope that this information has been helpful to you. Keep things general, because none of us knows what will appear on the actual tryout. It may be similar to last year's or it may not. Good luck.

Steve Meininger is president-elect of the Colorado MEA and associate director of the Colorado Chorale in Denver. Retired from teaching music in the public schools in Lakewood, Colorado, he is still active as an adjudicator and clinician. This article originally appeared in the Summer 1998 issue of the Colorado Music Educator. *Reprinted by permission.*

Preparing Your Choir for Adjudication
William J. Naydan

As an adjudicator at choral events this past spring, I listened to many elementary, middle school, and high school vocal groups. Unfortunately, the quality performances were more the exception than the rule. I think that you, as a conductor, need to see this process from an adjudicator's perspective.

Remember that I have never heard your group. I am really assessing your accuracy of performance as it compares to the written score. Dynamics and phrasing are vital and not optional. What else can I comment on other than interpretation and dynamics? Are the parts accurate? Have you changed voicings, doubled any parts, or changed dynamics? Have you written all changes in the score I am reading? Are the selections too hard for your ensemble? Remember that a bad arrangement of a classical piece is not better than a good arrangement of a nonclassical one.

Here Is a List of "Do's."
1. Be accurate, melodically and rhythmically.
2. Balance parts so that the harmonies can be heard.
3. Perform dynamics as they appear in the score or indicate changes.
4. Phrase as you would poetry. Use the text to define your interpretation. (A trick is to circle key words and ideas.)
5. Teach proper diction to your group.
6. Sing expressively! The singers need to focus on you for entrances and cutoffs. Be happy when it's happy and sad when it's sad. The facial expressions can really change a good performance into a great one.
7. Make sure your group can perform the piece well. Ask a colleague whom you trust and who will not offend you to give you an honest opinion and constructive criticism.
8. Record your group and listen with singers for mistakes and good things. Let your choir become the critical listener.

If you can do these things, your group will do wonderfully in competition. I am always thrilled as a judge when I hear a group that has taken care and effort to lift its performance to the level of superior.

William J. Naydan is music curriculum coordinator and director of choral activities at Hatboro-Horsham High School in Horsham, Pennsylvania, and adjunct professor of music education at Chestnut Hill College in Philadelphia, Pennsylvania. This article originally appeared in the Fall 1999 issue of Pennsylvania's PMEA News. *Reprinted by permission.*

Section 9

Inspiration

To teach music, you must have a tremendous love of music and need to share it with others. Sometimes though, you need a little inspiration, something to remind you of why you try to bring the joy of music to your students day after day. These articles range from thoughtful to humorous, but all will make you think.

 Section 9

Inspiration

No Excuses!
Leslie Guelker-Cone

As a young high school choral conductor, I attended a clinic one weekend to watch a master teacher at work. She explained and demonstrated the techniques she used with her choirs, which were among the finest ensembles in the state. As she spoke, instead of finding myself inspired, I began to feel more and more discouraged. "My students can't possibly sing that well," I told myself. "She's got all those great voices and they read so well. My students aren't nearly so accomplished."

At the end of the clinic, I spoke with her about my concerns. I expected that she would listen sympathetically and possibly give me some suggestions for improving my program. Instead, she looked me in the eye and said, "No excuses!" I suppose I must have looked shocked, so she continued, clarifying her statement. "You may not have control of what goes on outside your classroom. You may not have the power to influence scheduling, or budget, or a number of other things, but you do have control over what happens in your classroom. It's up to you to create a great choir within that classroom environment. Find a way to make it work. No excuses!"

I went home that day and began to develop a plan to stop making excuses and start building the program I wanted. Here are some of the concerns I began to address.

My students don't come in vocally trained.
    No excuses! Train them.
    Begin with your own personal training. Understand how the voice works. Read everything you can get your hands on about the vocal mechanism. Sign up for workshops, and take private lessons. Talk to other choral conductors and private teachers about what works for them. Take this knowledge into the classroom. Turn every warm-up into a group voice lesson. Reiterate the components of healthy, beautiful singing in every rehearsal. Split the choir up to work on the special vocal needs of each section. Work with students individually as often as possible. Help them prepare for solo/ensemble contests and other solo opportunities. Start an after-school voice class for your most interested singers.

My students don't have musicianship skills.
    No excuses! Teach them.
    Teach them to sight-sing. Choose a music-reading system and stick with it. Sight-sing in every rehearsal. Sight-sing to introduce new pieces. Pull appropriate pieces from your library just for reading purposes. Play "Name that interval" or "Clap that rhythm"—make sight-singing fun whenever possible. Get away from playing every part on the piano. Help students begin to gain courage as independent singers, even if you only begin with a few phrases a day. Teach theoretical concepts and test students on them frequently. Create a year-long plan and decide what students need to know at each grade/ability level: note names, key signatures, scales, etc. Highlight these concepts wherever they appear in the music you are rehearsing. Start a lunchtime or after-school theory class for your most interested students.

My students aren't musically sophisticated.
    No excuses! Train them.
    Teach them to be critical listeners. Give them a vocabulary they can use to express the things, both positive and negative, that they hear. Have individual students step out from the choir and critique what they hear in rehearsal. Have one section sing, and let the rest of the choir give feedback. Highlight a specific concept you'd like them to listen for—phrasing, intonation, tone, etc.—so that they have something to focus on. Continually urge them on to a deeper level of

understanding and response. Expose them to the musical world outside their classroom—play recordings of fine choirs, and take students to hear outstanding choirs in concert as often as possible. Discuss in detail what makes these choirs great.

My students aren't focused enough in rehearsal.

No excuses! Demand it.

Create a standard of rehearsal behavior and enforce it. Be consistent. Be sure that positive behavior is praised and that inappropriate behavior has clearly delineated consequences. Use student leadership to help create standards and model appropriate behavior. Talk to other choral conductors about what works for them. Create a sense of ensemble pride and ownership in which students know that excellence can only be achieved through discipline. Demand that excellence in every rehearsal.

No excuses! Though I first heard these words over 20 years ago, they have had a stronger and longer lasting effect on me than just about anything I've learned since then. Still today, when I become discouraged or I feel unsure about my choir's ability to meet a particular goal, I remind myself once again: No excuses! And I get back to work.

Leslie Guelker-Cone is director of choral activities and coordinator of vocal studies at Western Washington University in Bellingham. This article first appeared in the May 1999 issue of Washington's Voice. *Reprinted by permission.*

Looking to History for Colleagues
Anna Hamre

We music teachers have always known that colleagues are our greatest assets. They are our idea banks, our sounding boards, and our support systems. They have a suggestion for a great concert opener; they have an idea for recruitment; they have a method for building community support.

It was in my doctoral studies that I began realizing that we could also find colleagues in our history books. I realized that early music masters dealt with many problems we now encounter and many we'll never have to face. They had to perform at all kinds of civic and religious events, often with groups of unequal balance or abilities. Some early geniuses that we revere never dreamed of having the high-quality choirs that many public schools have today.

For example, for a long time the great J. S. Bach had to perform every week with what he considered to be inadequate forces. Each Sunday he did whatever was necessary to get through the services. Sometimes he conducted his group with his rolled-up music. Sometimes he played the first violin part. Sometimes he led while playing the organ.

One time, just as I was ready to take my high-school choirs to contest, my accompanist suddenly took ill, and I had to accompany my own groups during their competition performances. I quit feeling sorry for myself when I remembered that the great Bach, the composer I most admire, had to do the same almost every Sunday.

Surely the choirmasters working during the Thirty Years' War encountered enormous musical challenges in mustering performers. Composers the likes of Johann Hermann Schein and Heinrich Schuetz left us masterpieces that help with the modern "no-tenor" problem. Hundreds of years after his career we can thank Schein for the wonderful SSB sacred concertos found in his first *Opella nova*.

A first glance at the multichoir compositions by Giovanni Gabrieli might lead one to believe that well-matched unaccompanied choirs performed them. However, history tells us that a choir in such performances would perhaps have had only one soprano, while three trombones or three string instruments covered the ATB parts. Gabrieli used the performers and instruments available to him.

The genius of these men was found not only in their compositions, but also in inventive handling of their unique performing challenges. Simply by learning how they coped, we have new tools for our own situations, whether they involve groups with less-than-ideal balance or less-than-ideal abilities. This is not to say that getting through the notes in any possible fashion is acceptable. These early composers never imagined some sounds (such as those of a saxophone). Rather, these men were practical, and they had realistic solutions to challenges similar to those we face today. We can look at our great predecessors as colleagues, and they, too, are idea banks for us as we begin the new academic year.

Anna Hamre is director of choral activities at California State University, Fresno. This article first appeared in the Fall 2001 issue of California's CMEA Magazine. Reprinted by permission.

Getting It All Together
Howard Meharg

Unison! "One sound, the interval of a perfect prime, the state of being so tuned or sounded; akin to union, an act or instance of uniting or joining two or more things into one as in the formation of a single political unit from two or more separate and independent units, a uniting in marriage, something formed by the combining or coalition of parts or members, oneness, the growing together of severed parts." The line from Webster's is a shocker of sorts, but it is given in my dictionary as part of the definition of the word.

Unison, that illusive guiding principle which is the obsession of so many successful choral conductors. Unison provides the yardstick, actually a micrometer, for measuring tuning, for observing balance, for evaluating blend, and for deciding the presence of ensemble or precision in attacks and releases. In short, it helps conductors answer the question, "Are we together here?"

Once upon a time I attended a Paul Christiansen workshop at the University of Denver. Inevitably the question of vibrato or non-vibrato choral singing arose. Christiansen made it clear that vibrato wasn't the issue. Unison was the issue. He pointed out that the Philadelphia Orchestra string section didn't play without vibrato, but that they sounded as one instrument.

There is much more to be said about the use of the unison concept to guide us in choral musical endeavors, but there is even more to the concept of unison than the strictly musical. Choral directors have the unique position of being able to draw together much more than diverse tone qualities. We have the privilege of unifying hearts, spirits, ethnic backgrounds, cultures, economic classes, and people of differing political and religious beliefs. We have the most incredible and beautiful medium with which to make this happen, the one directly connected to the hearts and minds of individuals, music … made with the human voice.

Ninth-grade students often enter high school choral groups with hugely disparate abilities and backgrounds. Very often the ninth-grade year is the last school experience with choral music where there are little or no prerequisites or auditions required. That group is likely to be a cross section of the school population, and for that matter, of society itself. My observation was that, especially in the last several years of my public school work, economic differences, parental attitudes about school, and differing family values (or lack of a value system altogether to guide), created "classes" of students within my class which were given labels by the kids and were so distinct as to be more difficult to deal with than even racial issues. This kind of class discord makes choral music making considerably more difficult and, to the easily daunted, impossible.

Yet because the choral director seems to never give up, miracles happen. Because the music itself is so liberating, so unifying, and so emotionally satisfying, miracles happen. We endure and we deal with, at times, overwhelming animosities, fights and near fights, and the little "soap operas" of early adolescence. I pronounce no grand solution to society's ills through choral music, but, for a moment, the sharing of something beautiful unifies spirits and enriches lives. The music draws people together like virtually nothing else can do, and we know we've been part of something good. Maybe we are, indeed, part of a process which enables "the growing together of severed parts."

Some church choirs like to have a period of time during a rehearsal to share concerns and to pray together. Stop and think of the complexities, the sorrows, the hurts, the varieties of human experiences which the individuals making up such a group bring to it. Again, despite our disparate parts, there is strength derived from our unison … of voices and of spirits. Many times your singers come to rehearsal grudgingly, thinking, "Oh no, another night out." Many times I went to the rehearsals of my church choir tired and wishing I didn't have to do it. Invariably, I came away elevated and spiritually renewed by the music and the music makers. Such is the glorious nature of this art. Such is the power of true unison!

Retired after 30 years directing choirs in the public schools of Kelso and Longview, Washington, Howard Meharg is now editor of the ACDA Northwest Division newsletter Northwest Notes. *This article is reprinted from the Winter 1997 issue of* Alaska Music Educator. *It originally appeared in the Fall 1996 issue of the Washington ACDA newletter* Unison. *Reprinted by permission.*

Tell the Truth! Create a Disturbance! Make a Difference!
Fred Ritter

I was told something last year that has truly made a difference in my teaching. The following is a paraphrase with a Ritter twist on it, so unless you ask, it isn't necessary to mention the source. If you find this helpful, feel free to do the same. It wasn't offered specifically in the context of choral music, but it still applies very well. In essence, this is what I was told:

When you express yourself in speech, song, or actions, be truthful. In your voice, your body language, your facial expressions, in every fiber of your being, be honest and sincere. Tell the truth!

Telling the truth in this way will often create a disturbance in your listener. People often don't like to hear the truth, especially if they don't agree. It may expose us to something we know is right, but previously chose to ignore. The truth can be painful, stimulating deep personal emotions. It also can be refreshing in this world of gray colors, where half-truths are often the norm. Telling the truth can change the way people feel, act, or perceive something. It can create discussion where there was none. Communicating with sincerity and honesty can make a difference in people's lives.

I have found this life lesson to be very useful in my choral program. When I select a piece of music, I want to make sure the text has something to say that is relevant to myself and to my students.

Some music published today has content that can be trite in nature, with very little significance. A text that can make you laugh, cry, dance, be introspective, long for love, mourn lost love, or take you to heaven can be fulfilling and relevant to the lives of those involved. Music that has no personal significance to the performers or is unchallenging musically is easily performed but not satisfying for either you or your students.

The goal is to select music that has a significant text and is arranged musically in such a way as to deliver the message effectively. It doesn't have to be an eight-part a cappella motet. It could be written in unison. The challenge is in interpreting the music and communicating that message to your audience. I would rather hear one note sung sincerely with feeling than a thousand sung indifferently.

When presenting a chosen selection, begin by explaining your goals for the song and for the eventual performance. Focus on the central truth first, rather than pounding out notes and rhythms. If you have a recording or can demonstrate it, do that. Study the text. Speak it together. Have students offer their own interpretations. Have them discuss how it might apply to them or to others. Seek out help for literature with deep meaning from the English department. If it is a foreign language piece, write the literal translation in the music. When the students understand the message in the music and its relevance, they will put forth a better effort.

For the concert, adding movement to certain kinds of music, special lighting, or more instruments can enhance the songs. If it is a foreign language piece, print the translation in the program. Have someone read it aloud before your performance. If it is scriptural, use the Bible for a historical reference to put it in perspective. Don't take for granted that everyone knows these things.

A convincing performance requires excellent diction, tall vowels, proper phrasing, facial expression, proper breathing, and a careful interpretation of dynamics and tempos—all things to strive for in your singers. If it is sung truthfully and with full understanding, these vocal skills will finally happen naturally as a result of that truth. A crescendo is more than just getting louder—it is a strengthening of the moment to enhance the meaning of the song.

Watch the students. Have them watch each other. Are they convincing? Do you believe them when they sing a love song, a farce, a drinking song, a patriotic song, a sacred song? It's easy to tell when it finally comes together. You will hear it in the appreciative applause and the discussion it creates the next day downtown at the grocery store or in church on Sunday. Some of the talk may be favorable, while other discussion may be of a questioning nature. Either way, you will have made a difference by giving the audience something to think about.

This is also true of the performers themselves. Choir members will often begin to develop those things you strive for in your performance such as honesty, sincerity, compassion, trustworthiness, and a willingness to ask questions and be searchers of the truth—good lifelong lessons to be learned.

As a final note, selecting good literature is a never-ending search, and most important to the success of your program. Attend workshops and reading sessions. Go to the ACDA summer convention for new ideas and brain refreshers. Listen to other choirs and their performances. The best source of growth musically for your choir comes in sharing music with others. Sharing, not competing! But that is another article altogether.

I hope that you have a chance to share your music this spring with others. Tell your students that the most important goal is to find out what the music has to say, and then tell the truth to your audience. You may create a disturbance that will make a difference!

Fred Ritter teaches vocal music to grades 9–12 at Columbus High School in Columbus, Nebraska. This article first appeared in the April 2000 issue of the Nebraska Music Educator. *Reprinted by permission.*

Dear Denise
Beth Smalling

Dear Denise,

Congratulations! Your mom informed me that you'll graduate this spring from law school. You're all grown up and have become a beautiful, intelligent, and talented young woman, ready to meet the challenges of life. You are a very special young lady.

I wish I had known how special you were back in fifth grade. That was the year you auditioned for the fifth-grade chorus and didn't make it. I remember that your Mom visited me and wanted to know why you weren't chosen. I answered that the criteria for being in the chorus were to be able to match pitches and have a pleasing voice quality. According to my rating scale, your vocal ability did not rate high enough to make you a Wellington Singer.

Your mom accepted the answer, but I know she was disappointed and concerned because you were feeling left out. Even after becoming a cheerleader in high school, graduating from college, and then attending law school, your mom (now a good friend) said that you always remembered the disappointment of not being chosen to be in the fifth-grade chorus.

Teachers are always caught in a balancing act. As a music teacher, I was searching for a performing group that arrived with raw talent but would work with me to raise the level of musicianship. The previous year, I had chosen students based on the citizenship recommendation of the classroom teacher. They were a nice group of students, but I struggled all year just to get some of them to match pitches. The year you auditioned, I decided to choose on the basis of vocal ability. I ended up with voices that never reached their full potential because too many discipline problems got in the way.

The year after that, I decided on a compromise. The students would be rated by the classroom teachers for citizenship, work effort, and ability to work well with others. I would audition them and rate their voices according to pitch, volume, and quality. The students with the highest ratings would be chosen for the chorus. Students who came highly recommended by the classroom teacher could still be chosen, even if their vocal ability was not superior.

For most of the years that I used this system, my choruses sounded good and had only a few discipline problems. But interest in the Wellington Singers was high, and every year I auditioned over 100 students who wanted to be members. We met once a week after school, and, although I should have chosen only 64 singers, each year I added to the number so I wouldn't have to disappoint too many students. But there were always those who, like you Denise, were devastated to find their name wasn't on the list. Sometimes their moms, like yours, understood my process and helped their children deal with their disappointment. Other times their moms were very combative and the whole situation was very stressful.

So two years ago I devised a totally new system. Instead of a chorus that met once a week after school, I would have two sections of chorus once a week. Forty students would meet on Tuesday, forty would meet on Thursday, and for concerts they would perform as one group. There was only one requirement—the students had to love to sing. I told the fifth graders that I would take the first 80 students who signed up and brought in their parent permission slips. The Wellington Wildcat Chorus was born.

I discovered some beautiful voices and some that were at least enthusiastic. I worked with students who were a joy to teach and those who were a challenge. I've had to stretch my musicianship and class management skills to meet the needs of my students. But, because they all loved to sing, I've had two of my best years ever.

Denise, I wish I had known all this when you were in fifth grade. But sometimes it's the job of the student to teach the teacher. As you prepare to begin your career, I want to wish you well. I also have a small gift to recognize your great accomplishment. I hope you'll wear it with pride—a Wellington Wildcat Chorus T-shirt.

With thanks and affection, Beth Smalling, Music Teacher

(Note: Beth says there really is a Denise, although that is not her real name. She will graduate this spring from a Florida university, and she will get a T-shirt from Beth Smalling, her former music teacher.)

Beth Smalling teaches music at Wellington Elementary School in Wellington, Florida, where she also directs the Wellington Wildcat Chorus. This article originally appeared in the May 2000 issue of the Florida Music Director. *Reprinted by permission.*

Make Them Champions!
Carl Vuncannon III

Provide them a chance to be champions every day. Sounds great, doesn't it? It's actually a quote from one of my coaching colleagues, Mike Spiegel, at Lee's Summit High School. Mike is one of the most energetic people I have ever known. He is also tremendously committed to his teaching and coaching. The quote came in a clinic as I listened to him tell of his philosophy in the classroom and out of it. The quote rang a bell in my mind; it was also something that I had heard before from some others that I had known. I have a good friend in Erie, Pennsylvania, a math teacher, who has the same philosophy. He gets so excited about teaching, still after twenty-six years, that he can hardly wait to get to his classroom each day. It's the same philosophy that I experienced at home with my father, who taught choir for nine years before being a principal for the next nineteen years after that.

It's exciting to hear that we have people in the field of education who still have that philosophy and are very excited about the students that they teach, especially those teachers who have been at it for quite a while. Many of you across the state have that philosophy, maintain it in word and deed, and strive to give your students the opportunities and challenges every day that will make them champions, not only in school, but in life. It is the attitude that we need to take for our students and the success of our programs, if we are to be the kind of teachers and people that can change things, that can be trusted, and that can be relied upon. We must make children champions every day, somehow and some way, whether it be by the opportunities we give, the atmosphere that we make in the classroom, the time that we spend teaching, counseling, and listening, or the extra time that we find to take with students outside the classroom.

Are we giving our students every opportunity to succeed in school? Are we giving them all the outlets for performances that will enhance their high school experiences, making them feel positive about themselves and the abilities that they have? Are we making musicians for life, or rather young adults who, as they grow up, will relate to others and the children that they raise the wonderful experiences that they were given while in high school? The things that could shape the next senator, city council member, teacher, architect, doctor, or factory worker directly relate to the experiences that they have in high school, and we can provide them with the chance to be champions. What a wonderful thought that is!

You may think that this saying is only for coaches, but you need to know that you are a coach. You coach several hours a day. In fact, most successful music teachers would be fantastic coaches. There are so many things in common. You must pay attention to detail, you must be able to verbalize well and think on your feet. You must have compassion and be a good listener, organizer, and public relations master. You must take the negatives and make them positives along with being concerned with the well-being of each child in your care. This is what it takes to be a coach, and this is what it takes to teach children with the kind of passion that should consume us all. Make them champions and make them champions every day.

Success comes in many forms, as does the feeling of being a champion. Every child who walks in your classroom deserves to feel like a champion every day. This brings me to a wonderful practice that was first presented to me by Charles Robinson at UMKC in my Advanced Choral Techniques class. The rule is that if you criticize, you also praise positively. Not only do you praise once, but three times for every criticism. It's a tough one to follow, but if you are thinking about it while you are teaching, you will find that the practice becomes habit (heard that one before?).

Remember that teenagers are some of the best at recognizing fakes. Make sure that the praise is genuine and that they know and understand completely why they are getting complimented. The more they know about what they have done correctly, the more they will realize it on their own and strive for that positive reinforcement from you. Music organizations take on the personalities of their teachers. They will take on your values in music, attention or lack of attention to details, emotion, and, for some part, intellect.

Providing a chance for your students to be champions every day is a large responsibility, but you will be better for it, and your program will be better because of it. We must give to the children that walk into our classrooms a feeling of respite from the world; we must give them a place to understand emotions, feelings, and pas-sion. We need to give them chances to make mistakes and an understanding that to try and fail is much better than never to try. When our students realize the differences between right and wrong decisions in the classroom, it will give them the understanding and ability to make decisions outside the classroom. You will become a champion in your classroom, a better teacher, and an example for the future of the students that you teach.

Carl Vuncannon III is assistant activities director for performing arts, performing arts center manager, and director of choral music at Blue Springs High School in Blue Springs, Missouri. This article originally appeared in the Summer 1998 issue of Missouri School Music. *Reprinted by permission.*

Other MENC Choral Resources

Getting Started with Vocal Improvisation by Patrice D. Madura. 1999. 72 pages. #1638.

Getting Started with High School Choir by Steven K. Michelson. 1994. 64 pages. #1628.

Pronunciation Guide for Choral Literature by William V. May and Craig Tolin. 1987. 100 pages. #1040.

TIPS: The Child Voice compiled by Joanne Rutksowki and Maria Runfola. 1997. 44 pages. #1101.

Getting Started with Middle-Level Choir by Patrick K. Freer. 1998. 72 pages. #1637.

Movement in the Middle School Choral Rehearsal featuring Christine Jordanoff. 1992. VHS. 30 minutes. #3077.

Choral Music for Children: An Annotated List edited by Doreen Rao. 1990. 176 pages. #1502.

Teaching Choral Music: A Course of Study Developed by the MENC Task Force on Choral Music Course of Study. 1991. 64 pages. #1601.

Choral Triad Video Workshop Set featuring Christine Jordanoff and Robert Page. 1994. 6 tapes and workbook. #3096.

For complete ordering information on these and other publications, contact:

MENC Publications Sales
1806 Robert Fulton Drive
Reston, VA 20191-4348

Credit card holders may call 1-800-828-0229.